Political and Institutional Transition in North Africa

The year 2011 will go down in history as a turning point for the Arab world. The popular unrest that swept across the region and led to the toppling of the Ben Ali, Mubarak, and Qaddhafi regimes in Tunisia, Egypt, and Libya has fundamentally altered the social, economic, and political outlooks of these countries and the region as a whole.

This book assesses the transition processes unleashed by the uprisings that took place in Egypt and Tunisia in 2011. The wave of unrest and popular mobilisation that swept through these countries is treated as the point of departure of long and complex processes of change, manipulation, restructuring, and entrenchment of the institutional structures and logics that defined politics. The book explores the constitutive elements of institutional development, namely processes of constitution making, electoral politics, the changing status and power of the judiciary, and the interplay between the civilian and the military apparatuses in Egypt and Tunisia. It also considers the extent to which these two countries have become more democratic, as a result of their institutions being more legitimate, accountable, and responsive, at the beginning of 2014 and from a comparative perspective. The impact of temporal factors in shaping transition paths is highlighted throughout the book.

The book provides a comprehensive assessment of political and institutional transition processes in two key countries in North Africa and its conclusions shed light on similar processes that have taken place throughout the region since 2011. It will be a valuable resource for anyone studying Middle Eastern and North African politics, area studies, comparative institutional development and democratisation.

Silvia Colombo is Head of the Mediterranean and Middle East Programme at the International Affairs Institute (IAI) in Rome. She works on Euro-Mediterranean cooperation and domestic and regional politics in the Arab world.

Routledge Studies in Middle Eastern Democratization and Government
Edited by Larbi Sadiki
Qatar University

This series examines new ways of understanding democratization and government in the Middle East. The varied and uneven processes of change occurring in the Middle Eastern region can no longer be read and interpreted solely through the prism of Euro-American transitology. Seeking to frame critical parameters in light of these new horizons, this series instigates reinterpretations of democracy and propagates formerly 'subaltern' narratives of democratization. Reinvigorating discussion on how Arab and Middle Eastern peoples and societies seek good government, *Routledge Studies in Middle Eastern Democratization and Government* provides tests and contests of old and new assumptions.

EU Foreign Policy and Hamas
Inconsistencies and paradoxes
Adeeb Ziadeh

Politics and Revolution in Egypt
Rise and fall of the youth activists
Sarah Anne Rennick

Kurdistan in Iraq
The evolution of a quasi-state
Aram Rafaat

Political and Institutional Transition in North Africa
Egypt and Tunisia in comparative perspective
Silvia Colombo

Clientelism and Patronage in the Middle East and North Africa
Networks of dependency
Edited by Laura Ruiz de Elvira, Christoph H. Schwarz and Irene Weipert-Fenner

For more information about this series, please visit: www.routledge.com/middleeaststudies/series/RSMEDG

Political and Institutional Transition in North Africa
Egypt and Tunisia in Comparative Perspective

Silvia Colombo

LONDON AND NEW YORK

First published 2018 by Routledge

2 Park Square, Milton Park, Abingdon, Oxfordshire OX14 4RN
52 Vanderbilt Avenue, New York, NY 10017

Routledge is an imprint of the Taylor & Francis Group, an informa business

First issued in paperback 2020

Copyright © 2018 Silvia Colombo

The right of Silvia Colombo to be identified as author of this work has been asserted by her in accordance with sections 77 and 78 of the Copyright, Designs and Patents Act 1988.

All rights reserved. No part of this book may be reprinted or reproduced or utilised in any form or by any electronic, mechanical, or other means, now known or hereafter invented, including photocopying and recording, or in any information storage or retrieval system, without permission in writing from the publishers.

Notice:
Product or corporate names may be trademarks or registered trademarks, and are used only for identification and explanation without intent to infringe.

British Library Cataloguing-in-Publication Data
A catalogue record for this book is available from the British Library

Library of Congress Cataloging-in-Publication Data
A catalog record has been requested for this book

ISBN: 978-0-8153-4709-5 (hbk)
ISBN: 978-0-367-58990-5 (pbk)

Typeset in Times New Roman
by Apex CoVantage, LLC

Al mio Angelo custode
e ai suoi pastorelli
che hanno reso possibile tutto questo

Contents

List of tables viii
Acknowledgements ix

   Introduction 1
1 Debating transition, explaining institutional development 6
2 Looking back 30
3 Writing constitutions in time 56
4 It all comes down to electoral politics 94
5 The deep state fights back 117
6 Forward looking 142
   Conclusions 160

Appendix: list of interviews 168
Bibliography 171
Index 191

Tables

1.1	The institutional framework between engineering and development	24
2.1	Explaining Arab states' unsustainability	37
4.1	Distribution of seats in Egypt's Lower House	97
4.2	Distribution of seats in Tunisia's National Constituent Assembly (NCA)	107

Acknowledgements

Looking back over the past seven years, I am astonished to see what great changes have taken place in my life while drafting and re-drafting this book, which has been a constant feature of it. Sometimes life's circumstances have led me to neglect it, at other times enthusiasm and research creativity have made me progress beyond my own expectations. But I have never been alone in this endeavour. Lots of people have contributed to it from the substantive, intellectual, organisational, and, most importantly, emotional points of view. Some of them do not know how much they have been part of this journey. But I would like to take a moment to name and thank them all. Needless to say, all mistakes remain my sole responsibility.

I owe a big thanks to a group of people who have been a daily presence in my life in the past seven years and who have made my days busier but at the same time more stimulating and rewarding. All the members of the big 'IAI family' and Professor Leonardo Morlino have contributed to this book in many different ways, not least by pushing me to start this journey and by constantly providing me with a friendly and inspiring environment to discuss research and work problems. A great number of friends have shared with me the burdens, joys, frustrations, and achievements that are a part of any process of intellectual and personal growth. Some of them are the colleagues who – at different moments, in various places, and in a variety of forms – have provided me with their invaluable support and advice, have enlightened me with their remarks, have listened to my doubts, and have laughed with me. Similarly, my friends at home also deserve a special thank you for two very important reasons. First, because their friendship has made me what I am and, second, because their presence – near or far – their words, and their whole lives have taught me a very important thing, namely that drafting a book is not an isolated chapter in one's life. They might not know much about what is written here but I have greatly benefited from their friendship.

This research endeavour has also given me the possibility of travelling and spending some time abroad. Most of the empirical research for the book was conducted in the field in Egypt and Tunisia. Not only have these research trips been instrumental for collecting first-hand evidence and information, but they have also provided me with the opportunity to experience with my own senses the things I have talked about in this book, thus sharpening my understanding of the transition processes in these countries. I would like to thank here, in particular, all the people who agreed to be interviewed. Without their help, this book would never have seen the light. For anonymity purposes I cannot mention them, but they know who they are.

Last but not least, I would have not been able to write this book without the support of my family. Adele, Franco, Martino, and Agnese, as well as my extended family – including the little ones! – and parents-in-law have been a constant, albeit discrete, presence over the years. No words can fully express my sense of gratitude and my love to them. My grandparents, Angela and Giovanni, 'departed' in the middle of this journey. Their loving memory will always accompany me, while nothing can fill the emptiness they have left in my life. It is of great consolation though to know that they have been part of and can now 'see' the end of this endeavour. Finally, the most important thank you goes to my husband, Matteo, and our kids, Davide and Marta – the most precious things in my life. They have relentlessly been a source of inspiration, motivation, support, and encouragement throughout all these years. While this research has often kept us physically apart from each other, they have endured it all with patience, caring love, understanding, and generosity. There is so much of them, of their time, and of our love in this book.

Introduction

The sign appeared all of a sudden on the right-hand side of a busy street in downtown Cairo connecting Qasr El Nile to the heart of the shopping and evening stroll area that is July 26 St. The street was dark, like the building and the sign, only mirroring the glowing, blinking lights of the clothing shops on the opposite side. The severe and tidy sign clashed with the neglected and seemingly abandoned appearance of the building – a slagheap piled next to the entrance and cables hanging down all around, dangling in the late summer breeze. 'There was a time, many years ago, when buildings like this and the bustling life around them were the hallmark of downtown Cairo,' I thought while crossing the threshold. The sense of neglect and decay I felt in the entrance hall made me think (and hope) I was in the wrong place. There was nobody around, no noise to be heard except for the slightly sinister squeaking of the elevator. On the third floor, another sign, this time sparkling new, announced instead that I was in the right place: 'Welcome to Pension Roma!' The words echoed in the immense stairwell. At the very end of a carpeted hallway, a smiling figure behind a counter was waiting for me, a few pieces of paper in his hands. After opening my passport, Mustapha (the receptionist) smiled as if he wanted to reassure me: 'Welcome to our little Roman corner! I am sure you will feel at home here!'

From the very first time I entered this humble little hotel in October 2012, I immediately felt that it was like an oasis of peace and silence in the middle of Cairo's noisy, polluted, and often overcrowded streets. It was also a wonderful microcosm from which to gauge both the everyday lives of its inhabitants and the convulsive Egyptian transition. The waiters whispered comments on the political situation to each other while serving my morning breakfast and the questions about my daily meetings and discoveries were the best thermometer of the accuracy and relevance of my research. One evening, upon returning from a meeting-packed day, Mustapha greeted me with his warm, sincere smile and, while handing me my key, asked me what I thought of what he called Egypt's painful 'journey'. He warned me not to trust some of his fellow citizens who, blinded by the rhetoric about the greatness of the Egyptian people and its place in history, were led to think that a bright future awaits it around the corner. 'In every journey, it is important to know where you're coming from, your point of departure,' Mustapha told me as a smile crossed his not so young face. 'Of course it's also good to know where you're heading to, but the only thing that really matters is what lies in between. It's a journey, a process, the end of which I will most likely not see, but of which I am part and parcel,' he added. 'I am part of the change, and at the same time am transformed by what is happening,' he admitted sadly. 'Look, I was in Tahrir 20 months ago [. . .] it seems such a long time ago [. . .] I do not recognise our revolution anymore [. . .] the word itself [. . .] revolution [. . .] sounds empty and meaningless to my ears. It must be the wind, right? Aren't you annoyed by this stubborn wind too? That must be what has ushered in the failure of the revolution,' Mustapha told me on that still, hot evening in Cairo, almost presaging the coming 'winter'.

***

This book is about two journeys. It deals with the processes of transition unleashed by the uprisings that took place in Egypt and Tunisia in 2011. The wave of unrest and popular mobilisation is treated here as the point of departure of long and complex processes of change, manipulation, restructuring, and entrenchment of the institutional structures and logics that define politics. As such, this work contributes to exploring these institutional changes and continuities in the two countries taken individually and comparatively, as a way of advancing our knowledge both on a specific region, the Arab world, and on a set of processes that represent a key theme in comparative political analysis. Furthermore, this broad topic stems directly from the author's expertise in Near and Middle Eastern studies and interest in comparative politics. In fact, it provides an illustration of the possibility of combining and cross-fertilising area studies with theoretical insights developed through comparative political analysis.

As said, the point of departure of this research are the uprisings of 2011, a year that will go down in history as a turning point for the Arab world. The popular unrest that swept across the region and led to the toppling of the Ben Ali, Mubarak, and Qaddhafi regimes in Tunisia, Egypt, and Libya has fundamentally altered the social, economic, and political outlooks of these countries and the region as a whole. These events took many, especially external, observers and commentators by surprise (Bellin 2012). The Arab regimes that fell under the weight of sustained popular protests were regarded as stable, having been in power for decades (24 years in the case of Tunisia, 30 in Egypt, and 42 in Libya). Despite the apparent stability, however, these countries suffered from enormous political and socio-economic problems that had made the situation unsustainable. Growing inequalities, skyrocketing unemployment rates – particularly among young people – rampant corruption, and rising poverty levels compounded with political graft, increased repression, the lack of basic civil and political liberties, and entrenched authoritarianism to create an explosive mix (Colombo 2011). The tipping point was reached when the global financial and economic crisis hit the Arab states, albeit indirectly through their economic and commercial ties to Europe and the United States (Paciello 2010).

The analysis of the processes set in motion by the popular uprisings represents the core of this book. The timeframe chosen (2011 to the beginning of 2014), characterised by the often uncertain development of institutional structures and logics, corresponds to a very early phase of the transitions, as these are processes that usually span a much longer period of time. In addressing institutional development, this book adopts an open-ended definition of 'transition'. While this term is one of the key concepts in the democratisation literature, the way it is conceptualised in this work is different from mainstream approaches. The understanding and appreciation of the Arab transitions here underscores the open-endedness of these processes, which involve the (partial) destruction or revision of existing authoritarian power institutions without the necessarily linear attainment of a new democratic order. Further details about the definition and conceptualisation of key concepts, including 'transition', 'institutions', 'structure', 'agency', and 'institutional engineering', are provided in Chapter 1. All in all, these concepts represent the backbone of the book, the bulk of which is devoted to exploring processes of constitution making, electoral politics, the changing status and power of the judiciary, and the interplay between the civilian and the military apparatuses in Egypt and Tunisia. Breaking down institutional development into its constitutive elements enhances our ability to grasp complex processes of institutional change and continuity in that the incidence of these factors within transition processes varies across space and time.

In carrying out the analysis, an attempt was made to answer the following question: *what are the most significant factors that have influenced the transition processes in the Arab countries?* Investigating political transition processes lies at the very heart of the study of politics, which in Lasswell's ground-breaking definition means analysing 'who gets what, when, how' (Lasswell 1936). This overarching question can be broken down into four sub-questions. First, *in what direction does institutional development proceed?* Institutional development is a fundamental aspect in the life of an institution. Nevertheless, a number of neo-institutional scholars have shown that institutions tend to remain 'sticky' even when the political and economic conditions in which they are placed have changed dramatically in response to both exogenous and endogenous factors, and often become the object of contention themselves (North 1990). Debating change and continuity at the institutional level provides us with a tool for grasping the factors that lie at the core of transition processes. This question corresponds broadly to identifying the 'what' in Lasswell's terms. Linked to this, it is important to take into account the actors that shape institutional development, the initial 'who' in the definition above. The actors' preferences, strategies, and actions play a key role in shaping transition processes (this amounts to the 'how' as well). Against this backdrop, the second and the third sub-questions respectively ask *what role actors, and in particular old and new elites, play in transition processes* and *in what ways old institutions constrain or facilitate transition processes*. One of the advantages of addressing the issue of institutional development is that political agency and political choice can be taken into consideration along with institutional constraints.

Finally, by bringing together the threads of the empirical analysis, this book also compares the two countries in terms of the final outcomes of their transitions. By 'final outcome' I do not necessarily mean the end of these long-term processes, but rather of a short-to-medium term timeframe (from 2011 to the beginning of

2014), to assess whether Egypt and Tunisia are on the path to achieving democracy or not. This means moving from an open-ended understanding of transition processes to a closed-ended one, so that some attributes of democracy can be measured, namely legitimacy, accountability, and responsiveness. The last part of the book answers the following sub-question concerning the impact of temporal factors on political outcomes, the 'when' in Lasswell's definition of politics: *what impact have the different configurations of institutional changes and continuities, defined in terms of timing and sequencing, had on the short-to-medium term political development of the Arab countries?* By thoroughly assessing the temporal dimension of social processes, this analysis of the Arab transitions underscores the extent to which specific patterns of timing and sequencing matter, in that even when starting out from similar conditions, a range of outcomes is possible.

By answering this set of questions, this book sheds light on the complex processes that have taken place in the Arab world in the period 2011 to the beginning of 2014. In particular, it provides new insight into transition phenomena by contextualising the comparative analysis of Egypt and Tunisia into the broader narrative about transitions and democratisation developed in different geographical and historical contexts. In spite of a number of evident and important differences, the recent transformations in the Arab world are comparable to the profound changes that took place in Eastern and Central Europe in 1989–1991 (Masoud 2011; Springborg 2011a; Way 2011). This research thus engages the literature analysing such transition processes with a view to highlighting similarities and differences. Two theoretical contributions are also offered by this research. First, it contributes to establishing a productive dialogue across disciplines, namely Near and Middle Eastern studies and democratisation studies, deepening our understanding of the political development of the Arab countries and enriching the literature on (democratic) transitions. These two disciplines and the related literatures have had only limited chances of interaction so far due to the sheer absence of democratic experiences in the Arab world prior to 2011. In particular, this book challenges some of the theoretical frameworks that have been used thus far to interpret political development in the Arab world. I am referring here to the democratic transition theory, on the one hand, and the authoritarian resilience paradigm, on the other. Both have been partly challenged and partly reconfirmed by the transition processes unleashed by the Arab uprisings. While these theoretical frameworks have long been regarded as mutually exclusive or, at best, in competition, the research presented here arguably calls for combining some elements of both paradigms in order to account more effectively for the complex and dynamic processes of political development. The second theoretical contribution derives from the fact that it engages with some of the most state-of-the-art insights developed by the historical institutional literature. This literature provides both the intellectual boundaries and the methodological tools for assessing the impact of institutional development on political outcomes. Issues of timing and sequencing, path-dependence, and process tracing, stemming from the historical institutional literature, are used in this book to refine our knowledge of long-term historical phenomena such as transitions in general. Last but not least, the relevance of this research lies in its composite, multidimensional nature, whereby it is well placed to contribute to both the academic and practitioners' debates on the Arab transitions. While the book aims primarily at enhancing academic reflection on some specific issues pertaining to institutional and political development processes, its contribution in shaping the policy-oriented debate and in informing the policy-makers' decisions about contemporary political problems should not be underestimated.

This book is structured as follows. Chapter 1 provides the theoretical background for the analysis of institutional development in the context of the Arab transitions. It also discusses some key concepts, such as 'transition', 'institutions', 'timing', and 'sequencing', in addition to presenting the methodology. The remainder is then articulated in three parts. The first part, corresponding to Chapter 2, discusses the structural and agency-related factors that led to the outbreak of the Arab uprisings in Egypt and Tunisia in 2011. In it, legitimacy, accountability, and responsiveness are identified as the three main factors whose absence triggered the chain of events. The core of the book is made up of the central chapters (Chapters 3, 4, and 5), which present the original empirical analysis based on first-hand evidence gathered through extensive fieldwork and primary sources. These chapters point to and assess four constitutive elements of institutional development: the constitution-making process (Chapter 3), electoral dynamics (Chapter 4), and civilian-military relations and the role of the judiciary (Chapter 5). Changes and continuities in these institutions are thoroughly scrutinised in each of the two case studies. Finally, the third part of the book, corresponding to Chapter 6, mirrors part one in terms of both content and structure, but with the difference that part one looks backward while part three looks forward. In fact, Chapter 6 is devoted to assessing the relation between the constitutive elements of institutional development and political outcomes in a comparative perspective across time. The book concludes with a chapter that brings the empirical and theoretical threads together. It also further elaborates on the main findings, before drawing some implications for further research.

1 Debating transition, explaining institutional development

> We have institutions that have employees and budgets and paper work, but almost nonexistent output; we have a democracy, but that is only in so far as we have elections; [...] a judiciary that are above reproach or accountability despite their inefficiency and corruption; [...] a military with a huge budget and millions of soldiers and guns but can't protect our borders [...]. The Mirage State.
>
> from Mahmoud Salem. "The Mirage State of Egypt". *Daily News Egypt.* 31 July 2012

Questions about how different configurations of institutions influence political development have always occupied a central place in the discipline of comparative politics. If it is important to address such questions in times of relative institutional stability, it is even more crucial when institutions such as constitutional texts, party systems, and bureaucracies are the object of change. This is the point of departure of this book, which attempts to shed light on the institutional development processes that have taken place in the first three years since the Arab uprisings and to link them to political outcomes in the short-to-medium term. In 2011, the explosion of popular rage and frustration by mainly young people led to the destabilisation of the Tunisian and Egyptian regimes and ultimately to their collapse. Destabilisation occurs when the balance between political mobilisation and state capabilities becomes unsustainable and the pact between the state and the citizens is broken or at least severely undermined. People took to the streets in Tunisia, Egypt, Morocco, Yemen, Libya, Bahrain, Syria, and other countries in the Middle East and North Africa (MENA) with demands that ranged from political and socio-economic reforms to regime change. People protested against the lack of legitimacy and accountability, inclusiveness and equality, freedom, and transparency. Put simply, a great number of people in these countries expressed their resentment against the pervasiveness of the authoritarian system of power that tended to reduce them to subjects instead of treating them as citizens.

The most enduring and comprehensive definition of 'authoritarianism' – the starting point of this research – is the one provided by Linz. It spells out the characteristics of authoritarian regimes that distinguish them from totalitarian ones: presence of multiple groups, e.g., parties, trade unions, civil society groups, coercive apparatus; no ideology underpinning the power of the leader, e.g., president, leader of the party, monarch, etc.; no emphasis on the mobilisation of society in favour of the atomisation of society; manipulation of political institutions, such as parties and electoral laws; likelihood of succession problems due to the absence of a single party and a clear hierarchy; and some limits to the power of the leader (Linz 1964; Linz 2000). These features influence the transition process and its final outcome since the breakdown of the authoritarian regime and its institutions open the way to conflicts and negotiations among old and new elites. As a result of the sustained mass protests that have spared very few Arab countries, some of them have undergone a transition phase in which change and continuity have co-existed. Moving from similar causes and triggering factors, it would have been reasonable to expect some sort of convergence also in the short-to-medium term outcomes experienced by the countries undergoing transition. However, this is far from reality. The very circumstances that caused the eruption of popular discontent have been confronted through different measures, thus setting different countries on different transition paths, which in turn have had an impact on their short-to-medium term political development.

Patterns of change and continuity in the institutional development of transition countries are interesting to analyse in trying to pinpoint the most important factors and the direction of change (or lack thereof) that have influenced the transition processes in the Arab countries. Institutional development is a fundamental aspect of the life of any institution. While a number of institutionalist scholars have shown that institutions tend to remain 'sticky' even when the political and economic conditions in which they exist have dramatically changed in response to both exogenous and endogenous factors, they often become the object of contention in themselves (North 1990). Established institutions typically generate powerful inducements that reinforce their own stability and further development, while new institutions would often entail start-up and learning costs. This means that once in place, institutions – taken both individually and at the level of configurations of interdependent organisations and institutions – are hard to alter.

Treating change and continuity at the institutional level provides us with a tool for grasping the factors at the core of transition processes, which entails taking into account both structure and agency. One of the advantages of addressing the issue of institutional development is that one is encouraged to put the emphasis on political agency and choice next to and within institutional constraints. This ultimately means addressing the role of actors, and in particular of old and new elites, against the backdrop of the constraints and opportunities provided by the old institutions. This assessment would not be complete without taking into account the impact of temporal factors, namely time, timing, and sequencing, on the dynamics of institutional development and on their short-to-medium term political outcomes. Specific patterns of timing and sequencing matter a lot in that a range of outcomes is possible even when starting out from similar conditions largely as a result of the impact of temporal factors. All in all, this chapter outlines the analytical framework that is applied to the study of institutional development processes in the context of the Arab transitions, i.e., the articulation of different means of institutionalising and practicing new forms of political governance.

Institutionalising uncertainty[1]

'Fourth wave?' Not yet

Previous experiences in Eastern and Central Europe and Latin America reveal that the processes of '(democratic) transition' and 'consolidation' represent two different steps in the course of regime change. The distinction is based on both temporal and substantive factors. It is important to address both of them in order to clarify the theoretical approach adopted in this book, which tends to regard the process of regime change as a continuum made up of different dimensions that are intertwined but do not necessarily follow a temporal order. Transition and consolidation are generally seen as successive phases of the overall democratisation process, whereby one (authoritarian) regime is abandoned in favour of another clearly recognisable one. As such, according to the democratisation literature, consolidation is completed after transition, although it may start at one or more levels while transition is still in progress. The mainstream literature emphasises the more or less rigid benchmarks that, from the point of view of substance, signal the end of the transition phase and the beginning of consolidation. The first benchmark concerns the tasks that 'ought to be accomplished' by the transition. According to Pridham, 'transition tasks involve above all negotiating the constitutional settlement and setting the rules of procedure for political competition as well as for dismantling authoritarian agencies and abolishing laws unsuitable for democratic life' (Pridham 2001a: 5). This is a clear definition of democratic transition leading to a situation in which a new constitution is in place, the rule of law is secured, democratic structures are formally settled, and a certain consensus at the elite level has been reached. Thus, transitions are usually processes involving change at the political level. This process of change is ultimately driven by the interplay at the elite level (both old and new ones) that shape the new consensus and by a number of constitutional tasks. Constellations of actors at the elite level are widely regarded as decisive for the onset and evolution of transition processes. The transition literature argues that transition can only take place when a split in the regime elite takes place. Such a split is likely to occur after major events, such as an economic crisis, a lost war, or other critical events that undermine the legitimacy of the regime. Temporarily, democratic transitions can be – and indeed have been – accomplished in a limited period of time, around a half decade, although this is not absolute as some transitions have taken much longer, for example, in the Balkans (Olsen 2010).

Transition and consolidation are two distinct moments and may be separated by a significant time period during which uncertainty prevails. Empirical evidence shows that most democracies have made at least one false step towards democracy and then relapsed into undemocratic rule before subsequently succeeding in remaining democratic for at least two generations (Haerpfer, Bernhagen, Inglehart, and Welzel 2009: 19). Consolidation of the new democratic regime, characterised by more far-ranging economic transformations as well as, in a large number of cases, state and nation building, requires a longer timeframe – at minimum a decade – and has wider and usually deeper effects. Not only does it complete the tasks of the transition by eliminating the remaining uncertainties, e.g., in elite behaviour and civilian-military relations, but more importantly it leads to the internalisation of rules and procedures and the penetration of democratic values into the fabric of society via the emergence and/or consolidation of civil society. Consolidation thus involves a wider range of actors (Dawisha and Parrott 1997; Gunther, Diamandouros, and Puhle 1995). Juan Linz and Alfred Stepan (1996) argue that democratic consolidation is achieved when 'democracy is the only game in town'. Similarly, Larry Diamond (1999) treats consolidation as the process through which the democratic regime gains broad and deep legitimation to the point that any alternative is ruled out. From the discussion above, it emerges that the prevailing understanding of transition (and consolidation) is directly linked to the theories of democratisation that provide the conceptual framework for explaining the complex processes associated with regime change. The emphasis on democracy as the final outcome of the transition is the common denominator of a range of theories that assess regime change. Depending on the explanatory factors taken into account, these theories can be distinguished into four groups: the functionalist, the genetic, the interactive, and the transnational, according to the classification proposed by Pridham (2000a). The first group of theories draws from the modernisation approach claiming that economic progress provides a favourable milieu for democracy. Functionalist theories have been able to capture the interplay between the development of socio-economic conditions and the dynamics of political democratisation (Rustow 1970). The correlation between economic development and democracy was stated by Lipset in his original article and then reaffirmed through the 1980s and 1990s following the widespread shift to democracy in a number of regions in the world (Lipset 1959; Rueschemeyer, Stephens, and Stephens 1992). A sociocultural version of functionalist theories maintains that some social and cultural environments are more conducive than others to the establishment of democracy (Almond and Verba 1963). The Arab world and its prospects for democratisation have often been discussed through the prism of functionalist theories. This has led to an emphasis on the cultural and even religious limits to a home-grown process of democratisation (Hashemi 2009). This group of theories, and its ramifications, have invariably been criticised for being overly deterministic and for espousing a linear and unidirectional view of political development, almost exclusively stemming from material factors.

At the opposite end of the spectrum ranging from socio-economic structural conditions to agency lies the group of theories that goes under the name of 'genetic theories'. Many transitologists have identified themselves with and contributed to developing this approach (Karl and Schmitter 1991; O'Donnell 2001). It directs attention at the strategies and decisions of the political elites, which determine the pace and breadth of the transition itself. In a nutshell, genetic theories stress the central role of actors, particularly political elites, while structural preconditions, if considered, tend to be regarded as background factors. Various examples of this group of theories emphasise contingent elements, political crafting – including pactism and strategic calculations and choices – elite settlement, and the style and means of decision-making as a direct result of the quality of leadership. As such, they have been criticised on several grounds for being too elitist. The need to bring a wider array of actors whose behaviours concur in determining the outcome of the transition into the picture has led to the development of a broader framework for the democratisation process as a whole and not just the transition stage. 'Interactive theories' allow for a fruitful combination of functionalist and genetic approaches in that they try to address the following question: to what extent do historical conditions, e.g., specific socio-economic factors that are part and parcel of past legacies, impact on the present and shape the new regime and its actions? This approach also tends to widen the scope of the actors involved in the transition (and ensuing consolidation) beyond elite and state actors. State-society relations, including the nature of the conflict between the two, are brought back into the picture, and bottom-up pressures stemming from the society are treated alongside elite competition, conflicts, and pacts as fundamental drivers of the transition (Bermeo 1997). The emergence of civil society as one of the most significant forces in Eastern and Central European transitions has provided fertile ground for studies that are concerned with the interplay between top-down decisions and bottom-up mobilisation (Beissinger 2002).

Finally, transnational theories point to a complex array of actors, both domestic and external, to explain democratisation. One of the basic arguments developed by transnational theories concerns the extent to which the external environment, conceptualised as a wide array of actors and influences, can impose a set of constraints and opportunities onto domestic processes.[2] A number of concepts that have been developed by these theories, e.g., 'diffusion', 'contagion', 'waves' of democratisation,[3] 'demonstration effect', 'convergence', and 'conditionality', have proven useful for appreciating the importance of cross-national factors and influences on domestic change (or lack thereof).[4] The democratisation wave theory, with its two-way interactions between domestic and external factors, whereby individual transitions in the same period and geographical area are bound to impact on each other, has provided useful explanations of the events of 1989–1991 given its focus on the regional context. Nevertheless, transnational theories are less able than others to estimate cause and effect and to formulate generalisations about the relations between external and domestic actors, thus limiting themselves to developing ad-hoc explanations.

Transition of what? A multi-level analysis

The term 'transition' is usually considered synonymous with crossing over to democracy and is thus interpreted in a narrow sense. This is the case, for example, of the definition provided by Morlino:[5]

> transition can be said to commence when limited pluralism breaks down and the civil and political rights characterizing every democratic regime begin to be recognized. It can be considered over when the democratic direction taken by the transition is evident, and when the concrete possibility of establishing a democracy can clearly be seen.
>
> (Morlino 2011: 84)

At what point can we see the democratic direction signalling the end of the transition? The author answers this question by pointing to 'the first free, competitive, and fairly run elections held in the country, although the democratic turn is already evident before elections take place' (Morlino 2011: 84). However, looking at the electoral moment as the final act of the transition and the successful achievement of democracy obscures more than it reveals. Furthermore, the moment that separates the actual transition from the instauration of the new democratic regime is usually referred to in the literature as 'democratic installation'. Involving the complete expansion and genuine recognition of civil and political rights, as well as the drawing up and adoption of the main democratic procedures and institutions that will characterise the new regime, the concept of democratic installation, understood as an alternative or possibly subsequent process with respect to the liberalisation that characterises transition, introduces a further element of democratic determinism into the discussion of transition processes.

However, this is not the only definition that has been offered to this concept. Some authors have stressed the open-endedness of transition processes, meaning that democracy is not necessarily the end point (O'Donnell, Schmitter, and Whitehead 1986).[6] This comes from the revelation that authoritarian regimes can end without necessarily resulting in the attainment of democracy.[7] What matters is the process itself, here identified in terms of institutional development. Transition processes are indeed characterised by more or less profound changes at the institutional level. The beginning of the transition is therefore identified as being the beginning of institutional development processes. Evidence of this can be some change at the apex of the political system or the revision of the constitution. The unfolding of the transition and the different transition paths experienced by each polity have a direct impact on the prospects and outcomes of the process itself. In turn, transition styles are influenced by significant dissimilarities in the types of regime that collapsed, their structures and policies, and by the occurrence of forms of pre-transition liberalisation in some countries and not in others. Cross-national variation observed in the early transitions across Eastern and Central Europe shows that different systems responded differently to common dilemmas, chose different institutional arrangements, and proceeded at a different pace (Pridham 2001a: 2–3). All in all, this resulted in quite different forms of outcome. Although it is generally recognised in the literature that it is the first decade that is vital in determining regime change outcomes, it is in the shorter timeframe of two to three years that the bulk of the political and institutional transition is carried out.

By conceptualising transitions as open-ended processes, at least two dimensions of analysis can be accommodated by focusing on their dynamic qualities instead of treating them as qualitatively and temporally mutually exclusive. These dimensions interconnect backwards and forwards while change and continuity interact in a dynamic fashion. Drawing from Pridham (2001a: 10–19), the first dimension is that of authoritarian breakdown, the motives behind it, and the actors that made it possible. In almost all the transitions to democracy of the 1980s and 1990s, societal mobilisation occupied a significant position during the demise of the authoritarian regimes (O'Donnell *et al.* 1986). Thus, the literature analysing democratic transition processes emphasises the role of non-violent mass opposition in bringing them down. Ordinary people struggling against reluctant elites proved successful as they mobilised in such numbers and so ubiquitously that state authorities could not suppress them easily. This view seems to be confirmed by the Arab uprisings and their significance in paving the way for the transitions. These uprisings were spontaneous, mostly without leadership, and cut across different socio-economic and religious cleavages. According to the literature on social movements, four factors can explain what set the protests in motion: existing grievances – corruption, repression, economic hardship; emotional triggering factors/psychological empowerment; a sense of impunity; and access to new social media (Collier 1999; Beissinger 2007; Bayat 2009; Johnston 2011). A fifth factor that should be added concerns the role of the military in bridging the popular mobilisation phase and the transition phase.

None of these factors alone is sufficient to explain the incidence and outcome of mass protests, i.e., the collapse of the old regime or the sustained crackdown on demonstrators. Comparative democratisation literature oscillates between two positions: on the one hand, there are those who argue that authoritarian breakdown can take place only when changes do not impinge on the livelihood, interests, and influence of the incumbent elites. In other words, when the opposition succeeds in moderating its demands and in finding interlocutors within the regime, then a sort of 'conservative transformation' of the regime from authoritarianism to democracy is possible (O'Donnell et al. 1986: 69). Such a transformation is thus possible via elite pacts and bargaining between the regime opposition and the reform camp in the regime elite. According to this elitist view, mass anti-regime mobilisation is not only unnecessary for transition processes but even endangers them as it is likely to trigger the regime elite to close ranks and undertake repressive measures. On the other hand, others contend that chances for democratic transition are delivered 'from above' by elite interactions, but won 'from below' by mass mobilisation (Wood 2001: 863). These two perspectives can be reconciled when one takes into account institutional development processes in which both negotiations and conflicts take place.

The second dimension is that of the transition understood as institutional development. Despite marked differences in the patterns of mobilisation and self-organisation, a unifying trend in the democratic transition processes of the 1980s and 1990s was the successive shift of focus from the often spontaneous mobilisation of societal actors to old and new, generally traditional, political actors (parties, parliaments, bureaucracies) commanding the substantial legal, administrative, political, and economic resources needed to entrench themselves and to lead the transition through its various steps, i.e., the drafting of new constitutional texts, the establishment of new institutions, and the holding of elections. With existing power and institutional vacuums being filled by these actors, new constraints tend to be imposed on the actions of other intermediate groups that had participated in the phase of authoritarian breakdown. This reinforces the argument according to which it is important to decouple authoritarian breakdown from the process of transition, both in terms of the actors involved and the actions undertaken. Authoritarian breakdown and transition represent two distinct processes in the sense that the former can be understood as the point of arrival of the preceding configuration of power and its contradictions, while the latter is projected towards the unknown. As pointedly observed by Eva Bellin, 'while the elimination of autocracy must precede democratic transition chronologically, the two processes are analytically distinct' (Bellin 2012: 143). While popular mobilisation is sometimes important to precipitate changes in the existing regime and power relations, the actual transition takes place under the tutelage of the elites which, often through intense struggles and negotiations, influence the direction, pace, and final outcome of institutional development. The centrality of elites is asserted in light of their fundamental role in mobilising and channelling the action coming from the rest of the population. In this way the elites become the tip of the iceberg, representing larger groups and different claims and proposing solutions to the problems that emerge during the transition. Substantial attention is devoted to statecraft, namely to the purposeful action by political leaders and elites to shape outcomes. New institutional arrangements will only be adopted if they are compatible with the desires, beliefs, and technical and political opportunities of actors within the system. In light of their role, specific elites can emerge as 'anchors' in transition processes (Morlino 1998).

By 'elite' I mean people who are close to or command power or have a particular expertise. In this category I include the leadership of the traditional party organisations or other institutions such as the judiciary and the military establishment. So as to avoid too elitist an approach and to broaden the scope of this analysis, however, I also place in this category the leadership of all other groups, e.g., social movements, civil society organisations, and business groups, as well as influential figures that do not act on behalf of a group but are able to influence decisions. These elites act on different grounds and for different purposes.[8] During the transition, intra-elite behaviour produces a number of institutional outcomes that are based on interest calculations as well as unintended consequences. Intra-elite behaviour includes pactism,[9] co-optation, and confrontation (Linz and Stepan 1978; Przeworski 1991). At the same time, elites have to interact with a broad range of actors from society. The creation of a bond between political parties and society is a difficult task, particularly in countries where public authorities enjoy limited trust and legitimacy as a result of the authoritarian legacy. According to Collier and Collier (1991), distinct modes of incorporating civil society organisations into politics shape the political arena and the transition process itself. The role of elites and other societal actors in shaping the transition needs to be appreciated next to the constraints and opportunities provided by the set of institutions undergoing transition. The emphasis on institutions and their development is therefore functional in closing the gap between structure and agency, neither of which can, alone, explain complex social and political phenomena.

Institutional development

Transition is here regarded as entailing the transformation or manipulation of the old authoritarian institutions and the crafting and establishment of new ones. Any political, economic, and social system is made up of a broad range of structures, i.e., the institutions. Existing definitions of 'institutions' abound. According to Schattschneider (1960), institutions organise actors, issues, and resources in or out of politics and structure patterns of political struggle. Kiser and Ostrom define 'institutions' as 'the rules used by individuals for determining who and what are included in decision situations, how information is structured, what actions can be taken and in what sequence, and how individual actions will be aggregated into collective decisions' (Kiser and Ostrom 1982: 179). This definition emphasises the role of institutions as 'rules of the game' shaping any kind of action. Other definitions, for example the one provided by Terry Karl (1990), stress the understanding of institutions as social products, rules, and procedures, sources of constraints and opportunities that influence preferences and policy choices. Peter Hall's widely used definition speaks of institutions at a very high level of abstraction and generalisation in that he includes in this category 'the formal rules, compliance procedures, and standard operating practices that structure the relationship between individuals in various units of the polity and economy' (Hall 1986: 19). This wording is similar to another one of the most neutral definitions of 'institutions' available in the literature, the one developed by March and Olsen, which treats them as a 'set of routines, procedures, conventions, rules, strategies, organizational forms and technologies around which political activity is constructed' (March and Olsen 1989: 22). In a nutshell, institutions are the essence of politics as they regulate the allocation of power resources. Samuel Huntington in *Political Order in Changing Societies* assesses transition through the lenses of institutionalisation processes, namely the processes by which organisational structures 'acquire value and stability' (Huntington 1968: 12).

Attention to institutional factors has revived since the late 1970s out of a critique of the behavioural emphasis of (particularly American) comparative politics during the previous two decades. Latent, enduring socio-economic and political structures that play a role in moulding behaviours in distinctive ways in different contexts have been brought back to the surface. More generally, the emphasis has been placed on the extent to which any kind of political action is mediated by the institutional setting in which it takes place. The way in which institutions work is two-fold: on the one hand, institutions constrain or allow certain political actions by raising or reducing their costs and by setting the parameters for policy-making. On the other hand, institutions act as a constellation of incentives and constraints and thus shape the goals political actors pursue and influence their strategies by privileging some and putting others at a disadvantage (Hall 1986). This second, more complex channel through which the impact of institutions on political outcomes can be appreciated tends to emphasis the 'relational character' of institutions, i.e., the fact that one of the most important features of institutions is that they shape the political interactions through which power is constantly redistributed and traded (Hall 1986; Thelen and Steinmo 1992).

Explaining the persistence of cross-national differences in political outcomes and policies despite common challenges and pressures by assessing different configurations of institutions was a central theme for the authors of the neo-institutionalist school (Hall and Taylor 1996; Remmer 1997; Hall and Soskice 2001; Pierson and Skocpol 2002; Capoccia and Kelemen 2007). This research agenda has been broadly pursued by both rational choice models and historical institutional analyses with quite marked differences between the two (Pierson 2004). On the one hand, authors belonging to the rational choice current usually emphasise the rationality of actors as a precondition for the influence exercised by institutions over their actions through the shaping of strategies. They adopt an actor-centred approach and work backwards from extant institutional arrangements to develop an account of how these institutions have been rationally chosen (North 1990). On the other hand, historical institutionalists tend to explain political outcomes by taking a combination of agency and self-reproducing and self-sustaining structures into account, as well as the impact of social environments that are constantly changing. Drawing from the potential offered by the historical institutional approach, the role of structures in setting boundaries to human action is mediated by a strong focus on agency. Structural elements, in other words, are the outcome – unintended or conscious – of the actors' strategies, conflicts, and choices and ultimately influence them. This explains why battles over institutions occupy such a central stage in the various arenas of policy.

During the transition, new and old elites are constrained by surviving institutions – what Olsen identifies as institutional inertia or resistance to change (Olsen 2010: 119) – while actors create the institutional structures of the new regime. In cases of abrupt change, which can result from broad endogenous or exogenous socio-economic and political shifts, political actors adjust their strategies and goals to accommodate changes in the institutions. Changes in institutional arrangements are often unintentional and can produce unexpected consequences. This can be explained by three factors related to the nature of political agency, conflict, and power asymmetries. First, a high degree of turnover in elite configurations means that those who participate in changing the institutional framework are not necessarily the same individuals who will engage in later power struggles (Linz 2000). Second, the difference between short-term and long-term implications of institutional development cannot be discounted. While institutions are generally 'designed' to be difficult to overturn so as to reduce uncertainty and enhance stability, thus facilitating forms of cooperation and exchange that would otherwise be difficult to achieve, political actors, especially politicians, are usually motivated by their short-term interests and pursue actions that tend to discount long-term consequences (Pierson 2004: 41–44). Finally, learning processes would be useful for the actors to accommodate their actions to changing circumstances but they are hindered by the complexity and opacity of politics (Morlino 2011: 107–108; Pierson 2004: 37–40).

Institutional legacy

Although rejecting institutional determinism, the existing historical institutional literature tends to think of institutions as bureaucracies that are conservative and biased towards continuity. Yet, the importance of institutional formation and development in processes spanning time goes well beyond the fact that institutions matter in themselves to account for the ways in which institutions are the product of human action and as such can be changed over time. This dynamic factor in the analysis of institutional formation and development resonates powerfully with the research agenda set out by Paul Pierson in his *Politics in Time* (2004). Unpacking the claim that 'history matters' is fundamental for thinking more explicitly about the role of time in politics. With regard to the transitions from authoritarianism, it means illustrating how the meaning and function of institutions can change over time, producing new and sometimes unexpected outcomes. Since institutions are human products, they require continuously renewed collective confirmation and validation of their constitutive rules, meanings, and resources. As a result, all institutions tend to experience challenges and some turn out to be fragile and unable to reproduce themselves. This is when institutional development comes in. Some institutions are easy to change, for example some legal provisions can be declared null or a parliament dissolved. Others are more resilient to change and are thus more durable, continuing to frame the action of actors even when new and potentially conflicting institutions have been established. Examples of this kind of enduring institutions are traditional social structures and informal institutions.

The distinction between formal and informal institutions is thus a meaningful one. Formal institutional structures, including those spelled out in constitutional provisions, such as governments, parliaments, parties, and bureaucracies, do not exhaust the range of institutions that constitute the skeleton of a state (Shugart and Carey 1992; Stepan and Skatch 1993; Linz 1994; Sartori 1997). More enduring, informal institutions are equally important. I refer here to values, behaviours, and practices that, in order to be considered institutions, need to be shared, accepted, and repeated often outside of or in contrast to formal institutional architectures.[10] When talking of institutions, then, it is important to refer to both institutional structures and logics, i.e., socialised norms or behaviours. The concept of informal institutions recalls the notion of 'habitus' introduced and specified by Bourdieu (1984). Bourdieu sees power as culturally and symbolically created and constantly re-legitimised through an interplay of agency and structure. The main way this happens is through what he calls 'habitus' or socialised norms and tendencies that guide behaviour and thinking. Broadly speaking, habitus is the process by which a certain behaviour or belief becomes part of a society's structure when the original purpose of that behaviour and belief can no longer be recalled. The resilience of crony-capitalistic, neo-patrimonial, and clientelistic relations or specific religious habits provide an example of institutions shaping behaviours in a way that it is often difficult to dislodge (Lust-Okar 2008). Analyses of authoritarian systems must thus necessarily deal with informal institutions such as these 'hidden structures'. These are rooted in well-entrenched practices and balances of power that shape the preferences and goals of actors, and interact with formal institutions, often depriving them of content and meaning. In this light, informal institutions are 'critical to regime maintenance for authoritarian elites' (Cook 2007: 134). The distinction between formal and informal institutions becomes even more salient in the context of transition processes in which changes at the level of formal institutions may co-exist with continuities at that of informal institutions. Change of informal institutions is often a much longer process and during the transition phase new formal institutions may collide with remnants of the old informal institutions that take a long time to die out. However, sometimes profound changes in informal institutions may be precursors of long-sought transformations at the formal institutional level. The multi-faceted nature of institutions makes the process of institutional development complex and time-consuming. It is mainly a matter of changing behaviours, mentalities, procedures, and ways of working. It is often a question of more or less covert collisions between procedural reforms and actions of a repetitive and foreseeable nature – shades of 'we've always done it like this', positions of power, and vested interests.

By adopting a dynamic conception of institutional formation and development, i.e., processes of de-institutionalisation and re-institutionalisation, it is possible to account for variation in institutional frameworks and political outcomes across countries as well as over time. In other words, to explore how specific patterns of institutional development structure particular kinds of politics. So far, historical institutionalism has been especially helpful in pointing out cross-national differences and the persistence of institutional patterns. This is what Thelen and Steinmo have defined 'the study of comparative statics; that is, [the explication] of different policy outcomes in different countries with reference to their respective (stable) institutional configurations' (Thelen and Steinmo 1992: 14). By engaging with institutional development processes within individual countries – a rather rare kind of analysis due to the prevailing emphasis on continuity rather than change – this research thus contributes to filling the gap in the study of comparative politics and to moving from the 'snapshot' view of political life to 'moving pictures', in Pierson's words (2004: 2). While during periods of institutional stability institutions are independent variables and explain political outcomes, when institutions themselves are transformed they become dependent variables, whose shape is determined by the conflicts, negotiations, and pacts among the actors. However, even when institutions break down or are subject to reconfiguration, they are never entirely rebuilt from scratch. This is identified in the literature as 'layering', involving 'the partial renegotiation of some elements of a given set of institutions while leaving others in place' (Thelen 2003: 225). In some cases, layering may also suggest that existing institutional arrangements may remain intact, but other institutions are added, often modifying the functioning of the pre-existing ones. Finally, layering may also involve the creation of 'parallel' institutional tracks. All in all, both changes and continuities play an important role in explaining institutional development and impact on political outcomes.

In the context of transition processes, when institutions resist change and piecemeal adaptation prevails, continuities in modes of authoritarian governance can be observed. If this is the case, various authoritarian agencies are likely to retain substantial political and coercive resources. Alternatively, new actors come into play who pursue their (new) goals through existing institutions. This is what Thelen calls 'institutional conversion' (Thelen 2003: 226). Furthermore, since the meaning of formal rules must be interpreted and multiple interpretations are often plausible, the role performed by a certain set of institutions and/or the functions they serve may change even in the absence of formal revision. All in all, the Arab transitions best illustrate patterns in which changes in the institutional frameworks set in motion political struggles *within* the boundaries of the institutions themselves and *over* their meaning and functioning. In conclusion, a certain degree of continuity accompanying change is a central feature of any transition from authoritarianism. This continuity (or lack thereof) corresponds to the institutional legacy of the previous regime and creates the boundaries and parameters of the space in which elites operate (Hite and Morlino 2004; Pridham 2000b). As specified above, institutional legacies can manifest themselves under the guise of persisting social, cultural, and religious practices and values. More explicitly, these legacies can be reflected in untouched power hierarchies, with the same people occupying the same positions as under the previous authoritarian regime. The interplay between remnants of the old institutions' constraining top-down statecraft and bottom-up mobilisation and new institutions providing new opportunities and constraints for the actors' choices and actions represents the core of this research. Given the uncertainty, indeterminacy, and open-ended character of transition processes, the phase in which old and new structures and actors co-exist can vary in length, thus creating the conditions for contradictions, conflicts, explicit or tacit agreements, and competition at multiple levels. Drawing from a key work on transitions, uncertainty derives from the fact that 'it is characteristic of the transition that during it the rules of the political game are not defined. Not only are they in constant flux, but they are usually arduously contested' (O'Donnell *et al.* 1986: 6).

Time, timing, and sequencing

All this points to the fact that change and continuity are not in themselves homogeneous categories. In particular, institutional change can happen at multiple levels and in different forms. Even when dealing with long-term historical structures, i.e., the institutions, it is important to consider that change can be broken down into micro-change, on the one hand, and macro-change, on the other. Moving from the work of Penelope J. Corfield, the former corresponds to 'momentum' or gradual change, while the latter is defined as 'turbulence' (Corfield 2007). This allows a more nuanced understanding of the impact of time on long-term historical processes than the departing point offered by Braudel's seminal work on the *longue durée* (Braudel 1958). Distinguishing between micro-change and macro-change provides the ground to better appreciate the importance of contingency as opposed to path-dependence. Both are crucial concepts of historical institutional analyses (Thelen 2003; Lawson 2006). Applied to institutional development, the latter encompasses both continuity and micro-change, the argument being that institutions often generate slow, predictable reproduction or absence of change as a result of self-reinforcing mechanisms. In contrast, the former, i.e., contingency, entails that macro-change can happen as a result of unforeseen factors, thus causing turbulence over the course of institutional development. The importance of contingency in explaining changes (or lack thereof) in institutional development is also linked to the role of agency and of external factors. All in all, path-dependence and contingency are both at play during institutional development. As the following empirical chapters demonstrate, seemingly contradictory processes of institutional continuity and change happen together. To better appreciate them and the extent to which micro-change and macro-change co-exist in the context of transitions processes, questions of timing and sequencing are of great importance.

More than the duration of the transition – in itself an important dimension – it is the timing of the different steps of the transition that matters the most (Whitehead 2002). It is argued here that when an institution is transformed is at least as important as the direction in which it is transformed. This is relevant not only to processes that span a long period of time – such as the empirical analyses provided by Skocpol (1979) and others – but also, and particularly, to short-term processes. In the latter case, it is indeed one of the most significant factors explaining different outcomes. Similar institutional choices, tailored to the problems and needs of a given country undergoing transition, can have totally different impacts depending on the timing of these choices. Applying this argument to the actual processes that are the object of this research, one can claim that the Egyptian and Tunisian transitions, other differences notwithstanding, tend to confirm the importance of timing as a fundamental variable explaining their outcomes. Furthermore, the issue of timing adds substance to the very key point that there is no such magic formula that can work everywhere. Institutional choices can make a difference, but they do not make the same difference in all instances of transitions.

Similarly, when a particular event in a sequence occurs, it makes a big difference, meaning that early stages in a sequence can place particular aspects of political systems, including institutional arrangements, onto a specific track, which is then reinforced through time. The sequence of events constituting a transition can be split into different units. To some extent, they correspond to the dimensions identified above, i.e., authoritarian breakdown, followed by the actual transition. However, these units are not defined (only) by their temporal sequence. What matters is their substance. A fundamental concept of my research is that of 'turning points', which are similar to the 'critical junctures' that occupy a central position in historical institutional explanations (Capoccia and Kelemen 2007). Turning points are key ('critical') moments for the transition, moments in which the pace and direction of institutional development are questioned, institutions undergo radical transformations or preserve the status quo, and/or long-nurtured changes in the informal institutions manifest themselves, influencing the depth and direction of change of formal institutions. In other words, turning points tend to place institutional development on paths or trajectories that are then difficult to alter. Transition can thus be interpreted as a sequence of turning points. The substance of these pivotal units, for example the change and continuity associated with 'founding elections', and the sequencing of the turning points are essential factors to be taken into account in the analysis of transition processes. The relevance of the factor of time[11] in analysing transition processes also stems from the uncertainty mentioned earlier and the fact that institutions can undergo different changes at different stages of the process. To capture this, diachronic comparisons based on cross-temporal variations, namely comparing the same institution at different moments in time, are combined with synchronic comparisons,[12] defined by Stefano Bartolini (1993: 162) as 'slides of synchronic comparisons through time'. This makes it possible to appreciate the complexity and open-endedness of transition processes.

Overcoming the mirage state: developing inclusive institutions

Institutional engineering

Moving from the theoretical framework above, the following chapters assess the impact of institutional development on the short-to-medium term evolution of a political system undergoing transition. To accomplish this goal, they delve into the concept and substance of institutional engineering, which represents the central phase of the transition. Institutional engineering refers to the steps to craft 'appropriate institutions' (Vermeule 2007). In some works, the major concern is with the products rather than the process. It has been asserted that certain formats for organising power tend to provide advantages and better prospects for the successful delivery of the transition (Stepan and Skatch 1993; Bellamy 1996). The abundant literature on institutional engineering disqualifies this rigid view and indicates that the products of these processes do not have identical effects – be it in magnitude or in direction – in all polities (Zielonka 2001). This is due to the existence of different social cleavages, levels of economic development, and previous forms of autocracy and the impact of external factors. What can be tested in different contexts across time and space is the process whereby institutions are engineered, which corresponds to assessing changes and continuities in the institutional framework.

Institutional engineering can be broken down into a number of components. Each component interacts with the other in a dynamic way, and changes in one factor directly or indirectly influence the other components. The first component is the constitution-making process. The constitution contains the overarching meta-rules of a political system. It is the result of the attempt to bring coherence, order, and stability to the multitude of 'partial regimes' that compose the system itself. Not only does it lay out an explicit matrix of institutions and a formal distribution of their powers and competencies, but it also sets the norms that regulate transactions among a wide range of actors. While defining a comprehensive legal system delimiting the powers of the institutions is an important task, it is not enough, particularly in a phase of uncertainty. The drafting of a constitution entails a power struggle in itself involving decisions about the distribution of power. This is the dimension that holds the strongest potential for explanation, namely the way in which different groups, represented by parties, associations, movements, and clienteles, seek to influence the process of constitution making. Due to the ensuing conflicts among these groups, constitutions often enshrine a number of contradictions resulting from compromises. These contradictions also point to the complex interplay between change and continuity, since the resulting constitutional documents may fail to distinguish themselves from whatever remains of the old regime. The more protracted the constitution-making process, the greater the contradictions in the constitutional provisions (Zielonka 2001: 14). These contradictions can to a greater or lesser extent undermine the transition process or be accommodated into the system.

The second component regards the electoral law and the party system, and their impact on elections. Elite conflicts are mediated by political parties. Under authoritarian conditions, ruling parties play a fundamental role in sustaining elite coalitions for the sake of regime survival. Once the transition is underway, political parties play an equally important role in the phase of institutional engineering. They represent and aggregate interests and preferences, and institutionalise change. Two key variables in assessing the process of institutional development are the electoral formula used to allocate seats and the features of the party system.[13] Electoral laws are directly linked to the distribution of power and are therefore highly controversial. The main criteria for the evaluation of the electoral formula according to the research on comparative electoral systems are: '*representation* of votes from the population, *concentration* of the party system and the impact on voter *participation*' (von Beyme 2001: 141, emphasis in the original; Cox 1999). I would add that another important feature of electoral laws as far as countries undergoing transition are concerned is the legitimacy of the rules, or rather the perception of it (Taagepera 2002: 253). In turn, the party system can be measured in terms of such criteria as fragmentation, polarisation, and volatility. The features of the electoral law and of the party system can best be captured during the so-called 'founding elections' (O'Donnell *et al.* 1986). These elections represent a fundamental moment for the transition as they are the motor of party system development, with new parties emerging.

Founding elections and elections in general are an essential moment in transition, from both the procedural and substantive points of view. First, elections are instruments of administrative efficiency, which is needed to establish a register of eligible voters, define constituency boundaries, confirm or disqualify candidacies, set up polling stations, count votes, and apply the electoral formula. Second, they require and at the same time advance freedom of association and assembly, the rule of law, and a sense of political community. Furthermore, they are also the starting point of the chain of accountability. Free and fair elections are predicated upon the notion of subsequent electoral moments, ensuring that power resides with the people, providing them with the means to judge the quality and responsiveness of their representatives and to ensure the orderly succession of governments. As with the process of constitution making, the role of elections in polities undergoing transition is often unduly overemphasised. Excessive emphasis on elections risks falling prey to the 'electoralist fallacy' (Linz and Stepan 1996: 4). Elections may indeed provide a façade hiding the real locus of power. Linz and Stepan provide an illuminating example of this type of 'electoralist non-transition', namely when 'the military retains extensive prerogatives [so] that the democratically elected government is not even *de jure* sovereign' (Linz and Stepan 1996: 4).

In addition to these two components of institutional engineering, it is also important to consider other features of the institutional framework and its development in the countries undergoing transition. This is for example the case of the judiciary. A significant part of the transition process deals with the actions and institutions responsible for the control over the implementation, rather than the formulation, of rules. The judiciary is one of such institutions whose primary task is to grant all citizens unfettered access to justice for the redress of grievances, including complaints against the state itself and its agencies. The functioning of this institution involves a wide range of actors responsible for enforcing compliance with the law and punishing those who do not. The internal organisation of the judicial system includes a wide array of courts – ordinary courts, penal or criminal courts, constitutional and cassation courts – populated by judges, public prosecutors, attorneys general, and legal inspectors. While an articulated legal system often exists in authoritarian regimes, its effectiveness is quite a different matter, since, by definition, its autonomy should be paramount but often is not. Autonomy means that the judiciary is independent of any type of influence and control by political power. In the Arab countries, both the legislative and executive authorities have often undertaken actions aimed at curbing the independence and powers of the judiciary. Such intrusion has regularly been sanctioned by constitutional texts or ordinary legislation regulating appointments and transfers, freedom of expression, or salaries. Violations of the judiciary's independence has also manifested itself in the repeated renewals of the emergency laws that have been in place in most of these countries for long contiguous periods.

Deeply intertwined with the judicial function is the concept (and practice) of the rule of law. This is a central ingredient in the transition of any country trying to achieve democracy (Maravall and Przeworski 2003). At the same time it has had resonance with the Arab demonstrators protesting against the authoritarian regimes. The rule of law is seen as fulfilling two primary functions: a) protecting against arbitrary rule by imposing certain limitations, checks, and balances on the exercise of state power, and b) facilitating human agency by providing individuals with a predictable system of rules that allows them to calculate the legal consequences of their actions. In abstract terms, the rule of law posits predictability, certainty, and legal security both between the state and individuals (vertical) and among individuals (horizontal). The first attribute of the rule of law is particularly salient in the context of the countries undergoing transition from authoritarianism, and it requires that all citizens, including public officials, must abide by the law. A deficit in the rule of law in the interaction between public officials and individuals manifests itself through arbitrary treatment, unpredictability and inconsistency, discrimination, and a lack of access to justice. In some cases, a deficit in the rule of law emanates from problems inherent in the constitution, e.g., excessive powers granted to the executive or strong centralisation. This brings me to stress that the origin of the law is another fundamental issue to be addressed. In other words, where does the law come from? Where does the authority of the people in charge of drafting the law come from? Conflicts between different interpretations of or would-be monopolies over the rule of law are paramount during transition processes.

Finally, another important feature of the institutional framework pertains to civilian-military relations. Designing robust and legitimate civilian-military institutions is a fundamental step for countries undergoing transition. The literature on the matter stresses that the main goal should be to ensure that the military apparatus is capable of responding to internal and external threats, yet unable to disproportionately influence the civilian leadership. As demonstrated in the seminal work by Samuel Huntington, *The Soldier and the State: The Theory and Practice of Civil-Military Relations*, the military must be subject to the control of legitimate civilian authorities. According to the author, the solution lies in the establishment of 'objective civilian control' (Huntington 1981). Civilian authorities are responsible for devising national security goals and budgets, while the military, as an apolitical professional organisation, has the responsibility for determining the specific details required for their implementation. Moving from Stepan's (1988) thinking about the 'military as an institution', it – in the Arab authoritarian regimes, as elsewhere in the world, encompassing multiple branches – can be better understood on the basis of its professionalism and institutionalisation (Forster, Edmunds, and Cottey 2002). Professionalism entails clearly defined roles and a solid expertise by the military in its areas of responsibility. Military institutionalisation (in the Weberian sense), as opposed to patrimonial logics, is:

> where recruitment and promotion are based on performance rather than politics, where there is a clear distinction between the public and the private that forbids predatory behavior vis-à-vis society, where discipline is maintained through the inculcation of a service ethic and the strict enforcement of a merit-based hierarchy rather than cronyism and/or balanced rivalry between primordial groups.
>
> (Bellin 2012: 132–133)

The complexity and multidimensionality of the factors mentioned above is summarised in Table 1.1 with further specifics about the fine-grained elements that will be considered with regard to each of them.

Legitimacy, accountability, and responsiveness

By grasping these elements in the specific cases of Egypt and Tunisia it is possible to assess the impact of institutional development on short-to-medium term political development. By political development I do not necessarily mean 'democracy'. Given the lengthiness of some transition processes and the impossibility of anticipating their outcomes, it is more appropriate to focus on the conditions of unsustainability that were the causes of the Arab uprisings and to derive from them some factors to assess political development. These factors are legitimacy, accountability, and responsiveness. The literature on democratisation treats them as qualities of democracy based on the distinction between procedural and substantive attributes (Diamond and Morlino 2005). Legitimacy, accountability, and responsiveness can be included in the first category as they refer to the functioning

Table 1.1 The institutional framework between engineering and development

Factors of the institutional framework	Specific elements for analysis
CONSTITUTION-MAKING PROCESS	
Role of the constituent assembly/constitutional committee	– previous tradition of constitutional governance and features of the previous Constitution – emergence of claims from ethnic/religious minorities – election or selection of the members of the constitution-drafting body[1] – margin by which decisions are taken – ratification of the document, e.g., popular referendum
Form of government	– powers of the president, e.g., veto, legislative initiative, control over the budget, government formation, government dissolution, assembly dissolution, etc.
Degree of centralisation	– federalism vs. centralisation – powers of the regional governments, e.g., fiscal autonomy, law-making authority, etc.
ELECTORAL POLITICS AND PARTY SYSTEM	
Voters' participation and representation	– type of electoral law, i.e., single member district plurality voting system or proportional representation
Voters' concentration	– size of the constituencies – presence of geographically concentrated minorities – election thresholds
Party system fragmentation	– number of parties – predominance of clear-cut parties or loose coalitions
Party system polarisation	– level of institutionalisation of parties – typology of parties (ideology vs. patronage)
Party system volatility	– changes in the party system between one election and next – votes distribution
JUDICIAL SYSTEM	
Independence of the judiciary	– procedures for appointing or electing judges – duration of the judges' appointments – possibility for judges to hold other state offices or be members of political parties – existence of agencies to control the work of the judges and monitor their independence – level of remuneration of legal personnel and other civil servants
CIVILIAN-MILITARY RELATIONS	
Power of the military apparatus	– degree of professionalism of the military – degree of institutionalisation of the military – existence of economic monopolies and interests
Civilian control over the military	– civilian control over the military apparatus, e.g., over the military budget

Source: author's elaboration.

1 A further element concerns whether the members of the constitution-drafting body are automatically empowered to act as parliamentarians. This might be a problem since the drafters of the constitution would become its immediate beneficiaries, prompting them to grant powers and privileges that they know they will subsequently enjoy as members of the legislative assembly.

mechanisms of a democratic system. The linkage between these factors and the engineering and development of the institutional framework is stressed by the same authors when they argue:

> when we search for explanations for the different levels of democratic qualities, almost all the case studies point to similar factors, such as some socio-economic condition, the *legacy of the past, institutional design,* and the *modes of transition for countries that became democratic more recently.*
> (Diamond and Morlino 2005: xxxvii, emphasis added)

Since legitimacy, accountability, and responsiveness cannot be measured as such, the need for proxies arises. Quite succinctly, I define regime legitimacy at this stage of the transition as dependent on functional requisites, namely the government's performance in protecting the citizens' basic rights and in refraining from resorting to excessive violence against them. Accountability posits that officials must be responsible for their actions to other members of the political community.[14] Elections are the most obvious mechanism of democratic accountability, therefore the latter can be measured via regular alternation in power through the former. Responsiveness to the expectations, interests, needs, and demands of citizens is closely related to vertical accountability, and hence to participation and competition. At the same time, it also stems from the government's ability to make services, material benefits, and other symbolic goods available to its constituencies. As such and in light of the overwhelming socio-economic problems facing the Arab countries, proof of regime responsiveness in the short-to-medium term is sought in the government's ability to respond adequately to the problems of impoverishment, unemployment, and access to basic services of its citizens. Chapter 6 argues at some length that in order to achieve legitimacy, accountability, and responsiveness in the short-to-medium term, the trajectory of institutional development, i.e., the interplay between changes and continuities during times of transition, must go in the direction of developing inclusive institutions. The opposite of inclusive institutions are predatory/extractive institutions that enable the elites to serve their own interests even if they collide with, and prevail over, those of most of the population (Acemoglu and Robinson 2012). This is the single basic illness that has affected Arab polities in many domains over the past few decades.

Structure of the research, methodological note, and case selection

This research aims to cross-fertilise and establish a dialogue between two strands of the literature that have had only limited opportunities for interaction so far: on the one hand, the area studies on the political evolution of the Arab world and, on the other, the literature on democratic transitions. The reason for the scarce interaction between these works lies in the fact that most, if not all, Arab countries have not represented interesting terrain for the analysis of democratic transitions and the factors shaping them, mainly due to the authoritarian features of the regimes that have been in power until recently. The onset of more or less far-ranging transitions involving institutional development that kicked in during 2011 provided new stimuli to researchers to assess the political development of the Arab countries through the lens of (democratic) transition studies.

This research is composed of three macro-sections. The first part provides historical depth to the analysis of the Arab transitions by looking back at the last few decades, particularly the 1990s and 2000s. It considers the uprisings and the ensuing transitions as the point of arrival of long-lasting processes of economic dispossession and impoverishment, political brutality, and growing social inequalities. This evolution, which was enshrined in predatory/extractive institutions at all levels, is traced to identify the structural factors that can explain the uprisings and the end of the apparent stability of the authoritarian regimes, as well as the contextual triggering factors that made the onset of the transitions possible. To pursue these goals, it makes extensive use of the primary and secondary literature on the Arab world and on Arab authoritarianism, its strengths and weaknesses.[15] The second part delves into the processes of institutional development that have taken place in the Arab world, moving from the conceptualisation of 'transition' as a series of open-ended processes. For each case study, it assesses the interplay between structures and actors, change and continuity characterising the onset and development of each factor considered in the institutional framework. The timeframe is the period between 2011 and the beginning of 2014 and diachronic comparisons at different points in time are the main tool used to trace the development path of each institution. Finally, the third part explores the nexus between the institutions analysed in the previous macro-section and the factors linked to political development, i.e., legitimacy, accountability, and responsiveness. By comparing Egypt and Tunisia, the research highlights and discusses the different transition paths of the two countries and their impact on short-to-medium term political development. Special attention is paid to timing and sequencing in the transition processes by analysing synchronic comparisons of institutional development in the different countries.

This research is based on a combination of secondary (official and unofficial documents, newspaper and journal articles, reports, and the relevant literature) and primary sources, primarily elite interviews. The interviews were repeated, with the set of questions gradually expanded, two or three times over the course of the research period, depending on the availability of the interviewees. This is the best way to capture variation over time, bearing in mind that qualitative research (as is the case here) is often progressive. Given my focus on elites, defined using ample criteria, I tried to interview as many people as possible belonging to this group in order to obtain a comprehensive account of the issues at stake. My interlocutors ranged from party and public officials, business elites, and civil society representatives to local and foreign experts, researchers, people from the academic milieu, and journalists. The complete list of interviews is available in the Appendix of the book.

With regard to the choice of the case studies, namely Egypt and Tunisia, they have been selected on the basis of their different transition paths, as they are understood in this research. These cases have also been isolated to capture different levels of political development in the short-to-medium term. They are treated as individual macro-units in the second part of the research, and then the units of analysis – the institutions undergoing development – are further compared across the two cases in the third part. The analysis spans a timeframe of three years, from 2011 to the beginning of 2014. The starting point coincides with the onset of the transitions in Egypt and Tunisia after short-lived but repeated periods of protest. Setting the end of analysis at the beginning of 2014, which does not necessarily coincide with the end of the transition, makes it possible to isolate a three-year period encapsulating the core of these processes. Although the transition may continue for many years, the short-to-medium timeframe covered in this research is crucial as far as the number, pace, and direction of the institutional changes (or lack thereof) are concerned.

To conclude, it is clear from these spatial and temporal coordinates that this research does not aim at reaching universal conclusions. On the one hand, it tends to focus on macro-units (the case studies) that are relatively homogenous, all the important differences highlighted in the next chapters notwithstanding. On the other, as specified above, the timeframe considered is quite limited but at the same time rich in salient events for the future political development of the countries considered. This research can thus be considered a middle range analysis, establishing connections to similar analyses of transitions that have taken place in other geographical or temporal contexts. This is another strength of the historical institutional approach adopted here, namely the possibility of carving out a theoretical niche at the middle range level that allows combining explanations of the contingent nature of political development – with particular emphasis on agency, conflict, and choice – with path-dependence dynamics to advance our understanding of long-term patterns of political history.

Notes

1 Przeworski defines 'transition' as 'a process of institutionalizing uncertainty, of subjecting all interests to uncertainty' (O'Donnell *et al.* 1986: 58).
2 Bearing in mind the distinction between 'transition' and 'consolidation', it emerges that different stages in the regime-change process are prone to different types of external impacts (Pridham 2001b: 63). This means taking into account the way in which the interests of the external actors change as a result of the often disruptive transformations undergone by countries in transition, which sometimes also involve the reconsideration of external alliances and relations.
3 Samuel Huntington defines a 'wave' as 'a group of transitions from non-democratic to democratic regimes that occur within a specified period of time and that significantly outnumber transitions in the opposite direction during that period of time'. See Huntington (1991: 15).
4 For a comprehensive discussion of these concepts, see Schmitter (1995); Whitehead (1996); Pridham (2001a).
5 To be precise, a few lines before Morlino provides another, more dynamic, definition of transition:

> the intermediate period in which a regime has abandoned some key characteristic of the previous institutional arrangements without having acquired all the features of the new regime that will be installed. It is therefore marked by a period of institutional fluidity.
>
> (Morlino 2011: 83)

6 The authors define transition as 'the interval between one political regime and another' (O'Donnell et al. 1986: 6). Incidentally, it should be noted that the definition of 'regime' adopted by the authors stresses the role of institutions in that they claim:

> by it [regime], we mean the ensemble of patterns, explicit or not, that determines the forms and channels of access to principal government positions, the characteristics of the actors who are admitted and excluded from such access, and the resources or strategies that they can use to gain access. This necessarily involves institutionalization, i.e., to be relevant the patterns defining a given regime must be habitually known, practiced, and accepted, at least by those which these same patterns define as participants in the process.
>
> (O'Donnell et al. 1986: 73)

7 Broadly speaking, the literature on authoritarianism and the processes of departure from it has seen two prevailing schools of thought confronting one another. On the one hand, the literature on competitive authoritarianism underscores the durability and resilience of authoritarian structures of power; on the other, the transitologist literature posits a teleological path to democracy. Transitology tends to fail to differentiate between transition from authoritarianism and transition leading to democracy. In other words, it fails to recognise that the collapse of an authoritarian regime is one thing and the establishment of a democratic one another (Mahoney and Thelen 2010).

8 The behaviour of the elites has been assessed in various works. See, for example, Higley and Gunther (1992).

9 Higley and Burton (1989) distinguish between 'elite settlements' (involving an explicit agreement among competing elites) and 'elite convergence' (involving a reduction of conflict and increased cooperation without an explicit, comprehensive settlement). These processes feature an element of elite learning.

10 Douglass North defines institutions as 'humanly devised constraints that structure political, economic, and social interactions' (North 1991: 97). Constraints, as North describes, are seen as formal rules, e.g., constitutions, laws, property rights, and informal restraints, e.g., sanctions, taboos, customs, traditions, codes of conduct, which contribute to the perpetuation of order and safety within a market or society.

11 For insight into the treatment of time in comparative research, see Bartolini (1993).

12 By 'synchronic comparisons', I mean comparing the same institution in different political systems at the same time.

13 Taagepera (2002: 248–249) points to the meaningful distinction between the electoral system and electoral rules, and between the party system and the party constellation. Systems, either party or electoral ones, take many years and many elections to be shaped; what is generated in the early stages of the transition is, according to the author, a set of electoral rules and a party constellation.

14 For a taxonomy of the different interpretations of accountability, see Mashaw (2006). The following narrative on accountability brings together the pillars underlying this concept:

> democratic accountability begins with a sovereign national community of citizens who delegate governing authority to public officials. As an expression of their ultimate authority, these citizens then hold those officials to account for how well they have carried out their governing responsibilities. This they typically do by casting votes in formal elections. Exacting this accountability helps citizens control government officials to ensure they serve the public interest.
>
> (Borowiak 2011: 4)

15 This literature offers a number of explanations for the lack of democracy in most Arab countries. One of them is Arab exceptionalism, resulting from historical, cultural, and religious features that prevent democracy from taking root in the Arab world. This explanation draws from the modernisation theories recalled above (Brynen, Korany

and Noble 1998). Other explanations identify structural elements, both domestic and external, that make Arab authoritarianism robust. These include the impact of the ownership and distribution of natural resources, in particular hydrocarbons, on political development in the Arab countries, the so-called rentier-state theory (Beblawi and Luciani 1987). Other more recent explanations point in the direction of the neo-liberal economic and political reforms enacted under the pressure of conditionality from external actors, in particular the international financial institutions. These reforms, far from addressing the structural problems and imbalances besetting the Arab economies, led to the proliferation of crony-capitalist practices, clientelist networks linked to the mushrooming of a private sector co-opted or controlled by the regimes, and cosmetic political liberalisation measures that have protected the Arab regimes from external criticism while entrenching authoritarian practices. Some of these analyses have underscored the emergence of new forms of authoritarianism with respect to those prevailing under the populist and nationalist leaders of the 1950s and 1960s. This new form of authoritarianism has been named 'neo-authoritarianism'. See Chapter 2 in this book and the extensive literature available, such as Ayubi (1995); Hakimian and Moshaver (2001); Henry and Springborg (2001); Carothers (2002); Albrech and Schlumberger (2004); Bellin (2004); Heydemann (2004); Hibou (2004); Owen (2004); Perthes (2004); Hinnebusch (2006); Ehteshami (2007); Schlumberger (2007); Guazzone and Pioppi (2009).

2 Looking back

[F]irst we agitated on Facebook. We set a date, a time, and a venue for a big demonstration. Tahrir Square, yes. The riot police killed some of us, and we had an even bigger demonstration [...] protected by the Army. And what were we protesting? Brutality and bureaucracy, control and corruption. [...] When we realized something was happening we called it a Revolution, the second, must-see episode in the Arab Spring series.

from Yousef Rakha. "Thus Spoke Che Nawwarah: Interview with a Revolutionary". *The Kenyon Review*. 20 July 2012

In early 2011, the Arab world entered a revolutionary phase that would lead to the unprecedented unseating of an autocrat through peaceful protests. The self-immolation of the young street vendor, Mohamed Bouazizi, in Sidi Bouzid in Tunisia in mid-December 2010 triggered a wave of protests and demonstrations that in less than three months swept throughout the entire Arab world and led to the toppling of two of the most entrenched authoritarian regimes in the region. The uprising in Tunisia was buoyed by both its spontaneity and leaderless nature. It was also largely peaceful with thousands of people pouring into the streets of Tunis and other cities, chanting slogans against Ben Ali, his family, and his entourage, as well as the predatory practices that had characterised his tenure. The flagrant corruption of the ruling elite had tremendously expanded the chasm between the haves and the have-nots, breeding frustration and discontent. Despite this peaceful popular mobilisation, an estimated 300 Tunisians were killed, a strikingly high number in a nation of only 10 million people.

The revolution that had started with the least of revolutionary acts in its periphery quickly reached the centre of the Arab world, that is, the capital of neighbouring Egypt. In Cairo, the Tunisians' accomplishment lent drive to demonstrations acquiring unprecedented momentum and scale. Between 50,000 and 70,000 demonstrators took to the streets in Cairo on 25 January 2011, called – as in Tunisia – the 'Day of Rage'. The fact that the unrest broke out on 'Police Day' was not a coincidence (Interviewee 21). Over the course of the 18 days leading to the removal of Mubarak on 11 February 2011, an estimated 6 million Egyptians were seen in the streets taking part in the largest popular mobilisation in Arab history (Abu Dhabi Gallup Center 2011). According to a number of authors, Egypt's uprising could be better defined as a popularly inspired military coup (Hamid 2011b; Springborg 2011a). It was indeed the military that ultimately forced Mubarak from power, although the Supreme Council of the Armed Forces (SCAF) acted not only to protect its own interests, but also in response to the demands of the millions of Egyptians who had taken to the streets. As will be demonstrated in the following sections, this represented a unique case in the Arab world.

The goal of this chapter is not to dwell on the events of the so-called 'Arab uprisings'[1] and their extreme diversity in the different countries of the region but rather to pinpoint some of the undercurrents that are meaningful for the analysis that will be presented in the other parts of this book. The most prominent feature of the uprisings, representing a lowest common denominator of the countries' trajectories, which otherwise tend to have very little in common, is the fact that the wave of protests and demonstrations was by and large moved by urban-based, educated, Internet-savvy youth. In all the countries of the region, by initiating and leading a revolutionary movement, young people have proven to be a potential engine for long-needed change. The rapid and unexpected mass mobilisations of 2011, foreshadowed by the development over the last decade of youth-based activist groups and the spread of new communications technologies, can be described as the 'bubbling up' of a phenomenon that had been in the making for some time: the coming onto the scene of a new generation, united by the shared experience of the economic, political, and social failures of post-independence regimes and by new ways to protest and act. Arguing that the Arab uprisings were youth revolutions does not mean restricting the scope of the popular mobilisations to one specific age group. Quite the contrary, this concept is used precisely because it broadens the horizon by taking into account the full array of identities of the (young) people who participated in the uprisings and who do not necessarily fall into the category biologically defined as 'youth'. Regarding differences, although it is acknowledged that youth cannot be considered a homogeneous category owing to gender, class, and cultural divisions, it is equally true that Arab young people have developed and experienced a particular consciousness about being young and what this entails. As Herrera and Bayat (2010) have argued in the case of Mediterranean countries, schooling, mass media, urban spaces – public parks, shopping malls – and the new information communication technologies have played a crucial role in fostering a particular awareness of their youthfulness, facilitating mutual influence and peer interaction. Moreover, in the region, youth from almost all social classes have been confronted with seemingly desperate conditions of exclusion. As the transition to adulthood has become increasingly problematic, owing to the economic, political, and social failures of the system created by the older generations, a substantial social group beyond the 15–29-year-olds cohort has started to perceive itself as 'young' as well (Mulderig 2011). Therefore, being young in the Arab world in late 2010 was more than a biological attribute; it was the consciousness of a shared experience.

The composite and pluralistic identities of the youth who participated in the Arab uprisings were also responsible for the largely leaderless nature of the protests. Although some ad-hoc committees, such as the Revolutionary Youth Coalition in Egypt, were formed to coordinate actions in the squares, there was no structured organisation, let alone a hierarchical one. In some cases, this led to difficulties when negotiating with other groups and the regimes. This weakness of the youth movements has become even more apparent during the transition phase. As a result, they have played a marginal role and the fruits of the revolutions have been 'hijacked' by more structured and rooted organisations, namely the Islamist parties. Despite all these weaknesses and heterogeneity of the group, the youth represented the only truly revolutionary actor of the Arab uprisings. Although there were also members of the youth movements close to the Islamists, the behaviour of the central offices of the Islamist movements and parties differed markedly from the approach of the leaderless and spontaneous youth mobilisation, which cut across differences in education, class, and religion. In Egypt, for example, the Muslim Brotherhood only started to take part in the uprisings from 28 January 2011 onwards, purposely choosing to downplay their involvement and refraining, in Tahrir Square, from using any Islamic slogans. Furthermore, in the first days of their participation in the popular mobilisation, they did not ask for Mubarak's resignation, in keeping with the limited, albeit illegal opposition role they had played under the authoritarian regime (Hamid 2011c).

Overall, the Arab uprisings have represented a complex and multi-faceted phenomenon that altered the outlook of the Arab world once and for all. A flurry of explanations has been advanced to account for the unexpected, spontaneous, and largely peaceful youth protests that have shaken the Arab world from 2011 onwards. Needless to say, most of them have focused on a few causes or co-causes, stressing in particular economic factors, such as stagnant economic prospects and youth unemployment, rising social inequality and marginalisation, as well as other factors linked to the limited spaces for dissent and the penetration of the new communication technologies. Generally, explanations have failed to clearly differentiate between short-term, contingent triggering factors and more structural, long-term causes of the uprisings. In this regard, the Arab uprisings have to be considered the point of arrival of a number of processes that had been going on for at least two decades. This is the fundamental point to be stressed, namely that the Arab uprisings were the result of complex processes of transformation that took place during the 1990s and 2000s – processes that largely contributed to the development of the predatory institutions and the unsustainability of the state in the past two decades. At the same time, the Arab uprisings have marked the point of departure of transition processes in some Arab countries. No transition, understood as changes and continuities in the institutional framework, would have been possible in countries such as Egypt and Tunisia without the demonstrations against the Mubarak and the Ben Ali regimes. At the same time, the ousting of authoritarian regimes is a necessary but not sufficient condition for the beginning of transition processes.

Even though the Arab uprisings were the result of a number of processes, changes, and events that took place in the previous decades, most observers, both from the region and external, were caught off guard by their breadth and power.

However, whether it would have been possible to predict the Arab uprisings is not the right question to ask. It masks a rather simplistic way of looking at complex political phenomena, in which structure and agency, contingency and intention are complementary. The Arab uprisings tend to reinforce the view that, even with certain structural conditions pointing in the direction of growing unsustainability, the actual moment in which the tipping point is reached can be neither predicted nor anticipated given the overwhelming importance of human agency in setting these processes in motion.

Exploring the Arab uprisings: structural unsustainability and predatory institutions

The Arab states captured by neo-authoritarian regimes

Broadly speaking, the Arab uprisings are the result of the failures of neo-authoritarianism. The concept of neo-authoritarianism has made its way into the literature on Middle Eastern politics in recent years, dominating the more established frameworks that tended to explain political systems in the region with Orientalist or exceptionality-driven approaches. Examples of such frameworks include the numerous strands of the literature that deal with the study of change in developing countries. The Arab world has been regarded through the lens of democratisation theories that, according to Guazzone and Pioppi, can be viewed as a particularly fortunate offspring of the modernisation theory that provided the dominant paradigm of analysis of the developing world in western social sciences since the late 1950s (Guazzone and Pioppi 2009: 2).[2] Modernisation theories flourished during the 1970s and 1980s, providing accounts and explanations of the transition experiences of first Latin American countries and later Eastern European and former Soviet countries. The Arab world came late. It was not until the mid-1990s that the Arab countries started to be looked at through the lens of the democratisation paradigm. The Arab countries were considered as exceptional and/or latecomers (to say the least) with respect to the much more profound changes pointing towards democracy in other parts of the world (Salamé 1994; Brynen et al. 1998). Although many voices took part in this debate, the most common argument was that Arab political systems were inherently resilient to the 'third wave of democracy' (Huntington 1991).

Moving from similar premises, the theories that buy into the so-called rentier-state framework, starting from the ground-breaking work by Hazem Beblawi and Giacomo Luciani in 1987, tend to postulate a rather simplistic and unidirectional correlation between the wealth deriving from rents, either from natural resources or from man-made artefacts and infrastructures – the Suez Canal is a case in point as far as Egypt is concerned – and stability and continuity, i.e., absence of democracy, at the apex of the political system. Not only was an element of economic determinism introduced to explain political phenomena in 'rentier states', but this framework was also used to reify the state and to draw a rigid correlation between the rulers and the ruled, on the one hand, and between the distributive function of the state and the question of legitimacy, on the other (Beblawi and Luciani 1987; Luciani 1988, 1995; Chaudhry 1997).[3]

Going beyond both the democratisation and the rentier-state approaches, the neo-authoritarian theories, sometimes also called 'upgraded-authoritarianism' theories (Heydemann 2007a), focus on the modern character of the states of North Africa and the Middle East. Far from representing old-style political systems, the Arab regimes in the 1990s and the 2000s can be described as modern, dynamic forms of authoritarianism, heavily reliant on the repression of dissent, the de-politicisation and demobilisation of society, and recourse to adaptive mechanisms to cope with the challenges and opportunities provided to them by the neo-liberal economic policies often powerfully sponsored by external western powers. The neo-authoritarianism framework of analysis moves from the conceptualisation of 'authoritarian regimes' provided by Linz,[4] but goes beyond it and emphasises the mechanisms whereby robust authoritarian practices and systems of power are reproduced and thus reinforced, even while using democratic rhetoric and implementing cosmetic 'democratic reforms' when needed (Bellin 2004). In the scholarly debate related to this framework of analysis, the resilience of authoritarianism in the Arab world is linked to factors and mechanisms ranging from the weakness of civil society (Norton 1995; Hawthorne 2005) and the deliberate manipulation and co-optation of opposition forces through the distribution of rents (Zartman 1988; Brumberg 2002; Lust-Okar 2004, 2009; Heydemann 2007b; Wegner 2007), to the trap of economic liberalisation (Kienle 2001; King 2003; Moore 2004) and the effective manipulation of political institutions such as parties and electoral laws (Ayubi 1995; Pripstein Posusney 2002; Brownlee 2007; Blaydes 2011).

One of the key features of Arab neo-authoritarian regimes is the increased privatisation of political life, whereby only a restricted circle of people – among them relatives and co-opted technocrats – is allowed to participate fully in politics and benefit from it. This has been accomplished mainly through the proliferation of private or semi-private institutions, whose activities and reach lie beyond democratic oversight, and the parallel reinforcement of informal, mainly neo-patrimonial, and communitarian links.[5] Similar trends can be seen in the predominant economic relations, centred on the privatisation and liberalisation measures adopted by most Arab regimes during the 1980s under pressure from the international financial institutions – the World Bank (WB) and the International Monetary Fund (IMF). Economic liberalisation measures have been used mainly by incumbent elites as a strategic tool for restructuring external relations and for co-opting new social groups and excluding others through the redistribution of domestic resources. These measures have been adopted with different intensity by almost all Arab countries (Niblock and Murphy 1993; Henry and Springborg 2001; Hakimian and Moshaver 2001). In most cases they have resulted in a shift in patronage networks towards crony-capitalist practices, rather than in the formation of competitive markets able to create sufficient jobs to keep up with the steady increase in the workforce. Parallel to this, the reduction in state budgets under the constraints imposed by the structural adjustment programmes adopted during the 1980s and 1990s and the ensuing decline in the ability of the state to provide fundamental social services, including health, education, and welfare, have resulted in the increased marginalisation of large strata of society (Karshenas and Moghadam 2006).

The security domain with its idiosyncrasies, rituals, and policies has not been immune from this trend of growing authoritarianism. Here, it has taken the form of a relentless process of 'patrimonialisation', i.e., patrimonial forms of law and order, accompanied by the increased role in business of security institutions and personnel (Bellin 2005; Sayigh 2012). Two interlocking phenomena linked to the restructuring of security perceptions, conceptions, policies, and means have affected the relationship between the regimes and security institutions. The first is the increased securitisation of public policies, which can be defined as the construction of a policy subject in such a way as to legitimise the use of extraordinary means to solve what is perceived as the problem (Buzan, Waever, and de Wilde 1997). This reconfiguration has been particularly evident and pervasive with regard to a number of issues that rose to the top of the security agenda of Arab governments during the 1990s and 2000s, such as Islamism, migration, and trade (Storm 2009). The second, closely related to the first, is the banalisation of violence, which has been pursued by the proliferation of torture and routine physical intimidation of opponents or simply any individual perceived to be threatening the security of the state.

These are the factors most commonly identified with neo-authoritarianism in the Arab world. Some of them have a powerful explanatory potential for defining the features, although not unique or exceptional, of Arab political systems. This potential, however, has not been used to maximum effect because a number of significant factors related to human agency and learning have been overlooked. Therefore it is argued here that the Arab uprisings cannot be explained only by the structural conditions so clearly illuminated by the neo-authoritarian framework of analysis. These conditions are indeed not enough to explain why (and how) the political order that took shape with the rise of the Arab post-colonial regimes between the late 1940s and the 1950s has been broken apart by the upsurge of long-suppressed but unconsciously nurtured popular demands for freedom, inclusion, justice, and voice. A better and more complete explanation can only be provided if one considers the contingent and agency-related factors that have long been disregarded by the neo-authoritarian framework. With the benefit of hindsight, the Arab uprisings have cast new light on the neo-authoritarian framework, which has failed to see the limits of the 'upgrading' processes undergone by the political systems in the Arab world. In other words, it did not see the Arab uprisings coming. It somehow contented itself with highlighting the factors of adaptation and restructuring that allowed the incumbent regimes to remain in power throughout the region, but was not able to understand other possibly subtler trends that were taking root in Arab societies and starting to erode their relations with the states. In keeping with a framework that tends to perceive Arab societies as weak and passive, scholars belonging to the neo-authoritarian school focused their attention on power dynamics and the interplay between domestic and external factors that seemed to reinforce the political regimes in power.

Sustainability vs. stability

As argued above, the single major flaw of the neo-authoritarian framework rests in its inability to spot the unsustainability of a system of power, and therefore of a state, generated by the political, economic, and security-related practices of the Arab rulers during the two decades that led to 2011. The distinction between 'sustainability' and 'stability' is an important one and was elaborated upon by the author in November 2010, one month before the beginning of the Tunisian uprising (Colombo 2011). It critically underscores the extent to which, while a state can enjoy apparent or temporary stability domestically and externally without sustainable development, sustainability leads to a certain degree of order and stability in the long run, even though some instability can manifest itself in the short run. This is the paradox in which the Arab countries found themselves in the past decades – apparent stability and governability at the expense of increased unsustainability and state capture. In contrast, the processes triggered by the uprisings have attempted to move away from authoritarianism to build more legitimate, accountable, and responsive institutions.

Going back to the relationship between 'stability' and 'sustainability', the sustainability of any state is premised on its ability to preserve internal order, defend its power prerogatives, and safeguard its territory from external threats. This coincides with the concept of stability and the absence of or ability to curb threats from within and outside. However, as important as these features might be for establishing sustainable institutions, they are insufficient. Indeed, state sustainability also necessitates a bottom-up dimension that ensures the well-being, participation, and access to the civil, political, and social rights of its citizens. The predominant situation in most Arab states until 2011 was one in which power and sovereignty of the state were not questioned, but the standard of living enjoyed by the population constantly deteriorated, resources – be they natural, man-made, or human – were dissipated, and there was a backtracking on social, economic, and political reforms – all of this accompanied by the emergence of dissent and unrest, the radicalisation of opposition forces, and hence the risk of further destabilisation (Colombo 2011). My conclusion in November 2010 was exactly this: a number of countries of the southern Mediterranean region were likely to find themselves in this situation sooner or later unless major changes were undertaken to strengthen governance and foster inclusive political, social, and economic reforms.

The determinants of state sustainability

Given the complex and multidimensional nature of the concept of sustainability (and stability), a distinction has to be made between the sustainability and the stability of the state, on the one hand, and of the regime, on the other. The concepts of 'state' and 'regime' are widely used, together with that of 'political system', in the literature on neo-authoritarianism and (democratic) transitions in the Arab world. It is important to stress that these two concepts are not the same. The concept of 'state' is understood here as the set of institutions, processes, and relations that transcend the boundaries of governing bodies and involve society (Mitchell 1991). The concept of 'regime', in contrast, can be used interchangeably with that of 'state class', meaning the group of people who hold and administer power in the political and economic systems. This group is characterised by a 'blending of modern forms of association based on ideology, public issues and class interests [the dominant party(ies), the (organised) group(s) that control the allocation of material and ideational resources] with more traditional primordial and personal ties [the family, the circle of friends and clients]' (Hinnebusch 1990: 189). From this distinction, it should be clear from the outset that I am not concerned with the sustainability/stability of the regimes in power, whose survival and entrenchment has often been guaranteed at the expense of the people they purport to represent.

From this standpoint, the situation in most Arab countries prior to the uprisings could be defined as unsustainable and thus it comes as no surprise that it generated sustained popular protests that in some cases ultimately reached the tipping point of instability. Adopting the triple distinction elaborated by Marshall and Bottomore (1992) with respect to the concept of citizenship helps capture the core of the overwhelmingly unsustainable and predatory nature of the institutions and policies of the Arab states in the early 2010s. This amounts to identifying the root structural causes of the Arab uprisings. These authors consider citizenship the result of the gradual, progressive attainment of three types of rights: civil rights, followed by political rights, followed by social rights. According to the authors, without these three types of rights one cannot speak of citizenship or citizens. Consequently, when one or more of these rights are denied, one has to speak of 'subjects'. Looking at the situation in the Arab world through this lens, one can see that the majority of people in most countries in the region were treated as subjects, and not as citizens, as they were denied basic civil, political, and social rights. The denial of civil rights amounts to the constant obliteration of basic liberties as a result of growing authoritarianism and the very limited toleration of dissent. Political rights are not upheld as a result of bad political governance and restricted participation deriving from the capture of the state by a small group of people who maintain the control of power through corrupt practices and the lack of the rule of law. The denial of social rights corresponds to the lowering of the standards of living due to rampant inequalities and growing unemployment.

Table 2.1 below shows the three components of citizenship according to Marshall and Bottomore and their relationship to sustainability. A third column is

Table 2.1 Explaining Arab states' unsustainability

Components of citizenship	Determinants of state sustainability	Relationship between the rulers and their citizens
Civil rights	Basic rights and liberties	Legitimacy
Political rights	Political governance and participation	Accountability
Social rights	Citizens' well-being	Responsiveness

Source: author's elaboration.

added, introducing the concepts of legitimacy, accountability, and responsiveness that describe the resulting relationship between the rulers and the ruled.

The table can be read as follows. The unsustainability of the state derived from the denial of the components of citizenship. Basic rights and liberties were not respected and this deprived Arab citizens of their civil rights. This situation entailed a crisis of legitimacy in the relationship between the rulers and the ruled. Similarly, state unsustainability was the result of poor political governance and increasingly limited citizen participation. This deprived citizens of their political rights, producing a situation in which the interaction between the rulers and the ruled was not regulated by the principle of accountability. Finally, the third component of citizenship, i.e., social rights, was endangered since the state was no longer able to respond to the basic needs of its citizens, thus creating a situation in which the deterioration of citizens' well-being was widespread.

Predatory institutions in the neo-authoritarian Arab states: the denial of civil and political rights

While different in many respects, Egypt and Tunisia shared some features of neo-authoritarianism. Starting with Tunisia, President Zine El-Abidine Ben Ali took power in 1987 after dismissing as legally incompetent his predecessor, Habib Bourguiba. Following an early phase of political liberalisation, during which the new president released hundreds of political prisoners, including Islamists, from state prisons, recognised new political parties and negotiated a National Pact with the country's main opposition forces, abolished state security courts, put a ceiling on the number of presidential terms, and relaxed controls over television and radio, the true face of the president and his regime was revealed when he started to order the systematic repression of any form of opposition and dissent, significantly curtailing basic rights and liberties.[6] The main victims of these measures were human rights activists, journalists, and members of the opposition. They were placed under constant surveillance, harassed, and imprisoned; physical and psychological torture was also systematically practiced in police stations according to many accounts (Kausch 2009; EMHRN 2010). Freedoms of association and expression were almost non-existent. Citizens were not allowed to set up organisations or associations that were even remotely connected to political activity, with very few, albeit significant, exceptions such as the Tunisian League of Human Rights (*Ligue Tunisienne des Droits de l'Homme*), nor could they engage in any sort of public criticism of the regime (Kausch 2009).[7] Over the years, censorship and control was imposed on the media too, in particular the critical press and independent radio and television stations, as well as the Internet. The measures adopted by some agents of the Ministry of the Interior became increasingly capillary and sophisticated, entailing the routine monitoring of personal e-mail accounts, censorship of sensitive websites, and tight control of Internet cafes to discourage criticism and block potential forms of dissent from the outset (EMHRN 2010).

The situation in Egypt did not look much different from the point of view of the protection of civil rights (or lack thereof).[8] A case in point was the impact of the long-standing state of emergency, in place since 1981, which served to curtail freedoms of association and expression by prohibiting strikes, censoring newspapers, and constraining in the name of national security any activity of citizens that could be vaguely regarded as opposed to the regime. But it was in the political arena that the neo-authoritarian features of the Egyptian state were most evident. Politically, the Mubarak regime managed to control tightly political institutions and processes by alternating phases of relatively limited opening with phases of harsh repression and deepening authoritarianism. After taking power in 1981 following Sadat's assassination, Mubarak moved swiftly from a period of 'relative tolerance to neo-authoritarianism' (Beinin 2009: 21). During the 1990s, a number of measures were taken that went in the direction of deepening Mubarak's authoritarian rule. These included relevant constitutional changes to the Syndicates Law and the Non-governmental Associations Law, passed in 1993 and 1999 respectively, which curtailed the freedom of association by imposing strict governmental regulations and even harsher penalties for violations (Kienle 1998). At the same time the ruling party, the National Democratic Party (NDP), controlled by the president and his entourage, became the mechanism through which the regime created, re-created, and maintained its networks and clienteles which, benefiting from the favours and resources received, provided it with a limited but nonetheless real social base. Another piece of legislation, voted in July 1992, introduced amendments to the penal code and other laws that increased the sentences for a number of offences pertaining to public order and security. It also toughened punishment for terrorist crimes, whose definition according to the law was so far-reaching and general that it covered any use or threat of force that might upset public order or affect the security of individuals or property.

Other measures were the Amendments to the Party Law, voted in December 1992, which were instrumental in restricting the electoral process by barring founders of new parties from accepting foreign funds and from conducting any political activity in the name of their party until it was officially recognised (Al-Din Arafat 2009). Owing to these measures and to the systematic interference in the electoral process through vote-buying, fraud, intimidation, and arrests, the parliamentary elections of both 1995 and 2000 – small differences notwithstanding – resulted in an unprecedented majority for the ruling NDP (Abdulbaki 2008; Beinin 2009). These electoral competitions were all widely considered as less democratic than preceding ones. They were also clearly marked by a decline in the participation of registered voters as a percentage of those eligible with respect to the previous ones (Kienle 2001).

In solidarity with the Second Palestinian *Intifada* of 2000 and in reaction to the American-led invasion of Iraq in 2003, there seemed to be an upsurge in political dynamism and opposition in the early 2000s, often taking place beyond the strict confines of political activity. Demonstrators inside and outside the licensed and officially recognised opposition parties and movements, e.g., the *Kifaya!* Movement ('Enough!'), the 'Judges' Club', the *Al-Ghad* party, and the Muslim Brotherhood,[9] started demanding political reforms, including amendment of the constitution to allow competitive presidential elections, the end of the state of emergency, and the removal of restrictions on the activities of parties, civil society organisations, and the media. Faced with these pressures, the Mubarak regime did inaugurate a phase of temporary and limited concessions that were enshrined in a number of amendments to the constitution (Brown, Dunne, and Hamzawy 2007). While opening the road to direct popular election of the president, the constitutional amendments introduced very strict conditions for candidate eligibility, meant to ensure the NDP's control over the candidates for the position of president. For example, amended article 76 of the Presidential Election Law granted each licensed party the right to field a candidate, provided he or she had been a member of the party's executive committee for at least one year, thereby preventing parties from nominating a popular figure outside the small circle of mostly elderly, experienced politicians (Dunne 2006). Similarly, the party system was not liberalised, as the amended Political Parties Law effectively maintained the ban on parties with a religious identity, first and foremost the Muslim Brotherhood. It also altered the composition of the Political Parties Committee (PPC), the body in charge of supervising applications by new parties, by staffing it with an increasing number of NDP members (Dunne 2006). As a result, the first multi-candidate presidential elections, held in September 2005, saw the expected victory of the incumbent with 87 percent of the votes. Of the nine candidates who ran against President Mubarak, Ayman Nour, the leader of the *Al-Ghad* party, came in second with 7 percent of the votes but was sentenced to prison shortly after running in the presidential competition.

A rather different story seemed to emerge from the 2005 parliamentary elections. Muslim Brotherhood candidates were allowed to campaign more openly than in the past and, unlike in the previous elections, were not arrested in the run-up to the first round. So, while the NDP safely maintained its two-thirds majority, the Muslim Brotherhood candidates, running as independents, obtained 88 seats, 20 percent of the total. This was the strongest showing ever of the Islamist movement, prompting wide-ranging arrests of the Muslim Brotherhood's campaigners (Sullivan 2009). Since then, and in particular since early 2007, the Mubarak regime started to show signs of preoccupation, internal division, and weakness. Learning from the past and having to adapt to a partially changing political environment, the regime introduced a number of amendments that further constrained political rights and liberties. The powers of the president were extended, granting him the right to dissolve parliament without a referendum and the authority to refer civilians suspected of terrorism-related offences to military tribunals for trial, and those of the judiciary diminished (Kienle 2001; Brown *et al.* 2007). These were compounded by the extension of the state of emergency for another two years and by the not-so-masked violent crackdown on representatives or supporters of the opposition forces, i.e., civil society, bloggers, journalists, workers, students, and Muslim Brotherhood and *Kifaya!* members.[10] The brunt of the repression was borne by the Muslim Brotherhood, thousands of whose members were arrested and detained prior to the 2007 elections for the Upper House of parliament, the Shura Council, and the 2008 local elections. In the late spring of 2010, some activists claimed that there were more Muslim Brothers in jail than at any time since Nasser (Cook 2011). This neo-authoritarian surge in the Egyptian state culminated with the 28 November 2010 parliamentary elections, marked by unprecedented and widespread violations of basic civil and political rights, the arrest of hundreds of Muslim Brotherhood activists, and violence and intimidation directed at the media. The NDP won with an overwhelming majority, 420 seats, 81 percent of the total, as compared to the 14 gained by the opposition parties and the 70 by the independents.

Politically, the script followed by the Tunisian state did not differ much from the Egyptian one. The Tunisian political system was tainted by the same features of neo-authoritarianism that characterised the Egyptian regime, making it irresponsive to the demands of civil society. As in Egypt, the Tunisian political system was dominated by one ruling party, the *Rassemblement Constitutionnel Démocratique* (RCD). Even though limited pluralism had been introduced in the elections for parliament since 1994, and for the president since 1999, voting remained largely uncompetitive and marred by the regime's co-optation of the few legal opposition parties or the restrictions placed on them by, for example, a minority quota of seats for the opposition.[11] The result was that, even though parliamentary elections were regularly held in 1989, 1994, 1999, 2004, and 2009, the electoral system favoured and reinforced the hegemony of the ruling party controlled by the president. Going back to the issue of co-optation, of the nine legal parties that fielded candidates in the 2009 general elections, only three of them – the *Parti Démocratique Progressiste* (PDP), the *Forum Démocratique pour le Travail et les Libertés* (FDTL), and *Ettajdid* – were genuinely critical of the regime and could thus be regarded as independent and not co-opted. It is no surprise then that two of them – the PDP and the FDTL – did not obtain any seats.

Like the parliamentary elections, the presidential elections, although formally allowing for more than one candidate, were actually skewed in a way that left Ben Ali almost uncontested. Not only were opposition candidates, when not denied participation, banned from campaigning openly, but further restrictions were also introduced through constitutional amendments (Gobe 2009). In 2002, for example, the limit on the number of presidential mandates was lifted through a constitutional reform approved by referendum and the age limit raised to 75 years. These amendments opened the way for Ben Ali's fourth mandate, which started in 2004. In March 2008, before the presidential elections scheduled for October 2009, a new law stipulated that presidential candidates had to have been party leaders for at least two years, thus disqualifying prominent opposition leaders such as Mustafa Ben Jaafar from the FDTL and Nejib Chebbi from the PDP. Ben Ali ran almost uncontested in the 2009 presidential elections, obtaining an overwhelming 89.62 percent of the votes and thus winning his fifth term as president of the Tunisian Republic. To conclude, among the factors underpinning the growing authoritarianism of the Tunisian state was the widespread corruption, the frequent practices aimed at manipulating the judicial system, as well as the absence of the rule of law. The Tunisian judiciary was subject to constant interference by the regime that controlled the country's Supreme Council of Magistrates (*Conseil Supérieur de la Magistrature*), the highest supervisory body responsible for appointing, promoting, and sanctioning judges (Kausch 2009; EMHRN 2010).

Predatory institutions in the neo-authoritarian Arab states: social policy as a tool of control

The discussion of the status of social rights in the Arab world touches upon one of the most important root causes of the Arab uprisings. Throughout the region, from Morocco to Bahrain, issues of unemployment and inequality were among the factors enflaming the simmering discontent, mistrust, and frustration with the regimes' behaviours. Therefore, the processes that go under the name of the Arab uprisings and the ensuing transitions cannot be understood if one does not take into account the constant deterioration of social rights experienced by the people as a result of the predatory institutions and policies of the authoritarian regimes. In many respects, Tunisia was officially hailed as an economic success story, with sustained annual gross domestic product (GDP) growth, relatively high standards of living compared to neighbouring countries, and a sizable middle class.[12] Yet, in spite of this largely positive macroeconomic picture, Tunisia perfectly exemplified the situation of growing unsustainability at the socio-economic level – after a decade of impressive growth and development[13] – that was to lie at the core of the unrest and upheaval.

The first thing to be underscored is that social policy was, above all, an instrument of power and control in the hands of the regime (Hibou 2011). The relatively good level of social services and benefits the Tunisian middle class received was traded off against civil and political rights. As Ben Romdhane (2006) explains, social policy contributed to hindering the emergence of a democratic order in the country insofar as most Tunisians acquiesced in the lack of political rights and freedoms, considered the price to pay for socio-economic development and well-being. In addition, the market-oriented reforms, introduced under the aegis of the IMF and the WB, did not contribute to creating sustainable development. In particular, they failed to create sufficient employment opportunities for the burgeoning number of educated youth entering the job market and for the interior regions. The reasons for these shortcomings have been identified as the skewed nature of the export market, with most investments going to low-skilled sectors, such as apparel and agriculture (Hedi Bchir, Chemingui, and Hammouda 2009); the country's strong dependence on the EU for exports, tourism revenues, remittances, and foreign direct investment (FDI) flows and the consequent vulnerability to fluctuations in EU growth (Paciello 2010); and – no less important – the widespread corruption that characterised the provision of welfare. Indeed, social policy represented one of the regime's key means for distributing privileges and favours to the families of the president and his wife and protecting their vested interests (Godec 2010). The scale of corruption in Tunisia increased during the last years of Ben Ali's regime hand in hand with nepotism, and the lack of transparency and rule of law, thus fuelling increasing frustration, particularly among the youth. Before the outbreak of unrest in December 2010, this frustration had already found ways to come to the surface, for example in the wave of protests that roiled the Gafsa region in January 2008, sparked by the alleged unfair and fraudulent employment practices of the Gafsa Phosphate Company (GPC), the main employer in one of the poorest regions of the country (Amnesty International 2009; Allal 2010). As a result of these trends, Tunisia experienced a rapid and marked worsening of socio-economic conditions, thus making the tacit contract between the state and society increasingly unsustainable. Indicators of this unsustainability were the dramatic rise in youth unemployment, the pronounced regional disparities with a stronger incidence of poverty in the south and centre-west of the country (Harrigan and El-Said 2009; Mahjoub 2010), and the erosion of the middle class' purchasing power due to rising food prices and declining wages in the public sector. The issue of youth unemployment deserves to be further stressed in light of the tremendous implications it had in the popular uprising. According to the official estimates of the Ben Ali era, the unemployment among the youth, particularly those with higher education, increased from 8.6 percent in 1999 to 19.0 percent in 2007 (Mahjoub 2010). New figures released after the fall of the regime, however, revealed a far more dramatic rise, from 22.1 percent in 1999 to 44.9 percent in 2009 (Haouari 2011).

The socio-economic situation in Egypt in the last two decades did not differ to any significant extent from the one in Tunisia, when viewed through the prism of the retrenchment of social rights. In the period 2003–2007, Egypt experienced an economic boom with economic growth reaching a peak of 7.1 percent in 2006–2007, according to IMF statistics (IMF 2007). This was made possible by the substantial wealth and liquidity generated by the oil exporting countries as a result of the positive dynamics on the global oil market, which in turn translated into a steady increase in the flows of FDI and remittances from the Gulf Cooperation Council (GCC) countries. Against this backdrop, however, as in Tunisia, a growing segment of the population in Egypt, from the lower to the middle class, started to experience hardship. Four factors stand out in the Egyptian case that bear testimony to the underlying unsustainability of state institutions and policies under Mubarak, ultimately leading to his regime's demise: a) the incidence of crony capitalism and practices of economic governance profoundly rooted in the authoritarian, predatory, and coercive nature of the Egyptian regime;[14] b) the disproportionate recourse to expensive food subsidies and pay raises as a means of mitigating the negative impact of soaring food prices and inflation, which, however, only contributed to easing the plight of the poor to a limited extent while exacerbating fiscal problems (Klau 2010); c) the proliferation of the informal labour sector, with most new jobs created in the 1998–2006 period, characterised by extremely low wages, insufficient social security, and the lack of contracts (Assaad 2007); and d) the retrenchment of state welfare provisions in education and health services, both in quantitative and qualitative terms, engendering a sharp rise in poverty and extremely negative consequences for the education-job market nexus (Galal 2003; Bayat 2006; Tadros 2006).

Exploring the Arab uprisings: collective consciousness, empowerment, and learning

Beyond structure: the role of contingency in the Arab uprisings

At the core of the neo-authoritarian framework of analysis lies the concept of authoritarian upgrading or consolidation.[15] Both concepts stress the capacity of authoritarian regimes to adapt to changing circumstances through a series of transformations aimed at ensuring their durability and increasing the efficiency of their control over society. Most of the measures undertaken by the Arab regimes in the past two decades and described in the previous section can be read as part of a complex and multi-level game involving the regimes, their societies, and external actors. Based on processes of learning, emulation, and adaptation, the Arab regimes displayed an innate aptitude to develop strategies aimed at influencing the strategic calculations of their citizens, allies, and adversaries, to learn from past mistakes, to reinvent themselves, and ultimately to prevail. These behaviours testify to a certain degree of flexibility and manoeuvrability on the part of Arab authoritarian regimes, some of which have remained in power for an innumerable number of years.

Nevertheless, the momentous changes that have taken place in the Arab world since 2011 have revealed the ingrained limits of the authoritarian upgrading and adaptation, and of the frameworks of analysis based on such explanations. By focusing solely on institutionalised mechanisms of authoritarian governance, the paradigm underscoring the adaptability of the Arab regimes was unequipped with the tools needed to appreciate the resilience (or lack thereof) of regimes in the face of new political dynamics (Volpi 2013). The unintended consequence of these analyses was to generate a tendency to overstate the stability of the Arab state (Ayubi 1995). The limits of the alleged adaptive flexibility of authoritarian regimes are now self-evident. The measures, policies, and institutions meant to buttress the stability and durability of the regimes in power have contributed, instead, to creating a situation of state unsustainability that has made change and instability no longer a hypothetical possibility, but a reality. The hallmark of the regimes that have been displaced was an almost absolute focus on their survival at the expense of the rights of the citizens. It is thus not surprising that one of the core demands of the protests was respect and dignity (*karamah*) in opposition to the contempt and disdain with which the Arab citizens were for so many years treated by their governments. The limits of the neo-authoritarian framework of analysis lie in its inability to anticipate but, more importantly, to provide an explanation for the wave of popular unrest that, in only two months, led to the toppling of two of the most long-lasting and seemingly stable regimes in the Arab world. True, neo-authoritarian approaches indirectly underscore the existence of common grievances and demands throughout the region by pointing to the very similar causes of unsustainability dissected in the previous section. Above and beyond this contribution, though, it is impossible to gain a comprehensive view of the complex and multi-faceted processes associated with the Arab uprisings without taking into account the contingent and agency-related forces that have concretely made them possible at a specific moment in time and space.

Starting off with the role of contingency in triggering the Arab uprisings, the Arab countries thwart any attempts at reducing their complexity and differences by putting them in a single box. Thus, the appraisal of country-specific factors appears to be of the essence to overcome the limits of the neo-authoritarian framework and to gain a better understanding of the Arab uprisings in their manifold, concrete manifestations. Among the key contingent factors that triggered the unrest, particularly in Tunisia, was the impact of the global financial and economic crisis. When the crisis erupted in 2008, most countries in the Arab world were still enjoying high rates of growth. Within a few years, average economic growth dropped sharply, for example, in Tunisia from 6.3 percent in 2007 to only 3.3 percent in 2009 (WB 2010). Furthermore, countries like Tunisia, with their dependence on European markets and consumers for exports, tourism revenues, remittances, and FDI flows (Paciello 2010), were even more badly hit. Indeed, in Tunisia, where trade with the EU accounted for over two-thirds of total volumes at the end of the 2000s, the effects of the crisis were dramatic. Decreased industrial production translated into a drop in investments, negatively affecting private consumption and living standards, and increasing social tensions. The economic difficulties experienced by the Tunisian state directly impinged on its capacity to address the most prominent socio-economic challenges facing the country and to deliver solutions to them. Worsening socio-economic conditions made the social contract between the state and its citizens, on which the legitimacy and stability of the Ben Ali regime was premised, no longer acceptable, at least for large swathes of the Tunisian population.

A second factor that fuelled the uprisings and opened the way to a period of change in some countries was the question of succession. This was particularly true with regard to Egypt, where presidential succession represented one of the main drivers of the restructuring of power that took place with the outbreak of unrest (Collombier 2012). Although some states in the region had seen a generational change at the apex of their political systems around the turn of the millennium (Morocco, Jordan, and Syria, for example), most of them had been governed by the same elites for the past three decades. Given the extremely centralised nature and the limited pluralism of authoritarian Arab regimes, presidential succession constitutes a critical moment in which competition for power becomes more acute and potential splits within the ruling elite are likely to take place. In Egypt, this was definitely the case. The behaviour of President Mubarak and part of his entourage, as well as their decision to use the ruling party, the NDP, as the main instrument of Gamal Mubarak's bid for power, stirred the relatively calm waters within the party itself and other institutions. Although the succession of the president's younger son had been prepared for almost a decade, it soon became apparent that the strategy of transforming the ruling party into a coherent and efficient organisation geared towards Gamal's election was coming up against increasing obstacles. Below the surface of apparent unity and uncompromised support for the official presidential line, the party was already plagued in the mid-2000s by deep contrasts between different and sometimes competing power centres. First, internal opposition on the part of a number of party leaders, especially at the local level, started to emerge with protests against the monopolisation of the party by people close to Gamal Mubarak. Second, the strategy of acting through the party failed to take into account that it was a rather weak institution compared to others, such as the military, which were, incidentally, seen as harbouring strong opposition to the idea of Gamal Mubarak becoming president. The succession question can thus be seen as one of the factors behind the growing divisions within the Egyptian ruling institutions. Some scholars believe that the Egyptian regime was in the throes of a full-fledged internal crisis by the end of 2010, which can ultimately be regarded as responsible for the regime's inability to rein in the wave of popular mobilisation and avoid the ensuing collapse (Collombier 2012). These authors point to increasing tensions within the NDP. The parliamentary elections of November–December 2010, in which the ruling party won a landslide victory, obtaining 420 seats out of 508, and the Muslim Brotherhood, which had obtained 88 seats in 2005, secured only one, were indeed marred by conflicts that affected the cohesion of the party. Divisions, sparked by the decision of the NDP Secretary General and some close associates of Gamal Mubarak to field a disproportionate number of candidates from the party, thus preventing the legal opposition from obtaining fair representation, went beyond the traditional conflicts between the 'old guard' and the 'new guard' or between the 'conservatives' and the 'reformists'. Multiple circles of power, each distinguishing itself from the other by its degree of proximity and allegiance to Gamal Mubarak, became evident (Collombier 2012). Overall, the conduct and outcome of the 2010 parliamentary elections lifted the veil on the gap between the narrative sponsored by the regime and centred on its internal cohesion, and reality.

Notwithstanding the importance of such divisions and conflicts within the ruling party, the weakness of the Egyptian regime on the eve of the uprising derived also from the tensions that had started to emerge between the ruling party and other important institutions, notably the military. The attempt to exclude the armed forces from decisions concerning the succession, but also, starting in 2004, concerning the new economic policies masterminded by Prime Minister Ahmed Nazif and heavily influenced by neo-liberal theories,[16] proved troubling to say the least. It was ultimately the tension, at first hidden to outside observers, between Gamal's associates within the ruling party, on the one hand, and the military, on the other, that increased the vulnerability of the regime at the moment in which the uprisings broke out. Some diplomatic cables revealed by WikiLeaks showed that the military had sent unequivocal signals that they opposed Gamal's presidential election and that in case Hosni Mubarak were to die before the end of his mandate, the military would seize power. The possibility of a military coup had started to be rumoured as early as 2007.[17]

A number of analyses have rightly pinpointed the military's capacity and willingness to repress popular mobilisations as one of the most important factors determining the durability of authoritarian regimes in the region (Bellin 2004). The decision of the military in Arab countries to shoot at protesters or to refrain from doing so is considered decisive for the fate of the protests and the regime's chances for survival. Not only is this argument theoretically sound, but it is also empirically relevant in light of what happened in Egypt and Tunisia in January–February 2011. In Tunisia, Rashid Ammar, the Army Chief of Staff, refused to open fire on the demonstrators, as did Tantawi in Cairo only a few weeks later. Without key defections from within the higher echelons of the ruling elite or without military support, the popular mobilisations at the core of the Arab uprisings would have proved unable to accomplish their goals, as shown by the Syrian case. The military's willingness or unwillingness to use lethal force against civilians is in turn the result of its interests as an institution, including the need to protect its image and prestige as the defender of the people, to uphold internal cohesion and discipline, and to secure its economic interests (Bellin 2004: 131). What remains to be seen is the extent to which the behaviour of the military represented an important contingent cause of the uprisings and their final outcome. In order to answer this question, it is necessary to go back to the aforementioned divisions and contrasts between the ruling party and the military in the Egyptian case. Most of these contrasts derived from the fact that the Egyptian armed forces had a sense of corporate identity distinct from the regime since they were not linked by blood or ethnic ties to the Mubarak regime and family. This is not to suggest that the military did not have a stake in the political status quo due to its economic privileges and interests, blessed and protected by the regime. Ultimately, however, these factors were overshadowed by the military's fundamental opposition to the succession to the presidency of Hosni Mubarak's son. Not only had Gamal never served as an officer in their ranks, but his economic policies were also seen as potentially threatening to some of the officers' key economic interests. The interplay between these factors produced what may at first sight appear to be rather reluctant behaviour on the part of the military towards the shaky Mubarak regime (Albrecht and Bishara 2011).[18] After all, the Egyptian military decided to act to protect its role and autonomy by relinquishing any links to the Mubarak regime and by siding with the protesters.[19] According to some authors, '[Mubarak had become] a liability to [the military] and they were forced to push Mubarak aside; the officers would nevertheless seek to maintain the political system that had served them and their interests so well' (Cook 2011: 286).

A similar story can be told about the role of the Tunisian military in facilitating the success of the popular uprising. In the Tunisian case, it was the professional nature of the military and the fact that it was not the beneficiary of economic cronyism within the regime's networks that significantly reduced the margins of uncertainty on the part of the armed forces as to which stance to take. The Tunisian military did not play a relevant political or economic role under the Ben Ali regime, primarily due to the lack of investments in the military, as opposed to police forces. Furthermore, relations between the military and Ben Ali were known to have been tense in the past. The decision to distance itself from the regime and to side with the protesters was thus not a surprising development and greatly contributed to empowering the popular opposition against the Ben Ali regime. Both in Egypt and in Tunisia, the possibility that the military would not support the regime to the very end and that it would refrain from crushing the protests with the use of force entered the demonstrators' calculations. Once it started to become more concrete,[20] it no doubt had a strong impact on the demonstrators' actions and their resolution to go ahead with the protests until the collapse of the regime, on the one hand. The demonstrators increasingly saw their demands supported by the military, knowing that shooting the former could potentially be costly for the latter. On the other hand, the very decisions of the military stemmed from a careful weighing of different (and sometimes conflicting) imperatives, among which the scope, breadth, means, and, most importantly, potential outcome of the popular mobilisation played a central role. The fact that there were as many as 10,000 people protesting in Avenue Bourguiba in Tunis in mid-January 2011 and that they were relatively peaceful was of enormous importance in the Tunisian military's calculations.

Beyond structure: the role of agency in the Arab uprisings

At the core of the social mobilisations that engulfed the Arab world in 2011, there were agents – the people – seeking to precipitate change from the bottom. This in itself represents a significant novelty for the Arab countries, given the relative absence of political mobilisation at most levels of society over the past half a century. Until 2011, massive, cross-class mobilisation in the name of political, or even regime, change was relatively rare in the region. Although the history of independent Egypt, particularly after the Free Officers coup of 1952, had been marked by episodes of popular insurrection in the form of labour strikes, bread riots, and student protests, the most populous country in the Arab world had never seen the kind of sustained political mobilisation able to challenge the status quo experienced in early 2011 (Beinin and Lockman 1987). As a result, some descriptions of the Arab populations as apathetic could seem appropriate. The first protests in Avenue Bourguiba in Tunis and in Tahrir Square in Cairo have thus overturned some of these long-held truths, including the Arab people's lack of interest in political change. Needless to say, seeing tens if not hundreds of thousands of ordinary people pouring into the streets in Egypt and Tunisia at the beginning of 2011 was an enormous surprise for foreign and domestic observers alike. They did not have much time to understand and adjust their views on the region before the size and the cross-class character of the mobilisation revealed its unprecedented nature with respect to previous moments of unrest 'in ways that proved to be game changers in the region' (Bellin 2012: 153).

It is also important to acknowledge that this outburst of discontent and frustration did not take place in a vacuum and did not represent an isolated or unique case. Stating that the popular mobilisations at the core of the Arab uprisings were prepared by a decade-long process of growing awareness on the part of the people in the region does not mean to diminish the novelty and unprecedented nature of the protests. The 2000s were marked by a surge of protest movements in Egypt spurred by foreign policy as well as domestic issues. Initially, country-wide protests took place in support of Palestine and in opposition to the war in Iraq in

2003. With time, domestic politics and economic problems started to occupy centre stage and become the topics around which opposition to the regime started to coalesce. On the one hand, movements such as *Kifaya!* became the pole of attraction of the opposition to the Mubarak regime. Engaging in numerous public protests and demonstrations, its members and leaders were often brutally repressed or arrested by the security forces, particularly after 2005. Making its first appearance in the winter of 2004, the *Kifaya!* Movement was very active in 2005, but soon lost steam. In addition to the harsh repression of the regime, it was weakened by the fact that it did not manage to extend beyond a restricted circle of middle-class students and intellectuals in Cairo (Shorbagy 2007). Several of its demands, notably constitutional changes and opposition to Gamal Mubarak's hereditary succession, did not resonate with the Egyptian population at the time, many of whom were more concerned with socio-economic demands.

On the other hand, as of mid-2004 – coinciding with the inauguration of the Nazif government in July 2004 – social protests and demonstrations in the form of labour strikes became a prominent feature of Egyptian life. Reflecting the rising discontent of large swathes of the population with increased hardship, this wave of protests gained momentum and quickly became the largest social movement in Egypt, involving over 1 million workers in some form of collective action by the end of 2007 (Beinin 2009; Clément 2009). There were 265 strikes, sit-ins, protests, and demonstrations in 2004; 202 collective actions in 2005, 222 in 2006, and a staggering 614 in 2007.[21] In spite of their huge numbers, actions were more often than not uncoordinated, protests were dispersed, and gains few. Unlike the January–February 2011 protests, these demonstrations remained apolitical, focused on socio-economic problems (Hamzawy 2009; Ottaway and Hamzawy 2011). As a result of the traditional mistrust between workers and political parties, political and social demands did not merge in a potential spiral effect. Only on one occasion, in April 2008, did the latter try to establish a connection with the former, when the activists of the 6 April Movement, through their Facebook page, called on the Egyptian population to strike in support of the workers of the Mahalla factories, to no avail (Collombier 2012). This obstacle was overcome when workers, employees, youth from the middle class, peasants, political activists, and people from all generations and socio-economic backgrounds united to achieve the same goal, namely the removal of the Mubarak regime. The merging of political and social demands led to the successful outcome of the Egyptian uprising. Some authors have defined this as a 'multisectorial revolution', drawing on the term coined by Camau and Geisser with regard to the protests in Tunisia at the end of the 1970s. It refers to 'a situation where the benchmarks and constraints according to which the various actors operate their calculations and adapt their behaviours get blurred' (Camau and Geisser 2003: 185–186). It remains to be seen what factors contributed to making the benchmarks and constraints blurred, thus ultimately unleashing the role of agency.

A number of factors were essential in setting the protests in motion, above and beyond the long-lasting grievances about repression, corruption, and economic hardship. The first was the impact of events, which acted as catalysts or emotional triggers. In Tunisia, Egypt, and many other countries, people took to the streets in growing numbers feeling compelled by such emotions as anger, fear, or euphoria. In Tunisia, the emotional trigger that drove people to protest was outrage following the self-immolation of Mohamed Bouazizi. The humiliation inflicted upon this educated street vendor by state officials emblemised the disrespect and hopelessness felt by so many Tunisians, in particular young ones. In Egypt, a similar feeling of outrage was an important trigger sparking street protests, as the case of the regime's brutal murder of the human rights activist Khaled Said and the ensuing popular mobilisation showed.

Second, and related to emotional triggers, was the sense of empowerment felt by large strata of the populations in different countries following Ben Ali's rapid fall. It is known that, in order to increase the potential of collective social action for change, the sense of empowerment needs to be coupled by a sufficient threshold of social cohesion and shared sentiment for national unity among the people opposing a given regime (El-Din Haseeb 2012: 185). The unexpected unveiling of 'people power' contributed to heightening the feeling that, all of a sudden, the impossible was possible, empowering hundreds of thousands of people at thousands of kilometres from Tunis to act in the same way. To account for this, one concept that is well known in the literature on the politics of protest, namely the power of contagion, has to be brought into play (Volpi 2013; Bunce, Patel, and Wochick 2014). When talking about phenomena such as revolutions, contagion is driven by two different logics: the logic of deliberate diffusion and the logic of demonstration effect. As other historic examples outside the Arab world brilliantly demonstrate, the most important one probably being the wave of regime-toppling protests that led to the political transformation of Eastern Europe in 1989 and afterwards, the former concerns the conscious sharing of tactics and frames by activists who are linked by networks that sometimes take on a transnational nature (Caridi 2012). Clearly this leads to imitation. But in addition, the course of the Arab uprisings also provides evidence of the demonstration effect or the power of the precedent. A sense of commonality led people to 'make analogies' and 'read relevance into developments in other contexts' (Beissinger 2007: 263).[22] The demonstration effect favours patterns of emulation, which propels people to take actions they might never have considered before.[23]

Third and finally, the role of agency in the Arab uprisings cannot be understood in isolation from the combined role of social media and satellite television. The internationally dominant reading of the Arab uprisings is that they were driven by young, tech-savvy, educated members of the middle class. In this scenario, the social media (Facebook, Twitter, YouTube), mobile phones, and videos, and satellite television (in particular Al-Jazeera) enabled the mobilisation of collective action and contributed to creating a region-wide Arab public sphere, which amplified the demonstration effect of the first successful Arab uprising. By exploiting the anonymity, spontaneity, and lack of hierarchy made possible by social media, protesters were able to circumvent the control and repression of authoritarian states. In addition, these tools provided demonstrators with platforms for sharing stories and symbols, as well as for coordinating and synchronising thousands of people in the absence of a formal organisational infrastructure (Lynch 2011). But of the three factors discussed above, the role of social media is the least deterministic one. The contribution of social media to contentious collective action is rather of a permissive and facilitating kind.

The Arab uprisings as the point of arrival of a learning process

When Mohamed Bouazizi set himself on fire in the peripheral Tunisian town of Sidi Bouzid on 17 December 2010, he did not imagine that his flames would have enveloped the whole Arab world, reaching as far as the shores of Bahrain. He did not know that in less than two months, an ever growing wave of largely peaceful popular mobilisation would dislodge two of the most entrenched authoritarian regimes in the world and trigger a process of change that would dramatically alter the landscape of the Arab world. Bouaziz's act could well be regarded as an instance of 'radical contingency' which, according to Beissinger (2007), is a key element in processes such as revolutions or protests. What is meant by this concept is that small decisions and events early on can have huge and unanticipated impacts due to the interaction of different factors.

No better description of the dynamics at play in the Arab uprisings can be provided than the words used by Adam Przeworski to refer to the so-called 'third wave' of democratisation. In *Democracy and the Market*, he wrote:

> I know that hundreds of macrohistorical comparative sociologists will write thousands of books and articles correlating background conditions with outcomes in each country, but I think that they will be wasting their time, for the entire event was one single snowball. I mean it in a technical sense: as developments took place in one country, people elsewhere were updating their probabilities of success, and as the next country went over the brink, the calculation was becoming increasingly reassuring.
>
> (Przeworski 1991: 3–4)

By connecting all the dots of the Arab uprisings to one single event that took place in a remote area of Tunisia, the strong explanatory power of non-structural factors becomes apparent. Contingency and agency, with all the sub-dimensions whose impact has been assessed above, are two key factors in accounting for the outbreak of protests and their short-term outcome. They complement the explanation provided by structural factors, namely the existence of long-standing grievances about the policies adopted by the regimes. Nevertheless, as salient and vexing as they were, grievances alone do not shed enough light on the sudden surge in popular protest, its timing, and its location. In particular, by looking only at structural factors, it is hard to understand why the Arab uprisings started in Tunisia at the end of 2010. According to many authors, Tunisia was an unlikely candidate for revolution (Hamid 2011a). Corruption, repression, and economic hardship had plagued the country for decades, yet never before had popular protests emerged in a sustained way. Furthermore, political and socio-economic grievances had long afflicted other countries in the region, e.g., Libya and Syria to name just a few, to an extent that dwarfed the Tunisian experience (Bellin 2012). This does not mean overlooking the crucial importance of structural factors. Rather, the intention is to point out that structural conditions cannot be detached from contingency and agency if a sound assessment is to be made of the motives behind the outbreak of the uprisings.

On the one hand, structural factors together with certain elements of contingency, such as the succession question or divisions within the ruling elite in a country like Egypt, shaped the context in which popular mobilisation could take place. They provided the 'political opportunity structure' influencing the calculations of a number of actors, both in the regime and in the opposition. On the other hand, other elements of contingency, namely the self-immolation of 'martyrs' in each country, and the power of agency deriving from commonality, emulation, and the facilitating contribution of social media, provided other incentives and constraints for the stances of the different actors. These factors are an important constituent part of the 'discursive opportunity structure' that, according to the analysis conducted by Koopmans (2004), sometimes plays a more significant role than the 'political opportunity structure' in setting in motion processes such as protests or revolutions. Only by taking into account the context and the agency-related drivers of the popular mobilisations, but also the mutual interaction and impact they have had on each other, is it possible to grasp the turning point represented by the Arab uprisings.

The combination of context and agency-spurred mobilisation that led to the outbreak of the Arab uprisings was the result of a learning process among the Arab people. In the first part of this chapter, I talked extensively about the ability of regimes in power to learn from and to adapt to changing conditions. I also stressed how this adaptive capacity was, and still is to some degree, a defining attribute of authoritarian regimes in the Arab world. As a result of this process of learning and adaptation, the regimes managed to protect themselves from emerging challenges and problems for a long time, seemingly even reinforcing their grip on power through repression, co-optation, or selective liberalisation. While this learning process had its own shortcomings, making the situation in the Arab countries unsustainable and the status quo untenable, it was also increasingly faced by a number of challenges deriving from another learning process. It should be clear by now that Arab citizens themselves experienced a process of social learning – facilitated by the rapid diffusion of ideas, discourses, tools, and practices from one country to another and by their adaptation to local contexts – which started to bear fruit in 2011. In conclusion, the Arab uprisings can thus be seen as the point of arrival of two parallel learning processes going in opposite directions.[24] The former is the learning process of the regimes, which granted them apparent stability and ensured their survival for decades. The latter, going in the opposite direction, is the learning process experienced by the Arab people who were humiliated and reduced to powerless subjects in years of authoritarian institutions and practices. By learning from past mistakes and capitalising on the force provided by emulation and commonality, they were able to change the course of history in a number

Looking back 53

of Arab countries. What has happened after this intense, emotional, and unexpected turning point represented a different phase for the Arab world and will be examined in the following pages.

Notes

1. In this research, the terms 'Arab uprisings', 'Arab revolutions', and 'Arab spring' (sometimes in its plural form, 'Arab springs') are used interchangeably with a marked preference for the first, due to its neutrality.
2. One example of the application of modernisation theories to the study of Middle East politics is provided by Lerner (1958).
3. Rentier-state theories have been variously criticised for failing to take into account the specific socio-political contexts in which the use and distribution of rents take place and for overemphasising economic determinism. See the works of Okruhlik (1999); Nonneman (2001); Schlumberger (2006). These authors tend to stress that the relationship between rents and socio-economic and political development is circular rather than linear.
4. The constituent elements of the traditional definition of authoritarianism – the point of departure of this research – can be summarised as follows: authoritarian regimes are political systems with limited, not responsible, political pluralism; without an elaborate and guiding ideology (but with distinct mentalities); without intensive nor extensive political mobilisation (except at some points in their development); and in which a leader (or occasionally a small group) exercises power within formally ill-defined limits but actually quite predictable ones.
5. For an overview of the most common neo-patrimonial practices in North African and Middle Eastern politics and their relevance for the development of predatory institutions, see Gellner and Waterbury (1977).
6. For an appraisal of this early phase of political liberalisation, see Alexander (1997); Murphy (1999); Sadiki (2003); Erdle (2004); Brownlee (2007).
7. The Tunisian General Union of Labour (*Union Générale Tunisienne du Travail*, UGTT) cannot be considered an autonomous expression of society as it was co-opted under Ben Ali through government interference in the appointment of its members (Kausch 2009; EMHRN 2010).
8. On the co-optation of Egyptian non-governmental organisations and trade unions under Mubarak, see Moore and Salloukh (2007); Al-Din Arafat (2009); Guirguis (2009); Hopkins (2009).
9. For an accurate analysis of the role, strengths, and weaknesses of these organisations and movements in Egypt during the 2000s, see Hopkins (2009).
10. For a detailed account of the regime's repression during the 2007–2010 period, see Beinin (2009).
11. In 1994, the quota system allocated 12 percent of the seats to legally recognised parties other than the RCD. In 1999, this quota was raised to 19 percent and, in 2009, to 25 percent (Boubekeur 2009).
12. In 2008, the then managing director of the IMF, Dominique Strauss-Kahn, defined the Tunisian economy as an 'example for emerging countries', while the WB named it a 'top reformer' in regulatory reform. Quoted in Hamid (2011a: 111).
13. One of the indicators that pointed to sound macroeconomic performance and social policy in Tunisia in the last decade of the twentieth century was the level of public expenditure for education and health services, which doubled during the 1986–2002 period. In the same period, expenditure on social welfare increased by 214 percent. As a result, social security coverage reached approximately 85 percent of the Tunisian population according to some data (Ben Romdhane 2006). Poverty and unemployment were targeted by two social programmes, the National Solidarity Fund, also known as

'26–26', and the National Employment Fund, dubbed '21–21', established in 1992 and 2000 respectively (Harrigan and El-Said 2009). One major problem concerning these funds was that they were directly controlled by the ruling party and managed with little transparency.
14 For an excellent account of the impact of crony capitalism in Egypt, see Wurzel (2009).
15 The most widely read monograph on adaptive authoritarianism is *Upgrading Authoritarianism in the Arab World* by Stephen Heydemann (2007a). The concept of 'authoritarian consolidation' was developed by the French political scientist Michel Camau in his work on Tunisia under Bourguiba and Ben Ali. See Camau and Geisser (2003). See also the work of Jason Brownlee who stresses the importance of political institutions in processes of authoritarian consolidation. In particular, Brownlee (2007) underlines the crucial importance of institutional differences separating unstable authoritarian regimes from durable dictatorships. Institutional factors structuring elite relations and decision-making play a fundamental role in any regime and represent important elements explaining authoritarian regimes' durability or erosion and breakdown. Crucially, ruling parties are identified by the author as the most significant factor of regime survival.
16 The military's opposition to some of the economic reforms implemented since the mid-2000s derived from their deep involvement in the economy and, ostensibly, from their role as guarantor of national security. Some of the privatisation measures targeting public companies were indeed opposed by the military under the pretext that they would harm strategic assets. There is, however, lack of evidence that the reforms proposed by the technocrats close to Gamal Mubarak would have directly harmed the military's economic interests as most of the measures concerned sectors such as telecommunications and finance in which they are not involved.
17 See cable 08CAIRO2091 of 23 September 2008 and cable 07CAIRO974 of 4 April 2007.
18 The authors claim that the length of time that elapsed between the military's takeover of control of Egyptian streets (28 January) and the fall of the regime (11 February) provides evidence of the military's reluctant behaviour.
19 In the early days of the protests in Tahrir Square, the Egyptian military made use of tear gas and water cannons to disperse the protestors. Later on, as the balance of force started to tilt in favour of the demonstrators, they took on the task of protecting government buildings rather than intervening against the demonstrators.
20 In Egypt, this became evident when a YouTube video displayed the military not only refusing to shoot at a crowd of demonstrators but also appearing to protect them from the police, who were instead attacking the demonstrators (Bellin 2012).
21 These figures are quoted in Beinin (2009: 37–38) and are based on the activities of the Land Center for Human Rights. According to the same author, the most politically significant among the collective actions were two strikes at the Misr Spinning and Weaving Company in Mahalla al-Kubra in December 2006 and September 2007.
22 The author has developed the notion of 'analogic thinking' to refer to the driving forces lying behind the demonstration effect.
23 A form of emulation can also be read in the practice of turning public spaces such as Tahrir Square in Cairo, Pearl Square in Manama, Liberation Square in Benghazi, and Clock Square in Homs into symbols of popular defiance and podiums of dialogue for the multi-faceted popular mobilisation.
24 According to Heydemann and Leenders, a process of learning is still underway as far as the incumbent regimes that have remained in power in some Arab countries following the events of the Arab uprisings are concerned. By looking at the experiences of Syria, Bahrain, and other countries, the authors claim that patterns of the Arab regimes' counter-revolutions can be recognised, shaped by processes of learning and diffusion among regime elites, especially among those where protests began and gained traction at a later stage. While valid in many respects, explaining the absence of regime

change in countries such as Syria and Bahrain only by reference to the (new) strategies of repression and co-optation enacted by these regimes to prove that their countries are 'not like Egypt and Tunisia' obscures more than it reveals: it fails to account for fundamental structural differences in the makeup of the regimes themselves and their regional and external allies, and in the incumbent institutional arrangements compared to the countries where the uprisings have led to regime change (Heydemann and Leenders 2011: 649).

3 Writing constitutions in time

Q: The last three years have been very turbulent for Egypt, since the revolution that overthrew Mubarak. Looking back, what do you think have been the most important lessons from that time?

A: [. . .] That Egypt is totally unpredictable, and if you think you've got it figured out you're wrong. And we are doing a very, very good job being the soap opera of the world. We're drama queens of the news right now.

from Bassem Youssef's interview in the *New York Times'*
Lede Blog. 26 November 2013

The Arab uprisings represented a fundamental turning point in the political development of the Arab world. In light of its novelty and the far-reaching transformation it has brought about, many – largely unwarranted – parallelisms have been drawn between them and the changes that took place in Eastern Europe in the 1990s.[1] The Arab uprisings were a turning point also in another sense: they unleashed a long-suppressed feeling of empowerment and enthusiasm among the Arab 'masses', which had for so many years been subjected to brutal, oppressive, and illiberal authoritarian rule. It took the protest movements a decade and more to learn to overwhelm and physically defeat extremely capable coercive apparatuses in Egypt and Tunisia in January and February 2011. This result contributed to bringing the Arab world into the international limelight, thanks also to the role of unconstrained media duly covering the Arab awakening day and night. It was immediately celebrated in all corners of the world – particularly by surprised and astonished external observers and analysts – as the moment in which the Arab countries would enter a completely new, democratic phase. However, nowhere has the need to decouple the process of authoritarian breakdown from that of transitioning out of authoritarianism (and eventually replacing the old system with democracy) been so acute. Eva Bellin, among others, has drawn attention to the fact that simply because an authoritarian regime is unseated, this does not mean that a democratic regime will necessarily take its place. Looking back in history, one can easily see that the most common scenario has been for an authoritarian regime to be replaced by another authoritarian regime or a hybrid form of liberalised autocracy or competitive authoritarianism (Bellin 2011).[2] During the phase between

2011 and the beginning of 2014, political developments in Egypt and Tunisia all took place within the confines of an uncertain space, the space of the transitions from authoritarianism.[3] The end of an authoritarian system, through the collapse of the autocratic ruler, or its liberalisation through some ad-hoc reforms do not necessarily imply a progression towards democracy, but rather an uncertain 'something else' that can eventually give rise to a form of democracy, a new authoritarian regime, or the breakdown of the system into instability and chaos. This calls for an assessment of the transition processes that have been triggered by the events of 2011. The so-called Arab 'revolutions' have been primarily focused on individual political and socio-economic emancipation rather than collective transformation. Demands for full citizenship and for recognition of individual rights were powerful unifying forces across the Arab world during the uprisings. However, by focusing on these issues, the protests were self-limiting, and in some cases the initial gains have been rolled back during the transition processes that have followed.

All in all, every process of transition is likely to be shaped by both continuities and changes. On the one hand, the former exist both among the actors and in relation to formal and informal institutions. For example, elements of the old guard, including members of parliament, bureaucrats, judges, and military officers, have indeed remained in place. In the case of Tunisia, although Ben Ali's ruling party, the *Rassemblement Constitutionnel Démocratique* (RCD), was banned in March 2011, its assets seized, and its top figures barred from running for political office, some of the vestiges of the old party system have not completely disappeared. Some forms of continuity with the old authoritarian past could be seen in the extremely large number of parties that were created in the aftermath of the Tunisian revolution. In some cases, the functional or technical expertise accumulated by these elements of the old guard has turned out to be of great importance for the new (interim) governments. Not least because these actors and institutions sometimes have influence over large swathes of the economy, which they try to control through oligarchic and/or neo-patrimonial networks, even as the institutional system is being restructured. On the other hand, the continuing strong presence of adaptable and in some cases even evolving authoritarian institutional features should not divert attention away from the many significant ways in which the Arab uprisings have indeed led to some fundamental changes. These changes in turn challenge the long-standing and still persisting, at least within some strands of the literature on the Middle East, opinion that there is nothing new under the region's sun. In the words of Marc Lynch, a whole new 'texture of politics' has emerged in the aftermath of the popular uprisings of 2011 (Lynch 2011). Among the most striking features of this new texture of politics was the phenomenon of re-politicisation. This has taken various forms. The most obvious has been the rise in various expressions of contentious politics. In the Arab world, this has consisted of a 'complex collage of striking workers, trade unionists, unemployed university graduates, human rights and democracy activists, demobilized leftists and Islamists' (Beinin and Vairel 2011: 1). It has been reflected in countless examples of the 'quiet encroachment of the ordinary', to borrow Asef Bayat's expression, during these last few years of 'politics' taking place outside the confined spaces of political parties and institutions (Bayat 2009: 33; Alexander 2011; El-Ghobashy 2011).

Despite an opening-up of society in the initial stage of the transition, intra-elite behaviour is the key factor explaining the direction and pace of institutional development in the Arab world. Another form of the re-politicisation of the Arab world has indeed been the revitalisation of the formal political scene with the emergence of a whole range of new political parties and struggles over the definition and control of institutions (Valbjørn 2012). The scholarly literature on (democratic) transitions normally makes a distinction between the tasks of resistance within 'civil society' that help to deconstruct authoritarianism and the tasks of 'political society' that help to construct the new institutional system.[4] On the one hand, one example of the category of 'civil society' were the thousands of people who spontaneously took to the streets and squares at the beginning of 2011. Their main feature, i.e., their pluralistic and decentralised nature, represented an asset during the uprisings, but turned into a liability during the transition phase. Most of these groups remained trapped in their extremely value-ridden ideas and claims, unable to act pragmatically, and espousing short-term and purely negative messages and goals (Roberts 2013). On the other hand, the 'political society' made up of parties, parliaments, elections, and constitutions has gained a meaningful and central position in politics. A telling example of the powerful comeback of formal institutions on the political scene is the Egyptian Salafists' decision to found their own party and run in the elections, after years, if not decades, of rejection of participatory politics. All of a sudden, it has become meaningful, even for the Salafists, to be present on the formal political scene with a view to being part of and possibly influencing the political game (Valbjørn 2012: 32). One of the tasks of the 'political society' is to bring opposition leaders into agreement on plans for an interim government as well as elections capable of generating constitution-making authorities endowed with legitimacy (Stepan 2012: 94).

After the popular mobilisation of internally diversified, leaderless, and loosely structured groups of people that succeeded in bringing down some of the most entrenched authoritarian regimes in the region, political struggles turned to the restructuring, change, and manipulation of the existing institutions with a view to creating new ones. One of the most difficult aspects of post-'revolutionary' transitions is the task of turning the constituent power of the 'revolutionary' moment, its demands, and its claims into a constitutional form of (new) political order. Processes of constitution making or constitutional revision came to occupy the centre stage in Egypt and Tunisia, albeit to different degrees and with different implications. The importance of constitutions in defining the distribution and structure of power, i.e., how governmental tasks are distributed among different agencies and how conflicts are resolved among them, cannot be emphasised enough. Constitutional provisions define the identity and nature of a state and lay down the rules of the game that regulate the division of powers and the orderly conduct of business for the sake of predictability and efficiency. Another function performed by constitutions is to enshrine the protection of basic rights and freedoms in the most important document of the state, which is particularly pertinent in factionalised or deeply divided societies.[5]

Study of constitution making still has a frontier quality with respect to the broader field of comparative research, although it is growing fast as a result of the scholarly interest that has developed out of the break-up of existing polities, e.g., after World War I or the collapse of the Soviet Union (Hyden and Venter 2001; Samuels 2006; Blount, Elkins, and Ginsburg 2012). Any particular instance of constitutional design must deal with certain basic questions of organisation and process. These include designating *who* is to be involved; *when* that involvement takes place; and *how* the actors are to proceed in terms of formulating, discussing, and approving a text. As for the 'who' is involved in the process, institutional scholars usually think of actors as 'veto players' (Tsebelis 2002). The wide range of actors that participate in constitution-making processes can include expert commissions, legislative bodies or committees, the executive, the judiciary, national conferences, elite round tables, transitional legislatures, specially elected constituent assemblies, interest groups and non-governmental organisations, foreign advisors, and the population itself.[6] In order to correctly appraise the relative importance of each actor and its ability to influence the process, it is useful to think of them in terms of their power, understood both in its fixed/stock form and in its process/flow-based nature. By the former we mean the amount of power that each actor possesses at a specific moment in time, e.g., at the beginning of the constitution-making process. The latter instead conceives the actors' power as a much more complex, relational type of process, which is shaped by the (changing) features of the external environment and is subject to fluctuations. Furthermore, although constitution making is usually regarded as a largely homegrown, domestic process, forms of interdependence, borrowing, and influence from the international environment are not absent (Blount *et al.* 2012: 39–40). Other authors tend to appreciate the international impact on constitution making, both in terms of actors and ideologies, as the background against which domestic processes take place (Lang 2013: 352).

Regarding the 'when' dimension, time is universally acknowledged as an important variable in assessing the links between constitution-making processes and outcomes, albeit an under-researched one. It is widely acknowledged that decisions about timing and sequencing have a strong impact on political outcomes. How to sequence constitutional changes with elections will necessarily involve a tradeoff between the legitimacy ensured by early elections and the political and legal vacuum arising from establishing a new political order without the foundation of a clear basic institutional consensus. However, what some of the extensive debates on the topic of how to sequence the writing of a constitution and the election of a president and parliament have failed to grasp is the extent to which these decisions are the outcome of fundamentally political processes. In other words, constitution-making processes do not take place in a vacuum, but rather in political contexts that are characterised by actors wielding different degrees of power at a time when the basic rules of political life are uncertain. This means that constitutional engineering is shaped by political processes happening in time. Generally speaking, too rapid processes do not allow sufficient time for mobilisation of the public opinion and civil society, whereas too extended ones are unlikely to hold public attention for the duration of the process. Finally, with regard to the 'how', constitution making occurs in discernible stages, which can be identified as follows: drafting, consultation, deliberation, adoption, and ratification (Widner 2007).[7] The drafting phase is especially crucial as one can expect a fair degree of path-dependence in the later stages of the process.

The task of re-making the constitutional order in countries such as Egypt and Tunisia in the aftermath of the uprisings has been a daunting one. It cannot be reduced to the simple writing of the rules by which political choices will be made but it enshrines the making of important political decisions deriving from a compromise between conflicting political interests. In other words, making a constitution is not a pre-political or politically neutral enterprise but rather a supremely political process in which power is contested and stakes are high; it is often of tremendous symbolic and emotional as well as legal and practical importance. By the same token, constitutions should not be seen as 'ideal documents', but rather as contentious political projects, reflecting political realities, in which interests and conflicts are constantly negotiated. Thus, the focus of attention is not so much on the substantive provisions contained in the final document but on the process itself, which can be described as a 'struggle for power' that regards both the present day and the future. The process of constitution making is a contested endeavour that can bring to the surface deep-running societal rifts and, as a result, it is likely to trigger conflicts at multiple levels. During the transition, a great deal of the country's energies tend to be focused on the process of constitution making, often at the risk of heightening socio-political conflicts as a result of major disagreements on the content of the text itself. Some of the most contentious issues that need to be settled include the separation of powers, namely executive-legislative relations and horizontal accountability. Moving away from the tradition of strong executives in the Arab world, be they controlled by all-powerful presidents or monarchs, means setting norms that ensure effective guarantees against the abuse of governmental authority by providing 'checks and balances' through the functional interdependence of state bodies. Executive-legislative relations are a particularly difficult area of constitutional engineering as they are inherently interwoven with a number of issues that generally lie outside the constitutional framework, such as the party and electoral system, and that ultimately have an impact on the actual functioning of the system of government. This means, for example, that similar constitutional provisions would work quite differently in the presence of a fragmented party system or in one that is dominated by two strong parties (Brody-Barre 2013). It is also worth stressing that, even though constitutional provisions are fundamental in shaping executive-legislative relations, much of the evolution of these relations in practice depends on institutional logics and patterns of behaviour that develop informally, rather than on the strict application of relatively fixed texts. Another function of the separation of powers is to protect minorities from the tyranny of certain majorities. In this light, these norms would ultimately function as anti-majoritarian instruments.[8] Nevertheless, in as much as political systems coming out of authoritarian rule need to create more effective measures to remove bodies such as judicial councils, constitutional courts, and administrative courts from executive control, thus ensuring their autonomy from other political powers, there is also the need to make sure that these institutions are not beyond the mechanisms of accountability. The question of who guards the guardians, such as constitutional courts, is thus a relevant one. A second set of contentious issues that need to be settled during the constitution-making process in those countries where religion – in the case of the Arab world, Islam, given that this is the religion of the majority of the population – plays an important role not only in the private sphere but also in the public/political one has to do with the identity of the state in religious terms and the place of religious institutions within the architecture of the state. Finally, civilian-military relations represent crucial factors in political systems whose recent history was characterised by a substantial amount of political and economic power being under the direct control of the military and security apparatuses. The task then is to devise methods of real political oversight and civilian control, without undermining public security and the effectiveness of the military institution.

Egypt: the wrong sequence for a polarised process

Veto powers

The Egyptian institutional transition to a new constitution was the most significant issue of contention and conflict among the political actors in the aftermath of the fall of the Mubarak regime. Looking at the country's previous history of constitutionalism, one cannot fail to appreciate the significant amount of pressure and expectations attached to this step by a number of players willing to exercise their power to influence Egypt's development (Interviewees 1, 2, 10, 14). For the first time in the history of the country, the formal rules of the political game would be written by the people's representatives and not by an appointed body. Back in the 1920s, when Egypt achieved independence from Great Britain, a constitutional commission of 32 members, including law scholars, representatives of religious minorities, and other members of civil society, was appointed to draft the constitution. This decision was taken by the Khedive, the country's governor under the Ottoman Empire, under pressure from the British, despite the fact that they had formally transferred power over domestic affairs to the Egyptians. The establishment of the constitutional commission was fiercely opposed by the Wafd Party – the most popular and influential political party, of nationalist orientation, in the 1920–1930s period – which claimed that an elected constituent assembly would be the only satisfactory vehicle for drafting a constitution (Lufti Al-Sayyid Marsot 1977; Brown 2002). The result of the struggle between the unelected monarch and the largest and most organised political party of the time was the 1923 constitution establishing a constitutional monarchy, in which power would be wielded by a nationally elected parliament (Osman 2010). All the subsequent Egyptian constitutions, both during Nasser's revolutionary period and under Sadat, equally failed to include elected representatives in their drafting processes. This was due to the fact that these constitutions and their revisions were drafted under increasingly authoritarian conditions (Kassem 2004; Kienle 2001). This was, for example, the case of the already-mentioned constitutional amendments introduced by Mubarak in 2005, altering article 76 of the 1971 constitution that defined how the president of Egypt was elected. The need to change the approach to constitution making thus immediately emerged as one of the priorities in the aftermath of the 'revolutionary' moment. The ultimate goal was to make sure that the political system would cease to be separate from the social environment (Interviewee 4).

The whole process of constitution making was influenced by the nature of the actors who shaped it and by the timing and sequencing of the steps taken. There was considerable debate in Egypt about the sequence of the institutional steps that would follow Mubarak's departure. In particular, most of the attention was focused on whether writing a new constitution should come before holding elections. Finding the best sequence in abstract terms was not the problem (Brown 2013a: 46); but in practical terms this turned out to be a very contested issue and something that would influence the course of the Egyptian transition from that moment onwards.[9] The transition sequence was enshrined in the roadmap provided by the constitutional declaration engineered by the Supreme Council of the Armed Forces (SCAF) and approved in March 2011. The problem with that roadmap/sequence was that it was not the result of a broad agreement among all the elites on the rules of the transition but, rather, was passed by a majority vote reflecting the preference of one group over the others.

If one of the most difficult aspects of post-revolutionary transitions is to turn the demands, grievances, and expectations of the revolutionary moment into a new constitutional form of political order, it can be argued that the new Egyptian constitution was not the result of a competitive process. The whole constitution-making process did not unfold in a compromise-seeking atmosphere between conflicting political interests, rights, and responsibilities. This was mainly due to the fact that it was initiated and steered in a particular direction by an 'alliance' among established political forces, each of which had vested interests. I am referring here to the convergence of interests between the higher echelons of the military apparatus and the Muslim Brotherhood immediately after Mubarak's fall. While according to some authors talking about an 'alliance' is an exaggeration in light of the temporary nature of the agreement,[10] this does not change the most profound feature of the Egyptian constitutional revision process. It was driven by a number of different configurations of alliances among the actors depending on their relative power as a result of either electoral or street politics. The lowest common denominator of all these temporary alliances was the role played by the military, which acted as the swing force and was thus able to influence the pace and direction of the entire process.

The SCAF suspended the 1971 constitution two days after Mubarak's fall from power on 11 February 2011, thereby creating a legal vacuum that was to be filled with some interim provisions that would set out the principles for drafting the new constitutional text.[11] Upon assuming power, the SCAF appointed a committee of legal experts to draft amendments to the 1971 constitution. The result was not an open and participatory process. The SCAF excluded representation from all political parties and groups, save one member of the Muslim Brotherhood. The committee was headed by Tariq al-Bishri, a prominent jurist and public intellectual known for his outspoken criticism of the former regime. The constitutional reform committee unveiled a package of nine amendments to the 1971 constitution after ten days of closed-door meetings. This took place as early as 26 February 2011, thus allowing only a brief time for public debate. A national referendum on the proposed amendments was held just three weeks later, on 19 March.

There was no participatory process at all, and the only role for the main political parties and the public was a simple yes or no vote on the package of amendments (Interviewees 6, 11, 18). In detail, the most significant amendments involved paving the way for a new constitution after elections and were therefore important in determining the sequencing of constitution making and elections (art. 76); shortening the presidential term from six to four years and establishing a limit of two terms, which had been one of the opposition's main demands to Mubarak since at least 2004 (art. 77); and restricting the ability to impose a lengthy state of emergency as well as limiting the duration of the emergency period to no more than six months, which could be extended only by approval in a referendum (art. 148). As the population was summoned to the polls to approve the amendments that would build a new constitutional order, two opposing views manifested themselves, thus contributing to the emergence of fissures within the revolutionary groups that had participated in the popular mobilisation. On the one hand, the Muslim Brotherhood embraced the amendments, arguing that they were the best means of ensuring a quick transition process, which indirectly meant the withdrawal of the military from political life and the return to an elected parliament and president (Interviewee 27). Many people also took the referendum to be a vote on whether or not the provisions existing in the 1971 constitution that were in line with Islamic law would be preserved, and therefore voted 'yes' out of fear that they might be at risk if a completely new constitution were to be written.[12] Furthermore, most people who voted in favour of what were presented to them as constitutional amendments expressed their willingness for the creation of a new, stable institutional order that would guarantee them against failing public security (Interviewee 13). On the other hand, a sizeable amount of the Egyptian population opposed the amendments on the grounds that they did not provide for a sufficiently clear-cut break with the past. Most civic forces rallied around the idea that a new constitution would have to be written first, which would set out the principles and rules for crafting new state institutions. With political institutions largely unchanged and the population called to the polls to cast their ballots for elected institutions, the civic forces worried that it would only be a matter of time before remnants of the old regime or some other illiberal political forces would assert control over the state (Moustafa 2012). As much as they were equally worried that the strict timeline for new elections provided for by the constitutional amendments would not allow nascent political forces sufficient time to organise, the civic forces were unable to lay out a coherent, alternative plan for the transition, beyond calling for a broad and inclusive constitutional convention in advance of the elections. Among the groups and political forces that urged a 'no' vote in the referendum were a number of civil society groups, opposition parties, and youth groups, all of which had initiated and participated in the uprising alongside the Islamist opposition.

One of the most significant long-term repercussions of the referendum over the constitutional amendments was the wake of mistrust and polarisation over the rules and procedures to be followed for a return to an elected government that it left among the population. The absence of an agreed-upon, basic roadmap haunted the whole institutional development process, particularly as far as the making of the new constitution was concerned. At the same time, the process started off with the complete break-up of the anti-Mubarak 'alliance' and the establishment of a new one between the Islamists and the military. The Muslim Brotherhood chose 'the devil it knew' and decided to work with the SCAF to advance its interests instead of trailing a more uncertain path and joining the civic opposition forces. As a result of this alliance, the military found itself acting as the uncontested arbiter of the transition and was able to leverage on its privileged position within the Egyptian post-Mubarak political system. Against this backdrop and in the absence of any checks and balances on its power as well as any constitutional framework whatsoever, the SCAF purposely altered the timeline and process that was to guide Egypt's political transition several times to suit its own evolving interests. The extent to which the SCAF was actually controlling the transition was clear when the constitutional amendments, having been approved in the 19 March 2011 referendum by 77 percent, were not included in the old constitution. Instead, on 30 March 2011, only ten days after the referendum, drawing on its questionable 'revolutionary legitimacy', the military promulgated a new, temporary constitutional declaration consisting of 63 articles.

The March 2011 constitutional declaration issued by the SCAF was to serve as an interim constitution until a completely new text was drafted. In making this declaration, the military demonstrated the enormous amount of political control they had over defining the content, timing, and sequencing of the transition.[13] The interim constitutional document did not match the wording of the recently passed amendments and was drafted by people whose identity was kept secret. The fact that the constitutional declaration was written in secrecy and outside of a participatory process was in line with the country's past experience. As aptly recalled by Nathan Brown, '[p]ast constitutions have been drafted by committees working in private. The country has no tradition to draw on for a more protracted and inclusive process, such as an elected constituent assembly' (Brown 2011a). Furthermore, the declaration reopened the debate on how to sequence the writing of a constitution and the election of a president and parliament, a debate that once again aggravated political cleavages, with the Muslim Brotherhood and other Islamist groups wanting to have elections first, claiming that only a representative parliament would be able to create a legitimate and representative constituent assembly, and non-Islamists pushing hard for a new constitution in advance of elections.

As far as its contents were concerned, the document reintroduced some elements from the suspended 1971 constitution, but not others. For example, the mechanisms for parliamentary oversight of the government were removed from the constitutional declaration, which also failed to provide indications as to whether the to-be-elected parliament would be accountable to any authority other than the elected president. Even more problematic was that, in article 56, the declaration stipulated that the SCAF would be the only body that could legislate and govern, even after a new parliament had been elected (Lang 2013: 357). Thus, the declaration introduced severe limitations on the constituent and legislative powers of the new parliament. Another shortcoming of the 2011 constitutional declaration was its ambiguity – even if more by accident than by intention – surrounding the creation of the commission that was intended to draft the final constitution. While it was clear that the body would have to be selected by the parliament, there was no clear guidance regarding the composition of the assembly. Article 60 of the 30 March 2011 constitutional declaration read as follows:

> The members of the first People's Assembly and Shura Council (except the appointed members) will meet in a joint session following an invitation from the Supreme Council of the Armed Forces within 6 months of their election to elect a provisional assembly composed of 100 members which will prepare a new draft constitution for the country to be completed within 6 months of the formation of this assembly. The draft constitution will be presented within 15 days of its preparation to the people who will vote in a referendum on the matter. The constitution will take effect from the date on which the people approve the referendum.[14]

The provision was vague about whether or not members of parliament could be part of the constituent assembly, whether or not the assembly would have to include external figures, and who those figures would be, i.e., party leaders, technical experts, intellectuals, activists, or public figures. While this may sound like a secondary issue, in reality it was to become a major point of debate and friction in the uncertain and polarised post-'revolutionary' context. All in all, this ambiguous wording can be interpreted as a further sign of the military's unwillingness to include a wider constituency in the constitution-making process and to move forward by broad consultation and consensus. The way in which the constitutional declaration came to light, in particular, provided a good prediction of the fact that the constitution-making process was to be the outcome of unilateral choices.

Overall, not only did the military's decision about the timing and sequencing of the transition affect the electoral outcomes and the whole process, but it also undermined trust among the civilian political actors and increased their tendency to shun consensus-building methods. Nevertheless, the generals' management of the initial stages of the constitution-making process does not explain the whole situation. Rather, the lack of a consensus-based approach was mainly the result of the inability of the 'revolutionary' forces to unify around this notion and their tendency, instead, to pursue their actions through a narrowly defined set of principles and interests. In the absence of clear institutional rules, this led to the strong polarisation that was witnessed in the country during the transition phase. The main fault-line along which polarisation and conflict developed was between the forces that belonged to the Islamist camp and the civic forces.

Lack of consensus

In February–March 2011, it would theoretically have been possible to reach a consensus among all actors with regard to the steps to be taken to craft a post-'revolutionary' political order based on some basic matters of institutional reform. In other words, a consensual approach could have been devised based on the need to weaken the role of the presidency, provide stronger safeguards for freedoms and the rule of law, and ensure judicial independence. Nevertheless, many factors obstructed this evolution, including mutual suspicion, strengthened by the legacy of the former regime's anti-Islamist discourse and some actors' contradictory positions on political reform. Disagreements and fissures started to feed the tendency to view the generals as the only arbiter in the political game and thus the target of bargaining attempts. This was largely the result of decades of authoritarian rule that had left behind an unbalanced political scene,[15] unrealistic expectations regarding what could be achieved in the post-'revolutionary' phase, and the overwhelming fear and distrust between the competing camps.

As a result of the first parliamentary elections of the post-Mubarak era, the existing polarisation became palpable and started to undermine the constitution-making process. The new legislative assembly, elected between November 2011 and January 2012, was largely dominated by the Muslim Brotherhood and its party, the Freedom and Justice Party (FJP). This result was to be expected after their decades-long grass-roots work penetrating significant parts of the Egyptian society and heralding a new socio-political agenda based on an end to corruption and attention to the population's immediate socio-economic needs. The very biased nature of the newly elected Egyptian parliament, together with the lack of clarity about the procedures to be followed for appointing the members of the constituent assembly, coalesced to create a very confused constitution-making process.

Delving into the role of the constituent assembly means asking a number of questions concerning its origins, its composition, and its functioning. These features influence the process of constitution making and its final outcome, as the constituent assembly is a special institution, entrusted with a particularly important task in the transition from authoritarianism. Given its extraordinary nature and responsibilities – it is in fact created only in specific moments of a state's history and is not supposed to be in place for too long – it often becomes the locus of intense power struggles that shape the relationship among the most significant political actors during the transition. One of the more remarkable aspects of Egypt's constitution-making process was that it was the first to be carried out by an elected body – albeit indirectly – thus representing a significant accomplishment for a country whose previous constitutions had always been the product of secret sessions among unrepresentative and unelected political elites. On the basis of article 60 of the March 2011 constitutional declaration, parliament was responsible for naming the constituent assembly on 26 March 2012. The article was interpreted as stating that half of the members of the assembly would come from parliament and the other half would be non-partisan representatives of various institutions and organisations in Egyptian society. In practice, 64 of the 100 members of the constituent assembly were chosen among representatives of the Muslim Brotherhood's Freedom and Justice Party or had very strong Islamist connections. As a result, the 100-member Egyptian constituent assembly was dominated by the Muslim Brotherhood and other Islamist parties. Between 26 March and 10 April 2012 – the day in which the committee was dissolved – the constituent assembly began its proceedings, involving the creation of five internal committees, amid growing accusations of the lack of legitimacy particularly from the representatives of the civic forces and the Christians. The non-Islamist parliamentary forces went so far as to publicly accuse the Islamist ones of wanting to dominate the assembly by resorting to clientelistic practices such as drawing in relatives (Interviewee 1). Chiefly, the opposition stressed that since parliamentary majorities are transitory by nature, the assembly's makeup should reflect all parts of Egyptian society. The whole constitution-making process could have developed differently: had a deal over the constituent assembly been reached in the first months of 2012, a more consensual approach might have emerged. In the midst of all these tensions, the constituent assembly was annulled by a Cairo administrative court decision on two grounds. On the one hand, the decision to appoint half of the members of the assembly from among the elected representatives to parliament was regarded as flawed as those who are supposed to write the constitutional rules cannot be the same people to whom these rules will later apply.[16] On the other hand, the assembly was judged as unrepresentative as it had too few women and young people as well as no representatives of the workers and the minorities. The lack of legal experience of most of the members of the constituent assembly was also pinpointed as one of its main liabilities.

The second attempt to choose the 100 Egyptians, who under the terms of the constitutional declaration had six months to complete the task of presenting a draft constitution to the president, took place in a very tense political atmosphere. Throughout the spring and summer of 2012 a number of attempts were made to reach a deal between the Islamists and the non-Islamists over the membership ratio. However, an agreement did not materialise and, in the absence of consensus among the parties, the parliament ended up electing a very similar, albeit slightly more composite body to replace the disbanded constituent assembly.[17] The names of the new constituent assembly were unveiled on 7 June 2012 against the backdrop of a string of very significant decisions that would alter the course of the Egyptian transition.[18] The first of such political acts was the decision by the Supreme Constitutional Court (SCC) declaring the law under which the parliament had been elected unconstitutional.[19] The People's Assembly – the Lower House of parliament – was promptly disbanded the following day, raising doubts about the second constituent assembly's legitimacy, given that it had just been appointed by the now dissolved parliament. Furthermore, a lawsuit was filed against the second assembly on the grounds that some of its members had once again been selected from among members of the legislative body. The legitimacy of the second constituent assembly was further eroded by claims made by the civic opposition during the summer of 2012 that voting procedures had purposely been distorted to favour the solid Islamist majority that dominated the assembly (Interviewee 1).

The second political act was the issuing of a new constitutional declaration on 17 June 2012 by the SCAF. The so-called June declaration amended the March 2011 declaration in significant ways. First, it sought to alter the transition process in order to take into account the fact that the People's Assembly had been dissolved. The absence of a legislature required that some other authority had to assume legislative powers. Legislation was indeed one of the sub-powers and authorities listed in article 56 of the March 2011 constitutional declaration; article 56 bis of the June declaration set out that the SCAF would take it over until a new parliament was elected.[20] This provision greatly contributed to expanding the powers of the military over its civilian counterparts prior to the presidential elections. Second, the provisions related to the constitution-making process also granted the SCAF significant powers, chiefly by making use of vague wording and criteria. For example, article 60 bis of the June declaration provided that if the constituent assembly did not finish drafting the constitutional text in time, i.e., within the six-month timeframe, then the SCAF would appoint another assembly. This provision was quite detailed in that it specified that the SCAF-appointed constituent assembly would have three months, instead of six, to complete the constitution-making process. However, there was an absolute lack of clarity regarding what kind of circumstances could put the constituent assembly in the position not to be able to bring its task to an end. The use of the word 'obstacle' in the June declaration article was the contested point:

> If the constituent assembly encounters an obstacle that would prevent it from completing its work, the SCAF will form a new constituent assembly within a week to author a new constitution within three months from the day of the new assembly's formation. The newly drafted constitution will be put forward for approval by the people through a national referendum after 15 days of the day it is completed. The parliamentary elections will take place one month from the day the new constitution is approved by the national referendum.

Another example of the vagueness of the June declaration was the same article 60 bis, which provided that:

> [i]f the president, the head of the SCAF, the prime minister, the Supreme Council of the Judiciary or a fifth of the constituent assembly find that the new constitution contains an article or more which conflict with the revolution's goals and its main principles or which conflict with any principle agreed upon in all of Egypt's former constitutions, any of the aforementioned

bodies may demand that the constituent assembly revises this specific article within 15 days. Should the constituent assembly object to revising the contentious article, the article will be referred to the Supreme Constitutional Court (SCC), which will then be obliged to give its verdict within seven days. The SCC's decision is final and will be published in the official gazette within three days from the date of issuance.

While the assembly was previously expected to submit its work directly to the people with no other review or oversight envisaged, now a variety of actors, e.g., the president, the head of the SCAF, the prime minister, the Supreme Council of the Judiciary, or one-fifth of the members of the constituent assembly itself, could ask for any provision of the assembly's draft constitution to be reconsidered before submission to the people. Once more, the criteria against which the failure of the assembly's draft to comply with the 'revolution's goals and its main principles' or 'with any principle agreed upon in all of Egypt's former constitutions' was to be measured were extremely vague. The difficulty in correctly and univocally interpreting this provision revolved around the use of the term 'the revolution's objectives'. Although reference to the Egyptian 'revolution' in the June declaration was appropriate in that the country was undergoing a transition from authoritarianism, it also raised a number of difficulties given that no effort was made in the declaration itself, or elsewhere for that matter, to define 'the revolution's objectives'. The uncertainty around the core principles that should guide the establishment of the new rules of the game contributed to creating further polarisation as different actors defined these un-spelled principles in different ways. As we shall see, contrary to the draft of the Tunisian constitution, in which the preamble states that the constitution was drafted 'in response to the objectives of the revolution of freedom and dignity' and further elaborates on the core principles that lie at the origin of the constitutional text,[21] no constitutional, legal, or political document appeared in Egypt that defined, or even set out broadly, what might be legitimately considered the 'revolution's objectives'.

Adding to this climate of uncertainty, the first steps taken by the newly elected Islamist president came as another clear indication of the fact that the constitution-making process, and the country's transition in general, were advancing without any clear programmatic vision or any consensus among the major actors. A main turning point was indeed the election of the Muslim Brotherhood's presidential candidate in the balloting that took place in June 2012. Once elected, Mohammed Morsi tried to roll back some of the provisions enshrined in the March and June constitutional declarations that had been instrumental in securing the SCAF's hold on power during the transition process. He reconvened the disbanded parliament in defiance of the SCC's decision, before eventually bowing to the courts and acquiescing to its suspension. This decision was arguably the first visible act of what was to become an increasingly heightened animosity between the Islamist president and the Egyptian judiciary and which constituted one of the defining features of the first presidential term in the post-Mubarak era. Morsi was more successful in curbing the self-claimed powers of the military by asserting that the authority to issue constitutional declarations would belong to the president from that moment on. This decision was followed up by a presidential decree nullifying the SCAF's latest constitutional declaration and actions (Brown 2013a: 49).

Nevertheless, it was on the constitution-making process that most of Morsi's attention focused during the first semester of his presidency. Aware as he was of the precariousness of the Islamists' electoral gains, as attested to by the SCC's decision to disband the parliament, the president placed himself at the forefront of the effort to push forward the constituent assembly's work on the new constitution. Finalising and adopting it was seen by the Islamist president and government as the only guarantee for moving forward in the transition and preparing the ground for new elections which, in the Islamists' view, would further consolidate their hold on power despite the various pre-'revolutionary' institutions and powers attempting to curb it (Interviewee 27). The decision to speed up the constitution-making process in the midst of resignations and debates was taken against the backdrop of mounting criticisms of the Muslim Brotherhood's leadership, heightened political polarisation and tensions arising from the lack of stability, and the socio-economic grievances affecting the everyday lives of most Egyptians. The constitutional declaration issued by Morsi on 21 November 2012 significantly accelerated the constitution-making process. It clearly spelled out the president's new prerogatives aimed at ensuring that the constitutional revision process would not be disrupted by the judiciary. To this end, article 2 of the November 2012 constitutional declaration stated:

> Previous constitutional declarations, laws and decrees made by the president since he took office on 30 June 2012, until the constitution is approved and a new People's Assembly is elected, are final and binding and cannot be appealed by any way or to any entity. Nor shall they be suspended or cancelled and all lawsuits related to them and brought before any judicial body against these decisions are annulled.[22]

This was compounded by article 5 preventing any judicial body from dissolving the Shura Council, the Upper House of parliament, or the constituent assembly. In asserting absolute presidential powers – the declaration further stated that '[t]he president may take the necessary actions and measures to protect the country and the goals of the revolution' (art. 6) – use was made of the same vague language previously used by the military in their constitutional declarations. The two-fold aim was to complete the constitution-making process and avoid the potential dissolution of yet another Islamist-dominated constituent assembly by the judiciary, on the one hand, and to move quickly to the next parliamentary elections with a new electoral law that was to be drafted by the Shura Council, on the other. This assertion of absolute presidential powers, albeit only temporarily until the passage of the new constitution, triggered a new round of street protests and was strongly denounced by non-Islamist political forces and public opinion as an 'authoritarian' presidential move.[23] Many leftist, liberal, and independent political forces also insisted that the constitutional text that was being drafted – and would subsequently be put to a referendum – was 'void' as it was the result of the work of 'an illegitimate assembly that represent[ed] only one political current and [was] not representative of Egyptian society at large'.[24] The fact that the president agreed to meet the representatives of the civic forces to address their concerns, while also promising to take their views into account, did not contribute to easing the tension (Interviewee 30). The day after the meeting, the text of the constitution was unveiled with no changes whatsoever in its content.

A partially new beginning

The draft of the new Egyptian constitution was finalised on 29 November 2012 amid tensions and resignations from the constituent assembly by non-Islamist members. According to some sources, at least 40 liberal and leftist members withdrew from the 100-member constituent assembly, thus further heightening the opposition's fear of an Islamist-dominated constitution. The constitutional text was approved in a 14-hour marathon of voting in the constituent assembly and subsequently handed over to President Morsi to be put to popular referendum.[25] The round of voting took place between 15 and 22 December leading to the approval of the text with 63.8 percent of votes.[26] The turnout was far lower than expected, with just over 32.9 percent of the population making its way to the polls, which means that the constitution was approved by a mere 21 percent of eligible voters. According to a number of analysts, this poor showing laid the ground for the subsequent challenging of the constitution's legitimacy in 2013 (al-Ali 2012). The new Egyptian constitution entered into force on 26 December 2012.

Issues of substance and procedure are equally important for understanding how the constitution was received by Egyptian public opinion and the scenarios it opened up in the months following its approval.[27] Regarding the substance, it is worth mentioning that the text built upon, but also altered, the 1971 constitution. The existing constitutional tradition was thus embedded in the 2012 constitution. The effect was that while the new constitution claimed to be the product of the people's will, in some respects it was still influenced by the preceding provisions that had been in place under authoritarian rule – so much so that many articles appeared to be identical. Concerning the distribution of powers among state institutions, the constitutional text reinforced the role of parliament in line with what was probably the constituent assembly's most significant objective, that is to limit the president's powers in order to avoid the emergence of a new 'pharaoh'.[28] The 1971 constitution was heavily biased in the president's favour with respect to parliament, granting the former the right to choose anyone he wished to serve as prime minister without having to take the distribution of power within parliament into account. The 2012 constitution attempted to redress this unbalance by clearly introducing a new division of powers: the president would be restricted to two terms of four years each (art. 133) and would have substantial limits on his prerogatives.[29] For example, the president could declare a state of emergency only following approval by a majority of the members of each chamber and for a period not exceeding six months, which could only be extended for another six months upon approval in a public referendum (art. 148). The legislature would be composed of two chambers – the Council of Representatives (the People's Assembly) and the Shura Council, with significantly more extensive powers granted to the former than the latter – both responsible for the formation and dismissal of the government. Article 139 stated that the president must collaborate very closely with parliament during government formation and that the government must present its programme to parliament for approval. Furthermore, parliament was empowered to dismiss the government, the prime minister, or any minister by a simple majority of its members (art. 126). This was a major step forward compared to the 1971 constitution, whereby parliament could only dismiss the government after obtaining the president's approval or through a two-thirds majority vote of no confidence. These changes notwithstanding, some elements of continuity with the 1971 constitution still permeated the text in that, for example, the president still had the power to appoint one-tenth of the members of the Shura Council (art. 128). He could also name the heads of all the independent agencies in the country, including the audit institution and the central bank, thus limiting the independence of those institutions that are supposed to verify the executive's accountability (al-Ali 2012).

Other contentious issues in the text of the new constitution were the protection of basic freedoms and rights, such as women's rights and freedom of expression, addressed in articles 31 to 81, and the role of *Sharia*. It was on this issue that most debates took place, not so much among the members of the constituent assembly as at the level of public opinion. While some people interviewed in the framework of this research expressed concern that some provisions had purposely been included in the new constitution to establish a religious state in violation of the commitment to maintain a 'civic state', a closer reading of the text, as well as a better appreciation of the role of religious principles in the previous constitutional texts, does not support this claim (Interviewees 10, 18, 22, 28). Many constitutional experts have indeed underscored the extent to which Egypt prior to the uprisings was neither a secular state, at least not in the sense this word is usually used in the context of western liberal democracies, nor a religious state (Kienle 2001; al-Ali 2012). It was a state in which religion had always played quite an important role, such as in family law, due to the important functions attributed to *Al-Azhar*, one of the Islamic world's most influential and venerable institutions. In this light, Egypt's December 2012 constitution stands in quite strong continuity with this tradition.

First, the text retains the language of the previous constitution that stipulated that '[t]he principles of Islamic *Sharia* are the principal source of legislation' (art. 2). This quite undefined expression ('principles of Islamic *Sharia*') was regarded as a guarantee against too strict interpretations of the sources of legislation and therefore widely accepted by the civic forces. It is interesting to note that this provision was strongly advocated by *Al-Azhar*, which was thus sometimes regarded as belonging to the civic forces camp, in opposition to the Salafists of the *Al-Nour* party, who were instead in favour of replacing 'principles' with 'rules', a much more stringent term (Interviewee 1). However, the constitutional text saw two additions that had been supported by the Islamist actors and that were meant to change the way in which article 2 was understood. These additions were spelled out in articles 219 and 4. The former set out what the term 'principles of Islamic *Sharia*' means and, as such, widened the scope of article 2 considerably. 'Principles of Islamic *Sharia*' would include the entire body of Islamic jurisprudence that is accepted by Sunni doctrines, which is a complex and sufficiently broad set of jurisprudence rules including both moderate and more severe views. This broadening of the concept of 'principles of Islamic *Sharia*' would open the way to potentially conflicting interpretations, even in more conservative and severe terms, something that a number of non-Islamist members of the constituent assembly did not originally anticipate. Given that Islamic *Sharia* is such a broad set of principles, the question as to who is responsible for interpreting it becomes crucial (al-Ali 2012). Article 4 was indeed meant to resolve the matter by stating that 'Al-Azhar's Council of Senior Scholars is to be consulted in matters relating to Islamic *Sharia*'. It makes clear that the opinion of *Al-Azhar* must be sought by all bodies (including the courts and the parliament) and that this is mandatory. After decades in which authoritarian rule had completely deprived this institution of its powers, reducing it to a 'state's captive' (Barraclough 1998: 237), this constitutional provision formally entrusted it with the power to adjudicate on all matters related to *Sharia*. However, the role attributed to *Al-Azhar* and its Council of Senior Scholars also had the indirect effect of making this institution more exposed to struggles among the country's various camps for influence or control of it.

Another example of the strong continuity of the December 2012 constitution was that, under pressure to meet a short deadline, some provisions – including some of the ones most contested by public opinion – were simply copied and pasted from the 1971 constitution. This was the case, for example, of the much discussed article 10, which provides that '[t]he state and society oversee the commitment to the genuine character of the Egyptian family, its cohesion and stability, and the consolidation and protection of its moral values'. The same wording appeared in the previous constitution although, according to a number of constitutional scholars, this provision had no practical impact for decades (al-Ali 2012). The very fact that these issues were at the centre of the debate says a lot about the deep-rooted lack of trust and the polarisation of Egyptian public opinion, whereby unclear or neutral provisions were regarded as potentially threatening assertions of power of one part over the other (Interviewees 7, 11, 14, 25).

What most debates, even among informed Egyptian respondents, failed to grasp is the extent to which the section on the system for local administration largely replicated the old pattern of centralised forms of government to the detriment of true decentralisation of powers. Decades of authoritarian rule had resisted the ever growing trend towards greater decentralisation as one of the means of bringing government closer to the people. Throughout the Arab region, shunning decentralisation or implementing piecemeal local government reforms was justified by the argument that decentralisation would inevitably open the way to federalism, which was, in itself, portrayed as the precursor to the country breaking apart along sectarian lines. The result was that most Arab countries, including Egypt, maintained some of the most centralised forms of government in the world until 2011 (Moustafa 2002). A number of authors have explored the poor state of decentralisation in Egypt, arguing that most stumbling blocks have come from the central power itself, with very negative repercussions on the level of welfare services provided outside the capital (Mayfield 1996).

Upon the removal of the Mubarak regime, institutional reforms at the various levels of government appeared to be an important test of the new authorities' ability to break out of the old system of power and to pursue deep structural reforms. These expectations notwithstanding, the new constitution did not address the issue of decentralisation adequately and in this regard went along with the old trend of propping up a de facto centralised form of government. The structure of local government has remained highly hierarchical since 1960, when the country was reorganised into 26 governorates, with authority flowing top down. Following the reorganisation in 2011, Egypt had 27 governorates. The 2012 constitution called for local councils to be elected (art. 188), but allowed for their decisions to be overturned by the central government so as to prevent them 'from overstepping limits, or causing damage to public interest or the interests of other local councils' (art. 190). Similarly, the constitution did not specify how governors would be chosen (whether elected or selected) and remained silent about their powers (art. 187). As in the past, decisions about these crucial matters were referred to subsequent legislation, despite the fact that it appears from the literature on this subject that defining the powers of the central and local administrations should be one of the tasks of the constitution (Treisman 2007).

All in all, while the substance of the December 2012 constitution is characterised by both light and shadow, the procedural aspects of the newly passed constitutional text reveal a darker picture. In this regard, one of Morsi's greatest mistakes was to maintain the constitution-making process and schedule established by the SCAF in March 2011. The result was a vision for the country's transition that was heavily anchored in previous Egyptian constitutional and institutional logics, which in themselves were highly problematic in a 'revolutionary' context. This was the case, for example, of the six-month deadline that the SCAF had imposed, clearly too tight a timeframe for drafting a modern constitution for a country with a complex socio-political fabric, in which intra- and multi-party negotiations have to take place on every issue. When Morsi took power in June 2012, he chose not to revisit the March 2011 interim constitution, thus putting the entire constitution-making process in a difficult position.[30] In the end, meeting the deadline became a goal in itself, regardless of what it meant for the prospects for inclusiveness, legitimacy, and accountability. As a result, what can be regarded as the first phase of constitution making in the post-Mubarak period was a flawed experience with deep implications for the whole transition process, above and beyond the way in which the text was perceived by public opinion in terms of its (poor) ability to protect fundamental rights and freedoms and to provide a well-functioning framework to manage political conflicts.

Back to square one?

Having a new constitution, particularly one that saw the light in a hasty manner and amidst increased political polarisation, did not solve the everyday problems faced by the Egyptian population. In the face of mounting socio-economic difficulties, the Islamist-led government seemed unable to address the needs of an ever growing number of Egyptians, embattled against what they perceived as an unaccountable and seemingly-authoritarian government (Interviewee 16). Eleven months into office, President Morsi had not yet set out an economic plan and had not been able to build 'broad support' for the wide-reaching economic reforms requested by the IMF, whose proffered USD 4.8 billion standby agreement was on hold. Instead of addressing the subsidies issue head-on, the president and the Islamist-led government contented themselves with tweaking at the margins, simply raising a few customs duties and minor taxes. Plans to ration some hugely subsidised goods were neglected or swept under the carpet for fear of imposing austerity before the elections.[31] With the level of official foreign reserves down to USD 13 billion, from around USD 36 billion before the uprisings in January 2011, the Egyptian government started to borrow from external donors, particularly the Gulf States, Turkey, Iraq, and Libya (Interviewee 3).[32] The precarious financial situation affected the Egyptian population in various ways: increased inflation, burgeoning unemployment, particularly in the tourism sector, and a surge in unlicensed street markets, smuggling, and crime.

This situation of socio-economic malaise was only heightened by the feeling of exclusion experienced by the political and social actors who did not identify with the power structure created by the Islamists. Blaming the Muslim Brotherhood for the numerous socio-economic and security problems entangling Egypt became increasingly popular in 2013, further fuelling polarisation. Most civic and revolutionary forces started to accuse the Muslim Brotherhood of wanting to hijack the state by purging its apparatuses and putting its representatives in key positions. Talk of a gradual process of '*Ikhwanisation*' – the Muslim Brotherhood's attempt to capture the institutions of the state – started to circulate amongst the public and some parts of the decision-making structure. Evidence of this was that, since June 2012, 70 high officers had been fired from ministries, intelligence bodies, and the National Council for Human Rights (NCHR) and replaced with people close to the Brotherhood. Similarly, the appointment of ten new governors – four of whom were affiliated with the Muslim Brotherhood – in some of the movement's strongholds and strategic areas, including North Sinai, prior to the debate on the new constitution was also presented by some media as a Muslim Brotherhood takeover of strategic institutional positions.[33]

The main Islamist force was also accused of wanting to control the minds of the Egyptian population, including young people, through its penetration of the media – with the replacement of more than 50 editors in chief of some of the most influential newspapers, radio, and television stations – and amendments to school curricula, allegedly granting more space to the teaching of Islamic principles and precepts (Interviewee 1). But it was what was perceived by some parts of the public opinion as Morsi's attempt to 'Islamise' the justice sector that aroused the most deafening cries and accusations of a return to authoritarian practices. President Morsi's devious attempt in October 2012 to remove the prosecutor general, Abdel-Meguid Mahmoud, announcing that he was taking up the new position of Egypt's ambassador to the Vatican – despite his dismissal within hours of the announcement – was interpreted by some people in the non-Islamist camp as a further sign of the Muslim Brotherhood's intent to concentrate all powers in the president's hands.[34] In 2013, the conflict between the presidency and the judiciary – the executive power's attempt to 'massacre the judiciary' – became the single most important issue of contention.[35] These accusations, albeit greatly exaggerated by non-Islamist forces, were indeed not mitigated by the Muslim Brotherhood's inability to share power and develop a more inclusive transition process. In the end, as a result of the popular mobilisation staged by *Tamarrod* (which means 'disobedience, insubordination, revolt, and rebellion'), the situation precipitated. Between 30 June and 3 July 2013, the first democratically elected president in Egypt's history was ousted. This dramatic event had far-reaching consequences for the Egyptian transition.

With regard to the constitution-making process, the consequences were felt immediately. With the handing over of power to the military on 3 July 2013, the 2012 constitution was suspended with immediate effect. The entire framework for the constitution-making process imposed by the Islamist forces in 2012 was swept away with it. In the aftermath of the events of July 2013, there were accusations that what had taken place was a 'constitutional coup' and that 'constitutional pragmatism' was the best way to pursue the 'revolution's goals' (Interviewee 38). One of the first acts of the interim authorities was thus to issue yet another constitutional declaration, outlining the steps to be taken to move the country along the transition path. Once again, rather than a negotiated and consensual document, the constitutional declaration released by Adly Mansour, the interim president and former head of the SCC, was drafted by anonymous figures – from among the most conservative sectors of the Egyptian state, including senior judges. In terms of content, the declaration drew broadly on the previous SCAF document of March 2011 in that it granted the interim president many of the powers that the SCAF, and later Morsi, had granted themselves (al-Ali 2013b). Indeed, article 24 had granted the president virtually unlimited executive and legislative powers, including those to appoint and dismiss the prime minister, the ministers, and their deputies without seeking prior authorisation from parliament.[36]

The declaration outlined a three-step process for amending Egypt's constitution. The first step envisaged a ten-member technical committee, which according to article 28 was to be composed of at least six judges and which was to suggest amendments to the 2012 constitution within one month. This step was followed by a 50-member constituent assembly, mostly made of representatives of state institutions and civil society organisations, such as political parties, trade unions, and religious institutions, which would debate the proposed changes and submit a new draft of the constitutional text within two months.[37] Finally, the new constitution would be put to popular referendum for approval. All in all, the declaration imposed a very short and rigid timeframe for adoption of the new constitution. There was a three-month deliberation process, with limited or no consultation mechanisms in place, followed by one month of national debate. Given that the previous constitution-making process was not premised on a common understanding of the principles that should have been at the core of the institutional arrangement and the functioning of the state, the short timeframe imposed on the second round of constitution-making was again simply not enough to allow for a consensus on these things to be reached. The three-month timeframe amounted to around half the time the constituent assembly had had in 2012.

Going back to the composition of both the technical committee and the constituent assembly, it has to be said that all the most important existing institutions of the Egyptian state – ranging from the judiciary, to the military, the police, the political parties, the universities, *Al-Azhar*, and the state-sanctioned trade unions – were given a stake in the process. To different degrees, each of them was assigned some symbolic bargaining chips, which they could use to protect and advance their interests in the absence of a negotiated and consensus-driven process. Even political parties – with the noticeable exclusion of the Muslim Brotherhood's Freedom and Justice Party (FJP) – were treated like any other institution rather than as representatives of the people. In addition to the exclusion of the FJP, what appears more problematic is that any individual or group that did not wield significant power within the state's structure, including the majority of the Egyptian population, was excluded outright from the constitution-making process. No channels were provided for these individuals or groups to influence the rewriting of the constitution.

Working against time, the 50-member constituent assembly was able to accomplish its task within the short timeframe imposed by the constitutional declaration. The draft of the constitutional text handed over to the president on 2 December 2013 was put to popular referendum on 14–15 January 2014. Rather than looking at what is in the constitution, which in general terms drew heavily on the 2012 constitution, it is interesting to consider what has been removed from the text of the previous one.[38] First, the article in the 2012 constitution requiring that *Al-Azhar* be consulted on matters related to Islamic *Sharia* (art. 4) did not appear in the 2013 draft. Similarly, with regard to the provisions constraining the interpretation of article 2, which has remained unchanged, one of the major changes introduced into the 2012 constitution, i.e., article 219 defining what was meant by 'principles of Islamic *Sharia*', has been removed. Instead, the new constitutional text reaffirmed the authority of the SCC on this matter: with reference to article 2, the preamble stated that 'the reference for interpretation thereof is the relevant texts in the collected rulings of the Supreme Constitutional Court'. From an institutional point of view, the Shura Council, which acted as the Upper House of parliament and was long regarded as a useless and costly body, was eliminated. The single-chamber legislative body, the House of Representatives, was to be made up of 450 members elected for five years. Finally, the biggest absence of all was the recognition – implicit in the 2012 constitution – of any type of political activity based on religion (art. 74). According to the new text, parties such as the Muslim

Brotherhood's FJP and the Salafist *Al-Nour* party, which were created in 2011 after the ban on religious parties was lifted in the aftermath of the 2011 'revolution', were banned and were subject to dissolution simply by judicial order.

Reflecting on this important U-turn in the Egyptian process of constitutional revision, one cannot fail to appreciate that this was largely the result of the reassertion of the power and interests of a number of institutions and institutional logics that were temporarily sidelined during the first two and a half years after the uprising. The power struggles in Egypt in 2011–2013 prompted some actors, such as the military, the judiciary, and the police, to come back and re-assert their authority by leveraging the changed political circumstances. Indeed, the most interesting and far-reaching provisions in the new constitution were those concerning the military and the judiciary, which are analysed in Chapter 5. A final note concerns the way in which these actors have attempted to manipulate some important components of the state's institutional framework and bend them towards the protection and advancement of their interests. An example of this was the lack of clarity regarding the timing and sequencing of the presidential and parliamentary elections that were to follow the adoption of the constitution. While the July constitutional declaration called for parliamentary elections to take place first, to be followed – within an unspecified time – by presidential elections, the 2013 constitution remained silent as to whether the roadmap's electoral timing and sequencing would be applied in light of the main actors' calculations to maximise their power (Brown and Dunne 2013).

A few concluding remarks can be offered here about the complex constitutional revision process that took place in Egypt between 2011 and the beginning of 2014. This process was characterised by the failed attempt to transition to a new set of rules of the game – the new constitution – in the midst of an extremely polarising electoral process. As this process was supposed to be conducted according to democratic principles, over the course of the three years from the beginning of the transition, the Egyptian population was repeatedly summoned to the polls to express its will so that all matters would not be settled by closed-circle deals. This was an attempt to forge a participatory and democratic process even in the absence of agreed-upon rules and norms. Typically, elections – even when held within a clear institutional framework – tend to increase the polarisation between the different interests and positions. Although voting was not the cause of the country's institutional crisis and polarisation, elections contributed to bringing political fissures to the surface and aggravating them. In reality, one of the main goals of creating the new constitutional framework was precisely to overcome this polarisation and conflict by creating an accepted platform of principles and rules to guide the action of all actors. The conflicting dynamics between the majoritarian 'democratic' legitimacy stemming from the ballots, which is explored in greater details in Chapter 4, and the failure to include all the different constituencies in the making of the new rules have been a central feature of the Egyptian transition.

A number of factors in the constitution-making process itself further contributed to making the task of writing a new constitution an almost insurmountable challenge. Three factors are worth emphasising here concerning the nature of the actors involved, the timing and sequencing of the process, and the actual content of the constitutions that were debated and approved in the period between 2011 and the beginning of 2014. Regarding the first factor, the climate of strong polarisation was the result of the choices and actions of some powerful veto powers. The role played by the main political actors – the military, the political parties, the judiciary, and the security apparatuses – all of which had a stake in the transition process, significantly influenced the pace and direction of the constitution-making process. The Egyptian military, for example, played a key role in the transition, refusing to accept civilian oversight and attempting to monopolise key decisions, either directly or indirectly, throughout the whole three-year period. This led most other political actors to look at the military as necessary interlocutors and the gate-keepers of any institutional change (or lack thereof) and to seek an accommodation with them (Roberts 2013).

The second factor has to do with the management of time during the constitution-making process. That the six-month timeframe imposed on the drafting process of the 2012 constitution was not sufficient for reaching a negotiated solution has already been underscored. In addition to establishing that parliamentary elections would precede the constitutional revision process, the extremely vague provisions contained in the March 2011 constitutional declaration on the composition of the constituent assembly proved to be problematic because time was wasted easing tensions. Finally, the overarching factor that has emerged in the Egyptian constitution-making process, particularly in the final version of some provisions in the texts, is the persistence of underlying authoritarian patterns. The new Egyptian constitution was drafted on the institutional foundations that autocracy built and nurtured in the past decades. As already stated at the beginning of this chapter, getting rid of authoritarian rulers does not necessarily mean establishing a *tabula rasa* or levelling the playing field for all the actors, both old and new, who engage in crafting the new institutions. Both the 2012 and the 2014 constitutions, not to speak of the entire process of constitution making, were imbued with the authoritarian legacy of the past. Some parts of the authoritarian power infrastructure and old authoritarian logics have remained in place as they are deeply woven into both formal and informal institutions. The examples of the military and the security apparatuses, on the one hand, and the judiciary and the extended bureaucracy, on the other, are the most significant in this respect, and their institutional development or resilience are thoroughly assessed in Chapter 5. For example, not only has the autonomy and power of the judicial institutions been used to protect their vested and self-perpetuating interests, but they have also been in a position to withstand the new institutions, such as the presidency and the parliament, and their prerogatives, and to undermine them.

Tunisia: an inclusive process struggling against time

The shaping of a pact

In 1861, Tunisia adopted the first written constitution in Arab history. This was a remarkable accomplishment for the tiny North African country, in keeping with its history and tradition of moderation and modernity. In the words of the French social scientist Jean-Pierre Filiu, this constitution 'enshrined a political power distinct from religion: Islam was barely mentioned, only to stress that the text was not contradicting its principles, and it was not even explicit that the Bey [the ruler] had to be Muslim' (Filiu 2011: 142). Retracing Tunisia's past experience in constitutionalism, one cannot fail to notice the extent to which this country has been a laboratory for the entire Arab region. While still under the French protectorate rule, the *Dustur* (Constitution) party and other political forces were at the forefront of reforms, calling for the establishment of 'an elected deliberative assembly to which the government would be accountable. They also called for a separation of executive, judicial and legislative power' (Alexander 2010: 25). In the era of the *Neo-Dustur*, Bourghiba's nationalist party, a new constitution was passed in 1959 enshrining basic rights and freedoms (Murphy 2013). The importance attached to constitutionalism by the country's elites and public opinion, evident in the very names of the two most important political parties in the country's history, was to be revived in the aftermath of the uprisings that toppled Ben Ali's authoritarian regime. The entire Tunisian transition process has been crafted around the need to rewrite the basic rules that would govern the functioning of the state and its institutions.

In the immediate aftermath of January 2011, it was clear that the old constitution of 1959 would theoretically remain in force although a series of decrees made critical parts of it inoperative, while establishing a new, transitional constitutional order that was to lead to the adoption of a new text. Essential to this transitional constitutional order was the role assigned to the 'Supreme Organisation to Realise the Goals of the Revolution, Political Reform and Democratic Transition' (SORGR), also known as the Ben Achour Commission after the jurist that headed the body. Composed of a wide spectrum of political forces and representatives of civil society, the body was responsible for designing and ensuring the implementation of the transitional roadmap. One of the first steps of the SORGR was to agree on the steps that would lead to the election of a National Constituent Assembly (NCA), the body that, according to the roadmap drafted to endow the country with new institutions, was responsible to produce a constitution by October 2012. The roadmap stated clearly that the transition process had to begin with elections to a constituent assembly followed by general parliamentary elections once the text was ready.

The elections of the 217 members of the NCA were held on 23 October 2011 and were based on a closed-list, proportional representation electoral system with 27 constituencies.[39] As a result of a credible and fair electoral process, the Tunisian NCA enjoyed almost unquestioned legitimacy throughout the lengthy constitution-making period. This legitimacy was both procedural, being grounded in a widely accepted roadmap, and substantive, given that most discussions and decisions entailed consensus building and inclusiveness. The Tunisian constitution-making process was characterised by the emergence of a 'pact' among the major political forces as a result of their search for consensus and compromise. This is in line with what O'Donnell and Schmitter have called 'pacted transitions'. A pact is an agreement that defines the rules governing the exercise of power and provides guarantees for the vital interests of those entering into it (O'Donnell et al. 1986: 37). Pacts often occur when neither competing group can unilaterally impose its preferred solution on the other and are generally more conducive than either solutions to the establishment of democracy. Although the Tunisian constitution-making process was dominated by the so-called Troika, i.e., *Ennahda*, the *Congrès pour la République* (CPR), and *Ettakatol*, the need to strike a balance among the different positions within and beyond the ruling coalition has been addressed by consensus-building stances and compromises, thus avoiding potentially drawn-out battles over principles (Pickard 2012). The moderate Islamist party, *Ennahda*, which came out of the October 2011 elections as the strongest political force, was in itself driven by consensus. The party did acknowledge the legitimacy of established forms and logics of institutional organisation, including the old and new parties, and was in turn generally welcomed by them on the Tunisian political scene.

In terms of functions and internal organisation, even though there was no explicit requirement that the constituent assembly act as an interim parliament, in practice the body took on the role of interim legislator alongside that of drafting the constitutional text.[40] This was partly due to the precedent of the country's first assembly that operated in the late 1950s and to the absence of any other body that could claim legitimacy to legislate in the name of the people. As a result, the NCA established a number of constitutional and legislative committees, with membership distributed roughly in proportion to membership in the assembly as a whole and with most members sitting in both of them.[41] The six constitutional committees were organised around different subjects, with a coordination committee tasked to revise and structure the drafts of the individual articles in a coherent manner. This proved to be the space where most struggles to define the content of the new Tunisian constitution were fought.

Consensus-seeking actors

Some of the most heated discussions prior to deliberations took place in the second (rights and freedoms) and third (legislative and executive powers) committees (Allani 2013; Interviewee 42). Most of them revolved around the extent to which *Sharia* would be mentioned in the constitution. This issue turned out to be hotly contested not just in the rights and freedoms committee, but also among the public in general. While all secular parties, in both the ruling coalition and the opposition, were strongly against the word *Sharia* appearing in the constitution, *Ennahda*'s position was ambiguous and the object of internal dissent. An internal draft of the clause produced and circulated by *Ennahda* in February 2012 included a reference to *Sharia* as 'a source among sources' of legislation. This reference alarmed the secular forces and precipitated a heated debate with the president of the NCA, Mustapha Ben Jaafar from *Ettakatol*, who threatened to resign and withdraw his party from the ruling coalition, should the word *Sharia* appear in the constitution in any form (Pickard 2012).

Popular mobilisation around the issue was massive, with demonstrations taking to the streets to call, on the one hand, for the implementation of *Sharia* and, on the other, the establishment of a civil state. On 16 March 2012, over 4,000 demonstrators marched to the NCA demanding the *Sharia*.[42] This was followed four days later, on 20 March 2012, the 56th anniversary of the country's independence, by another peaceful march of some 15,000 protesters calling for a civil state.[43] On 26 March 2012, *Ennahda* finally made a formal announcement that it would no longer press for the inclusion of this provision, thus opening the way to the drafting of article 1 of the new constitution, which stated: 'Tunisia is a free, independent, and sovereign state. Its religion is Islam, its language is Arabic, and its form of government is a republic.'[44] A senior member of *Ennahda*'s political bureau later on admitted that this decision was taken in response to the increasing divisions the issue was causing and in light of the need to carry on with the drafting and approval of the constitutional text.[45] In addition to article 1, reference was made to Islam in article 73 of the June 2013 draft constitution, which stated that any presidential candidate had to be a Muslim, and in article 141, which provided that no constitutional amendment could remove Islam as the religion of the state. *Ennahda*'s behaviour with regard to the place of religion in the new Tunisian constitution is a clear example of the party's willingness to compromise and to engage in bargaining at a time when the rules of the game were being revised and institutional changes at multiple levels taking place. *Ennahda*'s decision to compromise on what is usually regarded as one of the pillars of its legitimacy as an 'Islamic movement' – the term that has been employed by the party leadership instead of 'political Islam' until recently – as well as one of the main campaign promises *Ennahda* made prior to the October 2011 elections can be better understood in light of the power struggle raging on other fronts where the party had to spend significant resources to achieve its goals.

Given that the various actors, i.e., parties and civil society organisations, that took part in the constitution-making process in Tunisia had different material and symbolic resources at their disposal, it is only natural to expect them to have used them in different ways to pursue the creation of different kinds of institutions. As highlighted in the literature on institutional development, institutions usually reflect the different contributions and often the conflicts between the motivations of the various actors (Mahoney and Thelen 2010). In the case of *Ennahda*, even though the issue of *Sharia* was important, the party found that it had to compromise on certain aspects of the institutional bargain, as a consequence of its relative power with respect to other actors and in order to be able to negotiate on other issues more fruitfully. This was, for example, the case in another much contested issue, pertaining to the organisation and division of powers among the different state institutions, which was debated in the NCA and in which *Ennahda*, like other political forces, had a stake. The most contentious issue of the whole constitutional revision process in terms of substance was not the place of religion in the constitution but the system of government, as it was perceived as directly affecting the distribution of power among the different actors. The debate about the appropriateness of presidential or parliamentary forms of government is an old one and has given rise to a prolific literature testing this assertion both theoretically and empirically (Linz 1990; Shugart and Carey 1992; Sartori 1997;

Cheibub 2007; Elgie and Moestrup 2008). While significant in the context of polities emerging from the collapse of long-lasting authoritarian regimes centred on the figure of a president (or monarch) enjoying almost unrestrained powers while depriving other institutions, e.g., parliament, of their functions, the choice between the presidential and parliamentary form of government in the Arab world was influenced by a vast array of factors pertaining to the institutional legacy and modern historical development of these nation-states and as such featured high on the list of priorities. The preferred option for *Ennahda* was to substitute the presidential system with a parliamentary one. The emphasis on the parliamentary system stemmed first and foremost from the political calculation that this form of government was more suitable for allowing the party to govern through a coalition entailing the diffusion of power but also of criticism. This was coupled with *Ennahda*'s confidence in its ability to control a plurality of seats in the parliament in the following years in spite of a deeply fragmented party system. The Islamist party's preference for the parliamentary system was also nurtured by its ideological affinity with the concept and practice of *Shura* – or consensus-based decision-making – which is widely perceived to be enshrined in the parliamentary system (Interviewees 51, 52). Conversely, secular parties widely expressed themselves in favour of a presidential or semi-presidential system, which they saw as the best way to put a cap on *Ennahda*'s power.

After endless discussions and a period of stalemate in the third constitutional committee, the issue was taken from the restricted group and discussed in a plenary session. In October 2012, the members of the ruling coalition, including *Ennahda* and two secular parties, were successful in reaching a partial compromise on the form of government. The Troika agreed that the president would be directly elected for a five-year period and would be responsible for 'representing the state [and] for outlining the general policies on the aspects of defence, foreign relations and national security related to protection of the state and the homeland from internal and external threats' (art. 76). The compromise also stipulated that the prime minister would be the leader of the party or coalition that wins the greatest number of seats in the parliamentary elections (art. 88). In addition, the prime minister would have to receive a vote of confidence in the Chamber of Deputies following the presentation of a short programme. Article 96 introduced the constructive vote of no confidence, which is the German-invented variation on the motion of no confidence that allows a parliament to withdraw confidence from a head of government only if there is a positive majority for a prospective successor. On the whole, the form of government provided for by the draft constitutional text was a semi-presidential one, which was what the secular forces had been aiming at from the beginning contrary to *Ennahda*'s preference for a parliamentary system.[46] This is another instance of *Ennahda*'s willingness to compromise on important points concerning Tunisia's future institutional arrangement.

These examples underscore the extent to which the actors had to engage in negotiations and compromises to be able to reach a commonly accepted level of power distribution in the new institutions. Overall, the Tunisian experience of constitutional revision following the demise of the Ben Ali regime corroborates one important point made by the historical institutional literature on institutional development. It concerns the importance of analysing the 'combined effects of institutions and processes rather than examining just one institution or process at a time' (Pierson and Skocpol 2002: 696). The final bargain in terms of institutional development tends to reflect not so much the goals and position of any particular actor on one specific issue but rather the result of the conflicts and compromises on a number of different matters. Digging further into the debates and deliberations of the NCA, it appears that the level of consensus on the distribution of power on substantive issues was the outcome of lengthy discussions and negotiations that took place within the framework of a timetable allowing all the actors a lot of time to familiarise themselves with the procedures to be followed, with each group's positions and preferred course, and with the public opinion's constant feedback.[47]

Playing politics?

As of December 2013, four successive drafts of the constitution had been released and subjected to public scrutiny and experts' comments. This very open, inclusive, and 'relaxed' process has been praised by a number of external observers as the best example of participatory constitutional revision implemented by a 'democratic coalition' (Landolt and Kubicek 2013: 9; Ottaway 2013). The downside of the transparency, inclusiveness, and electoral representativeness at the base of the NCA's legitimacy is that these were ensured at the expense of time-management and efficiency. Between 2011 and 2013, some of its merits as well as some of its drawbacks started to manifest themselves. On the one hand are the positive aspects of the Tunisian constitution-making process: the content of the constitutional provisions – the 'what' – has been agreed upon in a consultative and negotiated manner. No party felt that some provisions had been imposed on it (Interviewee 39). When a consensus on the constitution appeared to have been reached, the debate moved on to the procedural aspects related to enactment and implementation of the institutional revisions in the framework of the much broader and conflictual transition process – from the 'what' to the 'how'.[48] On the other hand are the negative ones: this consensus-driven process of constitutional revision failed to deliver clear results, i.e., the new rules of the game, within the expected timeframe (one year after the October 2011 NCA elections). Contrary to the Egyptian case, there was no exaggerated preoccupation with temporal deadlines in Tunisia. Nevertheless, after the first months of delay and continuous bickering over the 'what' and increasingly over the 'how', the issue of time started to haunt the Tunisian transition process. This happened against the backdrop of rising social tensions caused by pressing socio-economic issues, some of which had dragged on or even worsened since January 2011, such as unemployment, lack of security, and a tremendous drop in tourist revenues. The assembly's legislative functions and the enormous challenges facing the state have tended to delay the constitution-making process by diverting the members' attention, with the actors becoming increasingly impatient day after day and the tone of the discussions less and less reconciling.

The first signs of deadlock and institutional crisis appeared in October 2012 with the NCA's failure to draft the constitution within the one-year mandate. Anticipating the crisis, the Tunisian General Labour Union (*Union Générale Tunisienne du Travail*, UGTT), which had built up a reputation as the most important actor in contemporary Tunisia thanks to the role it played in the anti-colonial movement, convened an ambitious National Dialogue Conference on 16 October 2012 aimed at overcoming the crisis of interim institutions.[49] The rationale for this initiative was to lend the constitution-making process enough legitimacy to be able to move forward by incorporating additional civil society actors. All the political forces, as well as the main organisations from civil society, were invited to participate and provide their support for a new roadmap revolving around the need to set a realistic timetable for the completion of the constitution and the holding of parliamentary and presidential elections. All political forces, with the exception of *Ennahda* and the CPR, took part in the first National Dialogue. *Ennahda*'s refusal was mainly dictated by the fear that this would mean an endorsement of a new dynamic whereby the party would no longer be in full control of the transition. Some analyses have underscored that this was not the first time that *Ennahda* and the CPR blocked initiatives aimed at creating a level playing field and/or initiated by actors other than themselves. In July 2011, months ahead of the NCA elections, *Ennahda* pulled out of the SORGR.[50] Another point of contention that contributed to embittering the atmosphere during one of the most critical phases of the Tunisian transition was a bill on the 'political immunisation of the revolution' put forth by some of *Ennahda*'s hardliners on 29 November 2012. The proposed law appeared to be targeted at senior officials who had held positions in the former regimes between 2 April 1989 and 14 January 2011, among whom were some of *Ennahda*'s main political opponents, with the goal of excluding them from public office for the following ten years. The Islamist party's subsequent decision to postpone the discussion on this law until an unspecified date did not help ease the looming institutional crisis as many opposition members declared not to trust *Ennahda* to be in good faith and working for the good of the country (Interviewees 46, 47).

As was the case in Egypt, the constitution-making process in Tunisia has also been a part of the broader transition phase with its conflicts and uncertainties. The latter have significantly influenced the pace, direction, and outcome of the process. In Tunisia, the institutional crisis that erupted in October 2012 reached its climax with the political assassination of Chokri Belaid, leader of the opposition's left-secular Democratic Patriots' Movement, on 6 February 2013. This was followed by the killing of another opposition leader, Mohammed Brahmi, the founder and former head of the *Mouvement Populaire* (MP), on 25 July 2013. The event came as a further shock to the fragile Tunisian transition. While demands for a boycott of the constitution-making process intensified, the work of the NCA grounded to a halt after 60 of its members suspended activity.[51] The regional situation, particularly the developments that took place in Egypt at the end of June and the beginning of July 2013, did not help the Tunisian elites accomplish their task and overcome the legitimacy crisis of the interim institutions. The dismissal of Mohammed Morsi's presidency by a new round of popular mobilisation and the military's return to politics contributed to exposing the polarisation and faultlines dividing the main political actors in Tunisia in a way that had so far been tamed by the need to ensure a smooth and inclusive institutional transition.

Despite a number of opportunities missed and the protracted deadlock in the constitution-making process, there has always been an overarching agreement among the Tunisian political actors about what needed to be done in order to complete the transition. In this light, it is not possible to look at each single step, e.g., delivering the new Tunisian constitution, reforming the electoral framework and laws, and planning for the next elections, in isolation from the broader picture characterised by a number of interlinked stages. Constitution-making does not take place in a vacuum. From the beginning of the process of institutional transition, Tunisian elites planned it as if it were made up of a series of discrete steps to be undertaken in compliance with a long-term and clear temporal sequence. This has turned out not to be the case. The actors' inability to anticipate the consequences of an excessively protracted negotiation over the rules of the game, in a setting of political and socio-economic uncertainty, backfired on them and has risked endangering the legitimacy of the whole process.

In as much as there is a certain degree of path-dependence in the institutional changes initiated in 2011, there has always been much room for manoeuvre for the actors to make choices and change the course of the transition process. While agreeing on the steps to be taken to exit from the institutional stalemate – namely approving the constitution, forming a new technocratic government to lead the country until the new elections, organising both the parliamentary and the presidential electoral consultations by forming an independent electoral commission, writing the electoral law, and setting the polling dates – for reasons of political strategy, the main political actors harboured profound disagreements regarding the timing and sequencing of the steps. On the one hand, *Ennahda* made it clear that the coalition government had to remain in place until the constitution was passed, the electoral commission and the electoral law approved, and the election dates firmly set in early 2014 (Interviewee 51). *Ennahda* had a strong interest in holding the elections within a short timeframe (4–5 months maximum) in order to avoid losing too much support. On the other hand, the opposition parties, brought together in the National Salvation Front (NSF), wanted to put pressure on *Ennahda* to ensure that it actually delivered on its promises concerning the formulation of the new constitutional text. The opposition's fear was that if *Ennahda* managed to get everything it wanted before the government resigned, the party would have fewer incentives to do so. Quite understandably, *Ennahda*'s fears went in exactly the opposite direction: what would happen to the constitution and the elections once the government resigned? The opposition parties might indeed be shown to have an incentive to delay the electoral process long enough to allow themselves the time to get organised and campaign, as well as to purge the bureaucracy of *Ennahda*'s appointees (Interviewee 49).

It is clear that issues of timing and sequencing are crucial here and represent the main bones of contention. According to the roadmap proposed by the UGTT, and backed by UTICA (*Union Tunisienne de l'Industrie, du Commerce et de l'Artisanat* – the main employers' union), the Tunisian League of Human Rights (*Ligue Tunisienne des Droits de l'Homme*), and the National Bar Association – the so-called Quartet – and agreed upon by all political forces in September 2013, the NCA had one week to choose the new members of the electoral commission, two weeks to finalise the electoral law, three weeks to set a date for the elections, and four weeks to finish and pass the constitution. The roadmap also provided a clear timetable, partially overlapping with the NCA's four-week schedule for the creation of a technocratic government, starting with the selection of a consensus candidate for a care-taker prime minister, and the resignation of the *Ennahda*-led interim government.[52] As a result of the continuation of the institutional stalemate and the missing of the deadlines decided in the aforementioned transition schedule, growing distrust and disagreements on the substance of the steps to be taken started to emerge. The choice of the technocratic care-taker prime minister turned out to be a particularly divisive political issue with major conflicts between *Ennahda* and *Ettakatol*, on the one hand, and the majority of the other opposition forces, on the other. These conflicts were only solved in mid-December 2013 when a care-taker prime minister was finally appointed.[53] In addition to divisions about substance, issues of timing and sequencing have also been key. The timeframe provided by the UGTT roadmap proved to be unrealistic and far too ambitious to complete all the institutional transition stages. Some representatives of the political parties have even gone so far as to complain that it was imposed on the Tunisian transition by actors that were not 'knowledgeable enough about the lengthiness and intricacies of consensus-building and political negotiation' (Interviewee 50). This betrays a certain sense of uneasiness with the new speed 'imposed' on the transition process between September and October 2013. But while domestic factors were responsible for the change of pace, the regional situation, particularly what happened in Egypt during summer 2013, explains the widespread fear of possible derailment of the transition if it dragged on indefinitely.[54]

All told, the acceleration of the transition process in Tunisia has not been a mechanical development, but the conscious decision of the actors involved, particularly the powerful UGTT and, to a lesser extent, the political parties. The heated and fluid political environment created by the failed National Dialogue caused major problems for the transition process and put the country's future political development at stake. All this can be interpreted either as healthy dynamism – nothing more or less than a purely political process to determine 'who gets what, when, how', to quote Harold Lasswell (1936) – unseen in other parts of the region, or as a ticking bomb that has accompanied the country along a slow path to an unprecedented institutional crisis.

Notes

1 One of the main differences between the post-revolutionary changes that took place in Eastern Europe and those that unfolded during the Arab transitions was that in Eastern Europe institutional changes went hand in hand with the broader restructuring of

socio-economic policies. Quite to the contrary, given the different regional and international situations in 2011–2013, economic and social policies have undergone little change with respect to those enacted by the previous regimes in Egypt and Tunisia. On the interplay between political/institutional and socio-economic transformations in the context of the Eastern European transitions, see Karl and Schmitter (1991); Przeworksi (1991); Zielonka (2001). For a detailed account of the post-uprising socio-economic policies adopted in Egypt and Tunisia, see Paciello (2013).

2 For an account of similar views in the case of Egypt, see Brownlee and Stacher (2011) and Goldberg (2011).

3 Already in 2007, Steven Heydemann tellingly argued that:

> Democratic transitions in the Middle East are not likely to resemble those experienced in Eastern Europe or Latin America. Institutional rigidity, economic failures, and ideological exhaustion created the setting in which local civil societies and political oppositions could achieve rapid and decisive processes of democratization in Eastern Europe and Latin America. The unmaking of authoritarianism in the Arab world, if it occurs at all, will follow a different course. It will probably be less dramatic, more ambiguous, and slower. Efforts to achieve this end, moreover, must contend with regimes that have proven to be more adaptive and flexible than many might have believed possible.
>
> (Heydemann 2007a: 35)

4 The concepts of 'civil society' and 'political society' are used by Alfred Stepan in *Rethinking Military Politics* to distinguish the three important arenas of a polity: 'civil society', 'political society', and the state (Stepan 1988). By 'civil society' the author means the arena in which manifold social movements attempt to constitute themselves in an ensemble of arrangements to express and advance their interests. By the same token, 'civil society' is distinct from 'political society', meaning the arena in which the polity specifically arranges itself for political contestation to gain control over public power and the state apparatus. Finally, the state is the administrative, legal, bureaucratic, and coercive system that structures relations between and within the civil and political societies (Stepan 1988: 3–12).

5 Clearly, constitutional rights and fundamental freedoms may well remain ineffective if not backed by a strong and independent judiciary.

6 On the involvement of the population in constitution-making processes, see Elkins, Ginsburg and Blount (2008) and Samuels (2006). Horowitz (2002) discusses participation in constitution-making processes as a trade-off between design consistency and process legitimacy. In general terms, a substantial amount of evidence has recently been generated in the international debate on constitution making and has led to a set of 'norms' that can be used as a reference by countries undertaking this task. One such 'norm' is that, whereas in the past constitution making had a ritualistic participatory element, often entailing the election of a constituent assembly or the approval of the final text in a referendum, while the rest was seen mostly as a technical endeavour detached from public interest, today international practice underscores the extent to which constitutions should be written in a manner that includes all significant political forces, be truly participatory at various stages, and have a significant public element. See Samuels (2006).

7 Other authors, such as Banting and Simeon (1985), began even earlier to focus on what they call the 'idea-generating stage' during which the parameters are laid out and interests (and counter-interests) mobilised, prior to the preparation of the text.

8 This critical reading of one of the functions of the separation of powers is developed by Dahl in his *A Preface to Democratic Theory* (1965). A more recent analysis of the importance of anti-majoritarian provisions in the constitutions of the countries moving away from authoritarianism can be found in Alberts, Warshaw and Weingast (2012). The models developed by these authors imply that successful democracy, beyond

simply holding elections, requires attention to constitutional design, specifically the inclusion of anti-majoritarian features that protect one or more parties or minorities by constraining the policy discretion of the majority. Anti-majoritarian features must be tuned to the relative power of each actor. Examples of anti-majoritarian features are constitutional courts with powers of judicial review, legislative bodies with territorial representation or federal arrangements, and electoral requirements, such as that of a supermajority to pass certain types of laws. For a discussion of anti-majoritarian provisions and their classification in terms of their form (whether they create structures or procedures) and their scope (whether they protect diffuse interests or the interests of a targeted group within the population), see figure 4.1 on page 72 of Alberts et al. (2012).
9 To avoid political polarisation and conflicts in divided societies, the literature states that it is important 'to proceed to the phase of open electoral contestation only well *after* institutional reform has been instigated' (Afsah 2012: 495, emphasis in the original).
10 Author's conversation with Nathan Brown, Washington, 21 October 2013.
11 No substantial institutional reforms took place during the SCAF rule and most political power remained in the hands of the old regime's holdovers, particularly in the Interior Ministry. Overall, the military council's ad-hoc transition management was marked by the lack of transparency, participation, and coherence (Landolt and Kubicek 2013: 13).
12 There were some allegations that the Muslim Brotherhood had engaged in activities of vote-rigging by convincing the sizable ranks of their (in some cases illiterate) supporters in the vast rural areas of the country that it was their religious duty to vote for the amended constitution. See "Islamism in Egypt: legitimate concerns?". *Ahramonline*. 20 April 2011. http://english.ahram.org.eg/NewsContent/4/0/10405/Opinion/Islamism-in-Egypt-legitimate-concerns.aspx.
13 Elster develops the distinction between 'upstream' and 'downstream' constraints in the constitution-making process. Upstream constraints are imposed by the powers setting up the constitution-drafting body, whereas downstream constraints result from the anticipation of preferences of those involved in later stages (Elster 1995: 373–375). The constraints introduced by the SCAF in the constitution-making process through the March 2011 constitutional declaration are an example of upstream constraints.
14 The unofficial translation of the 30 March 2011 constitutional declaration can be found at the following link: www.constitutionnet.org/vl/item/egypt-constitutional-declaration-march-2011.
15 The impact of the authoritarian practices on the Egyptian political scene during the Mubarak era is assessed in Chapter 4, dealing with electoral politics.
16 As aptly argued by some authors, '[t]o reduce the scope for institutional interest, constitutions ought to be written by specially convened assemblies and not by bodies that also serve as ordinary legislatures. Nor should legislators be given a central place in ratification' (Elster *et al.* 1998: 117). The main distinction here is between 'constituent assemblies', which are elected especially to draft a constitution, and 'constituent legislatures', which are legislatures that take on the added task of constitution making. The 'constituent legislating assembly' refers to an intermediate category of cases in which assemblies elected purposely for constitution making transform themselves into sitting legislatures. See also Elster (2006).
17 The second constituent assembly included members from the following groups: 39 representatives of political parties from the People's Assembly; six judges; 13 representatives of labour unions; 21 public figures; five representatives of *Al-Azhar*; four representatives of the Coptic Orthodox Church; one representative of the Ministry of Justice; one representative of the Ministry of Interior (in charge of homeland security); one representative of the armed forces; and nine legal scholars. Judge Hussam Al Ghariani, President of the Supreme Council of Justice, was elected by the members of the assembly to oversee the constitution-making process. According to the figures quoted in Landolt and Kubicek, the second constituent assembly closely resembled the first in that 60 – rather than 64 – members had Islamist connections (Landolt and Kubicek 2013: 15).

18 "Official: The 100 members of Egypt's revamped Constituent Assembly". *Ahramonline*. 12 June 2012. http://english.ahram.org.eg/News/44696.aspx.
19 The Arabic version of the verdict can be found at the following link: http://blogyaacoub dotcom.files.wordpress.com/2012/06/24-efbfbdefbfbdefbfbdefbfbd-efbfbd.pdf. The English translation of the main motivations behind the disbandment of the Lower House of parliament reads as follows:

> There is no doubt that establishing this competition had a definite impact and reciprocal effect on the two-thirds allocated for closed party lists, since if political parties were not competing with independents over that other portion, then a rearrangement would have taken place within the party lists, taking into account the priorities within each party. Furthermore, political party members had the choice between two ways to run for the People's Assembly, the closed party-list system and the individual candidacy system. Independents were deprived of one of these ways, and their rights were limited to the portion allotted for the individual candidacy system, in which political party members also competed.

Quoted in Tavana (2012). Historically, the People's Assembly had been dissolved three times, namely in 1987, 1990, and 2012. See also "Saving Egypt's Supreme Constitutional Court from itself". *Ahramonline*. 15 June 2012. http://english.ahram.org.eg/NewsContentP/4/45009/Opinion/Saving-Egypt%27s-Supreme-Constitutional-Court-from-i.aspx. The political significance of the SCC decisions to disband the first elected parliament of the post-Mubarak era is assessed in Chapter 4.
20 See the unofficial translation of the June constitutional declaration at the following link: "English text of SCAF amended Egypt Constitutional Declaration". *Ahramonline*. 18 June 2012. http://english.ahram.org.eg/News/45350.aspx.
21 According to the draft preamble, the purpose of the new Tunisian constitution is to:

> build a participatory, democratic, republican regime, where the state is civil and is based on the law and institutions; where sovereignty is granted to the people through peaceful rotation of power on governance and free elections, and on the principle of the segregation of authorities and balance between them; where the right to govern is based on plurality, objectivity of administration, and good governance representing the basis of the political race; and where the state ensures freedoms, human rights, independence of the judiciary, justice, equality of rights and duties between all male and female citizens and between all groups and regions.

See the unofficial translation of the fourth draft of the Tunisian constitution, released on 1 June 2013, at the following link: www.constitutionnet.org/vl/item/unofficial-english-translation-fourth-draft-tunisian-constitution.
22 The unofficial translation of the November 2012 constitutional declaration can be found at the following link: http://english.ahram.org.eg/News/58947.aspx.
23 Another constitutional decree was issued on 8 December 2012, after the constituent assembly had presented the constitution draft to the president, which annulled the first declaration of 21 November, but provided that '[c]onstitutional declarations, including this one, shall not be appealed against before any judicial body. All legal lawsuits on this regard before all courts shall be void' (art. 4). See "Translation of President Morsi's latest constitutional decree". *Ahramonline*. 9 December 2012. http://english.ahram.org.eg/NewsContent/1/64/60116/Egypt/Politics-/Translation-of-President-Morsis-latest-constitutio.aspx.
24 "Egypt's opposition protest on Friday to reject constitutional declaration, draft constitution". *Ahramonline*. 29 November 2012. http://english.ahram.org.eg/NewsContent/1/64/59476/Egypt/Politics-/Egypts-opposition-protest-on-Friday-to-reject-cons.aspx.
25 "Constituent Assembly okays draft Egypt charter in night-time session". *Ahramonline*. 30 November 2012. http://english.ahram.org.eg/NewsContent/1/64/59505/Egypt/Politics-/Constituent-Assembly-okays-draft-Egypt-charter-in-.aspx.

26 Most of the civic forces interviewed for this research prior to the constitutional referendum expressed their strong concern that the vote would favour Islamist forces, as was the case in the March 2011 referendum on the SCAF-issued constitutional amendments (Interviewees 8, 11, 18).
27 A number of drafts of the constitutional texts were circulated in the fall of 2012. Although these drafts were largely incomplete and provisional, they triggered a lot of controversy and debate, thus signalling a return of attention to politics on the part of the Egyptian population. For example, the draft circulated in October 2012 was harshly criticised by some people as too conservative and as putting too much emphasis on representative structures, for example the parliament, while failing to provide for adequate participatory channels. The system, based more on representation than participation, was regarded as being in contrast with the aspirations and claims of the protests (Interviewee 4).
28 According to some views, the constitution introduced some dysfunctional elements in the distribution of powers between the president and the prime minister, as it assigned more authority to the former and also introduced some significant obstacles to their exercise (Interviewees 3, 5, 13). On the past history of strong Arab presidents and the origins and evolution of 'presidential security states', see Owen (2012).
29 The unofficial translation of the December 2012 constitution can be found at the following link: www.constitutionnet.org/vl/item/new-constitution-arab-republic-egypt-approved-30-nov-2012.
30 Even though the November 2012 constitutional declaration issued by Morsi contained an article purposely amending the duration of the constitution-making process, from six to eight months, the constituent assembly had to rush to finish its task at the end of November 2012.
31 Afraid of igniting popular unrest, for more than a decade Egyptian governments shied away from tackling a system that provided consumers with such items as bread, petrol, and cooking gas at a fraction of the actual cost. On the subsidies system in Egypt, see Harik (1992).
32 See "Egypt and Qatar negotiating interest on $3bn bond sale: Planning minister". *Ahramonline*. 28 April 2013. http://english.ahram.org.eg/News/70296.aspx.
33 "Egypt's new regional governors: A who's who". *Ahramonline*. 4 September 2012. http://english.ahram.org.eg/News/52010.aspx.
34 "Morsi politely 'asks' defiant prosecutor-general to stay on". *Ahramonline*. 13 October 2012. http://english.ahram.org.eg/NewsContent/1/64/55526/Egypt/Politics-/Morsi-politely-asks-defiant-prosecutorgeneral-to-s.aspx.
35 "Egypt's judicial authority bill: A 'purge' or 'massacre' of judiciary?". *Ahramonline*. 7 May 2013. http://english.ahram.org.eg/NewsContent/1/0/70873/Egypt/0/Egypts-judicial-authority-bill-A-purge-or-massacre.aspx. The conflict between Morsi and the judiciary is analysed in greater detail in Chapter 5.
36 The unofficial translation of the constitutional declaration dated 8 July 2013 can be viewed here: www.constitutionnet.org/vl/item/unofficial-english-translation-constitutional-declaration-egypt-july-08–2013.
37 Article 29 of the constitutional declaration was silent on the procedures that each state institution and organised group had to follow to select their representatives, as well as the number of representatives that each of them was entitled to. As far as the parties are concerned, the declaration did not specify whether their relative proportions had to be determined on the basis of the previous parliamentary elections results.
38 For an analysis of the constitution drafted in 2013, including some provisions that limit the power of the president, such as article 161 that allowed two-thirds of the parliament to call for a public referendum to end the president's rule and organise early presidential elections, see "Inside Egypt's draft constitution: Checks and balances mediate presidential power". *Ahramonline*. 12 December 2013. http://english.ahram.org.eg/News/88274.aspx. The unofficial translation of the text of the new

constitution can be found at the following link: www.constitutionnet.org/egypt-draft-constitution-dec-20133.
39 The electoral process and results that led to the creation of the NCA are analysed in Chapter 4, devoted to electoral politics.
40 It is worth recalling the distinction between 'constituent assemblies', 'constituent legislatures', and 'constituent legislating assemblies' presented in footnote 16 of this chapter.
41 The distribution of posts in the NCA reflected this tendency towards inclusiveness, with *Ennahda* controlling three of the six constitutional committees.
42 "More than 4,000 people descend on Constituent Assembly to call for Shariaa Law". *Tunisialive*. 16 March 2012. www.tunisia-live.net/2012/03/16/more-than-4000-people-descend-on-constituent-assembly-to-call-for-shariaa-law/.
43 "Tunisians celebrate Independence Day in the thousands". *Tunisialive*. 20 March 2012. www.tunisia-live.net/2012/03/20/tunisians-celebrate-independence-day-in-the-thousands/.
44 All the texts of the articles are taken from the 1 June 2013 constitution draft, which can be consulted at the following link: www.constitutionnet.org/vl/item/unofficial-english-translation-fourth-draft-tunisian-constitution.
45 "Tunisia's leading party reaffirms commitment to Arab-Muslim identity". *Tunisialive*. 26 March 2012. www.tunisia-live.net/2012/03/26/tunisias-leading-party-reaffirms-commitment-to-arab-muslim-identity/.
46 Some of the powers and prerogatives of the president appear to be considerably limited to the benefit of those of the prime minister. For example, article 76 specified that the head of state was to develop the policies of foreign affairs and defence 'in compliance with the general policy of the state'. Another example is article 69, which granted the prime minister the prerogative to legislate by decree 'in the event of the Chamber's dissolution or during its recess'.
47 Regarding the NCA's willingness to engage and consult with citizens, a number of people complained that there was a disconnect between the constitution-making body and the public due to the lack of formal mechanisms for incorporating its feedback, in the form of protests, petitions, strikes, and messages, into the draft text (Interviewee 41).
48 The procedural part of the constitution-making process revolves around the methods for approving the constitution. In the case of Tunisia, this was a two-step process. The first step was for the assembly to approve each article with a majority vote. The second step was for the plenary session to approve the constitution by a two-thirds majority. If the assembly failed to achieve a two-thirds majority twice, then the draft constitution would be put to a public referendum to be approved with a simple majority.
49 The unfolding of events was to demonstrate that the role of the UGTT, which has always had a political dimension over and above its basic identity as a labour confederation, was less one of an impartial mediator than one of an ideologically motivated broker (Interviewee 38).
50 The UGTT initiative was matched a few months later by another one launched by President Marzouki aimed at involving all the ruling parties as well as the opposition represented in the NCA, including *Nidaa Tounes*. This time the dialogue was boycotted by the parties from the socialist and social-democratic side of the political spectrum and by the UGTT.
51 "Tunisia's constitution in limbo". *Tunisialive*. 29 August 2013. www.tunisia-live.net/2013/08/29/tunisias-constitution-in-limbo/.
52 Upon accepting to disband the interim government, *Ennahda* was keen on reassuring its constituency that it would give up government but not power (Interviewees 38, 52).

53 "Mehdi Jomaa chosen to become new Prime Minister". *Tunisialive*. 14 December 2013. www.tunisia-live.net/2013/12/14/mehdi-jomaa-chosen-to-become-new-prime-minister/.
54 Some provisions in the draft constitution were likely to further contribute to increasing the deadlock as they maximised the uncertainty by extending the interim period. For example, article 146 stipulated that the new constitution would enter into force gradually and that recourse to the Constitutional Court to verify the constitutionality of laws would not be permissible in the first three years of the court's operation.

4 It all comes down to electoral politics

> Once again [. . .] Egyptians woke up on the morning after an election to find the conflicts tearing at their society deepened rather than assuaged. [. . .] If democracy failed to develop in Egypt, [. . .] it was not for lack of voting. The problem was not that elections came too early or too often: [. . .] better-timed elections might have helped.
>
> from Nathan J. Brown. 2013. "Egypt's Failed Transition".
> *Journal of Democracy* 24 (4): 48 and 50

The actual functioning of constitutional provisions is influenced by a number of factors including the party system, elections, and the rules regulating them, i.e., electoral laws. This part of the research thus completes the analysis of constitution-making processes in the Arab world in the aftermath of the Arab uprisings by introducing another set of variables related to institutional development. The study of electoral politics in the Arab transitions context has to tackle the issue of electoral authoritarianism. Prior to the Arab uprisings, autocrats in countries like Egypt and Tunisia, while displaying markedly authoritarian features, made extensive use of elections to sustain and legitimise their rule.[1] As aptly stated by Andreas Schedler, '[a] large number of regimes in the contemporary world [. . .] have established the institutional façades of democracy, including regular multi-party elections for the chief executive, in order to conceal (and reproduce) harsh realities of authoritarian governance' (Schedler 2006: 1). The notion of electoral authoritarianism places electoral contests at the core of the dynamics of change and durability of any regime. Arguably, in electoral authoritarian regimes elections are recognised as playing an important role in contrast to what happens in other types of autocracies. This feature identifies electoral authoritarian regimes as one point on the continuum between full democracies and closed autocracies, and distinguishes them from other types of authoritarian regimes.[2]

Nevertheless, elections in authoritarian regimes are only minimally pluralistic, minimally competitive, and minimally open. Usually, and unsurprisingly, elections tend to reinforce and prolong authoritarian rule. As aptly claimed by Brownlee, 'election results in authoritarian contexts tend to ratify rather than redistribute the power that competing groups wield' (Brownlee 2007: 9). This is due to the existence of significant barriers to the access to the electoral contest and thus to power. In other words, electoral authoritarian regimes are able and indeed have an interest in manipulating electoral processes by making use of a number of barriers that block the full participation of some actors in it. 'Gate-keepers' in electoral authoritarian regimes have a number of different functions, ranging from the discriminatory, such as manipulating electoral laws, excluding opposition parties and candidates from entering the electoral arena, and infringing upon their political rights and civil liberties, to the more subtle controlling, such as restricting their exposure to media campaigns through indirect boycotts or financial crackdowns. In the presence of a ruling party, such as the Egyptian National Democratic Party (NDP) and the Tunisian *Rassemblement Constitutionnel Démocratique* (RCD), elections should be viewed as symptoms, rather than causes, of deeper trends that originate in the institutional organisation of the state. Since authoritarian regimes are characterised by limited pluralism, the extent to which 'limited elections' allow the opposition to gain some space to contest the regime's dominance is indicative of either the regime's full control of the political arena or the beginning of the erosion of its power. This contrasts with what some authors have claimed about elections being the 'death of dictatorship' (Huntington 1991: 174).

Against this backdrop, the challenges for Egypt and Tunisia when moving away from authoritarianism have lain in developing a new role for fully pluralistic, fully competitive, and fully open elections. Political parties arguably have had a major stake in tackling these institutional challenges, although they had proved largely irrelevant during the 2011 uprisings. Removed from organised political structures, leaders, or ideologies, the mass mobilisations were possible thanks to the use of new communication technologies (Achcar 2013: 159–168), horizontal links, common framing, and emulation.[3] Traditional opposition parties, including the Islamists, were not at the forefront. Decades of electoral authoritarianism had produced a deep mistrust among the people about the ability of formal political options and structures to promote change. This feeling triggered the overwhelming sense of the need to promote people's agency in the form of strikes, protests, and demonstrations as a way of subverting the ossified structures of power in place. This is what Pace and Cavatorta have called the 'anti-political flavour of the uprisings' (Pace and Cavatorta 2012: 134), meaning people's dissatisfaction with traditional modes and institutions of political representation and channels of policy implementation.

Nevertheless, the role of political parties gained relevance immediately after the uprisings and during the transitions from authoritarianism, consistently with their traditional function of representing citizens' interests, channelling claims into an institutionalised political consensus, fostering participation, structuring political choices, and forming governments. Contrary to what is stated in Thomas Carothers's seminal work on the role of parties in young or struggling democracies (Carothers 2006), parties have been held in high regard during the Arab transitions as they have typically been seen as the main agents of institutional development. As an extension of this argument, it can be contended that the party system – which can be assessed in terms of its fragmentation, i.e., the number and shape of parties (the presence of clear-cut or loose coalitions); its polarisation, i.e., the extent to which parties are institutionalised and built on ideology or patronage; and its volatility – provides useful information about the political system as a whole. At the same time, parties and party systems are shaped by societal features and the actions of political actors (Brody-Barre 2013: 221–225).

Egypt: the phantom of 'electocracy'

Too many elections?

The period between 2011 and the beginning of 2014 was characterised by the repeated summoning to the polls of the Egyptian population (Brown 2013a). It seems redundant to state here that, in themselves, elections are neither a step forward towards a more democratic type of polity nor the cause of a country's failed political transition. In the case of Egypt, electoral politics in the initial phase of the transition had an unprecedented bearing on the whole process of institutional development, particularly with regard to the relationship among the main political actors – the political parties, the military, the judiciary, and the 'revolutionary' movement. The way in which the voting process was shaped and the results it produced contributed to throwing the growing fissures in the Egyptian political architecture into stark relief and sometimes aggravated them.

In late 2011 and early 2012, Egyptians were called upon to vote in three rounds for the Lower House of parliament. This was met by unprecedented enthusiasm. The three voting stages ran from 28–29 November 2011 to 10–11 January 2012. Voters were supposed to elect 498 representatives in the People's Assembly, to which would be added ten seats appointed by the Supreme Council of the Armed Forces (SCAF).[4] The elections for the Upper House of parliament, the Shura Council, followed in three stages between 29 January and 22 February 2012.[5] These elections resulted in a resounding Islamist majority (Table 4.1). The newly constituted Freedom and Justice Party (FJP) was one of the protagonists of the electoral contest. Established in April 2011 as a direct spinoff of the illegal but tolerated Muslim Brotherhood organisation,[6] FJP members initially suggested that they would seek to win only a third – and to that end put up candidates in only half – of the seats in the People's Assembly.[7] Nevertheless, before the elections they went back on this and eventually ran for two-thirds of them. According to some views, this was triggered by the decision of the Salafists – traditionally a quietist and apolitical movement, squarely hostile to the very notion of political parties as they allegedly divide the community of believers – to launch their own political parties and enter the electoral arena (Roberts 2013). The FJP's decision to run for two-thirds of the seats might superficially seem to have been vindicated by the elections' outcome. The Democratic Alliance for Egypt, the FJP-dominated coalition of 11 parties, obtained 37.5 percent of the vote and 225 seats, i.e., 45.2 percent of the total, followed by the Salafist *Al-Nour* party and its allies, which came in second place with 27.8 percent of the vote and 125 seats (25.0 percent). The secular, liberal, and centre-left political parties and coalitions followed.

Table 4.1 Distribution of seats in Egypt's Lower House

Coalition/Party	Number of seats	Percentage of seats
Democratic Alliance	225	45.2
Freedom and Justice Party (FJP)	216	43.4
Al-Karama	6	1.2
Al-Hadara	2	0.4
Labour Party	1	0.2
Islamist Alliance	125	25
Al-Nour	109	21.8
Building and Development Party	13	2.6
Al-Asala	3	0.6
Al-Wafd	41	8.2
Egyptian Bloc	34	6.8
Al-Tagammu Party	3	0.6
Egyptian Social Democratic Party	16	3.2
Free Egyptians Party	15	3
Reform and Development Party	10	2
Al-Wasat Party	9	1.8
Revolution Continues Alliance	8	1.6
Egypt National Party	5	1
Egyptian Citizen Party	4	0.8
Union Party	3	0.6
Freedom Party	3	0.6
Al-Adl Party	2	0.4
Democratic Peace Party	2	0.4
Arab Egyptian Union Party	1	0.2
Nasserite Party	1	0.2
Independents	25	5
Total	**498**	**100**

Source: author's elaboration based on the information provided for by the dossier "2012 Egyptian Parliamentary Elections". *Carnegie Endowment for International Peace.* http://carnegieendowment.org/2015/01/22/2012-egyptian-parliamentary-elections-pub-58800.

All in all, the sweeping victory of the Islamists – both the Muslim Brotherhood and the Salafists – represented an earthquake for the still fragile post-Mubarak political system.[8]

Majoritarian tendencies

When attempting to explain the Islamists' resounding victory, one needs to take into account the decades of authoritarian rule that shaped an unbalanced political scene tilted in their favour. By 2011, most non-Islamist political forces had grown completely disillusioned with participation in formal politics to the point that, according to Nathan Brown, they had 'become little more than dried-out husks' (Brown 2013a: 52). At the same time, they had been unable to cultivate and enlarge their electorate by resorting to the mechanisms of informal politics, something the Muslim Brotherhood (and to a lesser extent the Salafists) had been very successful in doing by drawing on their broader social agenda (Rubin 2010). The very timing of the elections, taking place less than one year after the fall of Mubarak, and the sequencing of constitution making and elections worked out in the March 2011 constitutional declaration added up to an electoral advantage for the Islamist forces.

It is worth reflecting in greater detail on the implications of the Muslim Brotherhood's victory in the 2011–2012 parliamentary elections with regard to two issues: the intra-Islamist bloc dynamics and the relationship between the FJP and the non-Islamist political actors. Regarding the former, the significant, and to some extent, largely unexpected emergence of the Salafists as the second political force in the parliamentary elections increased the pressure on the Muslim Brotherhood to come to terms with their more conservative rivals, which in turn made it exceptionally difficult for them to seek alliances in parliament with non-Islamist parties without putting their own internal unity under strain (Robert 2013).[9] Overall, this meant that the Muslim Brotherhood's leadership started to take on increasingly conservative connotations. Turning to the latter, i.e., the relations that developed between the Muslim Brotherhood's party and the civic forces, the Islamists immediately displayed their unwillingness to engage with non-Islamists out of fear that this could jeopardise their own internal cohesion. This was ultimately the result of the Muslim Brotherhood's strategic 'miscalculation' when they decided to file candidates to run for two-thirds of the seats in the People's Assembly. The decision shattered any possibility to develop a relationship based on mutual trust with the civic forces, and ultimately heightened the latter's fear of the former's majoritarian ambitions, and led to reciprocal alienation.

Some scholars convincingly ascribe the Islamists' inability to deal with the civic forces to the inherent and persisting nature of the Muslim Brotherhood, despite its post-Mubarak's attempt to refashion itself into a national governing party. According to Brown, the Muslim Brotherhood, which dominated its party and kept it on a short leash, 'had been built not for open democratic competition but for resilience under authoritarian pressure. It was tight-knit, inward-looking, and even paranoid' (Brown 2013a: 57). With the benefit of hindsight, a certain degree of paranoia could have been justified, not towards the rather toothless civic forces, but rather towards the military. Indeed, the Islamists discovered quite soon that their parliamentary majority meant little because the military had purposely enshrined in the June 2012 constitutional declaration a number of provisions barring the new parliament from exercising some significant powers, namely the power to oversee the government or to pass legislation without the generals' approval. On 14 June 2012, another blow to the Islamists power was dealt by the Supreme Constitutional Court (SCC) when it found that one-third of the seats in the Lower House of parliament were invalid, in that the seats reserved for independents had been contested by party members. According to the court, this called for the dissolution of the entire People's Assembly voted in less than six months earlier. The court's authority on this issue was contested by many players, in particular the Muslim Brotherhood, on the ground that in the absence of the constitution, nobody had the right to dissolve the parliament or that dissolution had to be decided by popular referendum. While acknowledging the alleged irregularities in a number of constituencies, the FJP argued that election results should be invalidated only in the constituencies concerned. However, this argument was rejected and the SCAF followed up with an administrative decree dissolving the assembly. The SCC's decision immediately translated into a reinforcement of the military's power as the June 2012 declaration conferred legislative authority, in the absence of a sitting parliament, to the SCAF.

In the middle of the first round of the confrontation between the Muslim Brotherhood and the judiciary, the first Egyptian presidential elections of the post-Mubarak era took place. These elections and the way in which they were managed by the Islamists opened up another front in the struggle for power, this time pitting the Muslim Brotherhood against the military. Despite having made clear as early as March 2011 that they would not put forward a candidate for president, in late March 2012 the FJP backtracked again and fielded its own candidate, namely the Supreme Guide's deputy and prominent businessman Khairat Al-Shater.[10] Once again, the Muslim Brotherhood's decision appears to have been influenced by the dynamics within the Islamist camp (Roberts 2013). Immediately after the establishment of the FJP, one of the Brothers' most prominent members, and one of the leaders of the movement's liberal and progressive wing, Abdul Moneim Aboul Fotouh, broke ranks and declared that he would run for president as an independent.[11] With the presidential elections approaching and *Al-Nour*'s enthusiastic endorsement of Aboul Fotouh's candidacy, the Muslim Brotherhood decided that the least bad option would be to reconsider their previous position and field their own candidate. Here, too, issues of internal discipline and coherence – the result of years and decades of the movement's acting as a secret organisation under authoritarian rule (Farag 2012)[12] – were responsible for the Muslim Brotherhood's misguided decision to run in the presidential elections in the way they did.[13] As aptly argued by Roberts (2013), in the years 2011–2012, the deep-rooted crisis within the Islamist movement, which dated back to the last years of Mubarak and of which Aboul Fotouh's split from it was one of the most telling signs, came to the surface.[14]

Voting for the presidential elections took place in two rounds, the first on 23–24 May 2012 with the run-off on 16–17 June. In the first round, with a voter turnout of 46 percent, the results were split between five major candidates: Mohammed Morsi (25 percent); Ahmed Shafiq, the last prime minister under deposed president (24 percent); Hamdeen Sabahi, a prominent dissident during the Sadat and Mubarak regimes (21 percent); Abdel Moneim Aboul Fotouh (18 percent); and Amr Moussa, who had held positions under the Mubarak regime (11 percent). The run-off saw a slightly higher voter turnout (around 52 percent) and Morsi reportedly won by a narrow margin over Ahmed Shafiq. The official figures released by the Supreme Presidential Electoral Commission (SPEC) declared that Morsi had taken 51.7 percent of the votes versus 48.3 percent for Shafiq.[15] Morsi was sworn in on 30 June 2012.

The elections arguably set the stage for and deepened existing divisions between the Islamist and civic forces, on the one hand, and those opposing them and thus supporting the former political elite, on the other. As a result, some authors tend to qualify the Egyptian political system that took shape after the events of 2011 as 'bipolar' (Abdul-Majid 2013: 20). This description appears to be convincing only in as much as it identifies the main fault-line running through the party system, namely the Islamist vs. non-Islamist one. A more accurate picture of the party system in the 2011–2013 period, however, would describe it as fluid in nature. In addition to the FJP, with all the schisms and divisions within it, a great number of non-Islamist, leftist, and fledgling liberal parties and groupings saw the light.[16] Given their lack of clear platforms or plans, their reliance on a small core of elite supporters, and their downplaying of ideology, this jumble of political groups were often hardly distinguishable from each other. Their actions in the initial phase of the country's transition revealed the extent to which they lacked the capacity to form solid and viable political platforms and were plagued by internal conflicts and divisions, while betting on the SCAF to create a sort of balance with the Islamist parties.

The pitfalls of the electoral law

According to the new Egyptian constitution, approved in a referendum at the end of 2012, Egyptians were still not done with elections. Article 229 provided that preparations for elections to the Council of Representatives, the successor to the People's Assembly, would begin within 60 days of its adoption.[17] In January 2013, the Shura Council, the Upper House of parliament, which according to article 230 of the new constitution had interim authority to legislate until the new Council of Representatives was formed, drafted a law amending two of Egypt's myriad electoral laws with some far-reaching changes.[18] The new provisions on elections provided for a mixed electoral system that was made up of individual first-past-the-post candidate districts and proportional representation (party and independent) lists. These provisions were regarded as too complex and confusing for voters, of whom about a third were illiterate.[19] An added complication was the provision that allowed independents to form their own lists or be on a party's list. Accordingly, the country would be divided into two different types of districts for the individual candidate voting and the proportional representation voting. Furthermore, some seats would be reserved for 'workers' and 'farmers'. The bill was overwhelmingly read as favouring Islamist parties and biased against many segments of society, including the Copts (no positive, even temporary, discrimination provisions), women (no quota for female candidates), and Egyptians residing abroad. For one thing, the large size of the districts would serve Islamist parties the best, in particular the Muslim Brotherhood's FJP, as they could draw on greater financial resources and, thus, were likely to be able to launch bigger electoral campaigns both nationally and locally, outcompeting liberal and leftist parties with more limited financial resources. In addition, the draft law imposed a constituent-based threshold that required every party to secure at least one-third of total votes in a district for its candidates to enter parliament and at the same time removed the 0.5 percent national threshold. The law also stated that the remaining seats in the list system would go to parties with the most remaining votes.

All in all, the bill sparked controversy and most liberal and leftist parties, particularly the umbrella National Salvation Front (NSF),[20] opposed it. First of all, the opposition complained about the clause determining the size of the electoral districts as this would increase the chances of the Islamist forces to the detriment of small parties to take all remaining seats. Also related to districting procedures, the opposition lamented that the distribution of seats under the bill was skewed in favour of the countryside and against Egypt's major cities. The assumption was that the ruling FJP received most of its support in Egypt's poorer rural districts and thus favoured those areas by granting them proportionally more seats in the parliament's final makeup. Second, the draft adopted the closed-list proportional representation system, which violated the NSF's main demand to adopt an open-list system. Finally, according to the bill, parliamentarians could change their party affiliation during their term and independents could join parties following their election. This provision would, in the opposition's view, serve the Islamists' strategy of fielding as many (partisan and independent) candidates as possible in order to secure the majority of seats. As a result of these very politically charged circumstances, with the polarisation between the Muslim Brotherhood and civic forces heightening day after day in the wake of the adoption of the new constitution, the opposition NSF went so far as to state that the bill was unfair and that it would boycott the elections if the rules were not amended.[21]

In addition to the long list of disagreements and criticism of the new Egyptian electoral law, suggesting a repetition of the controversial 2012 constitution-making process and marking another cycle in the ongoing struggle between the Islamist and civic forces, the prospects for it seeing the light were further frustrated by procedural issues. Apparently in an attempt to lessen the risk of the next parliament being dissolved once again, the 2012 constitution required the SCC to review the constitutionality of the electoral laws prior to its passing in parliament. This was enshrined in article 177:[22]

> The president of the Republic or the speaker of the Council of Representatives shall present draft laws governing presidential, legislative or local elections before the Supreme Constitutional Court, to determine their compliance with the Constitution prior to dissemination. The Court reaches a decision in this regard within 45 days from the date the matter is presented before it; otherwise, the proposed law is considered approved. If the Court deems one or more parts of the text non-compliant with the provisions of the Constitution, its decision is implemented. The laws referred to in the first paragraph are not subject to the subsequent control stipulated in Article 175 of the Constitution.[23]

An important turning point in the Egyptian institutional transition process came in mid-February 2013, when the finalised electoral bill was referred to the SCC in accordance with article 177 of the new constitution.[24] In response, the SCC ruled that five articles in the draft law were unconstitutional and requested changes to a further eight. While some of the issues raised by the SCC included relatively small technical matters, others were much more controversial and difficult to handle. For example, on 18 February the SCC found that the bill's proposed distribution of seats within electoral districts was in violation of the constitutional principle of equality.

At the same time, the Shura Council revised the draft law, but decided not to resubmit the text to the SCC. Instead, it was sent to the president for final approval and published in the Official Gazette, thereby giving it legal force. On 21 February 2013, President Morsi announced that the elections would be held in four phases starting on 27 April and ending on 27 June. It was only at that point that the first real controversy arose. Once again, it was triggered by the vague wording of the constitutional provision that failed to anticipate the legal implications of the SCC's decision.[25] On 7 March 2013, a Cairo Administrative Court, after receiving more than a dozen requests to intervene in the matter, ruled that the text of the revised amendments to the electoral laws should have been returned to the SCC to enable the court to review its compatibility with the constitution. It also cancelled the president's decree and suspended the holding of elections.[26] In addition to arguing that the FJP's interpretation of article 177 was incorrect as sketched out above, the Administrative Court formulated a second reason to explain its decision. This had to do with one of the articles in the new constitution establishing a semi-presidential system of government, according to which the president had to share executive authority with the government. More specifically, the court referred to article 141, according to which all the president's powers, aside from a small number that were specifically listed, were to be exercised through the prime minister. Given that the list of exceptions did not include electoral matters, the court found that the president no longer had exclusive authority to call elections. This had a momentous impact on electoral politics, but also on the balance of power between the president and the prime minister, altering it in some significant, largely unanticipated ways, which did not however manifest themselves to the fullest extent because of subsequent events.

The fast pace and the deep resonance of these vicissitudes threw the Egyptian political system into disarray. Although the SCC's decision appeared to be well reasoned from a number of important standpoints, the very vivid experience of having the most democratic parliament in living memory dissolved on a technicality was immensely frustrating for many Egyptians and at that point concerns were raised that if the amended law was not deemed fully compatible with the SCC's ruling, then the next electoral results could by the same token also be declared unconstitutional. In addition, the SCC's ruling pulled the court into the political dispute between the Islamists and the civic forces and unveiled the institution's partisan nature. On 25 May 2013, Egypt's SCC rejected on several grounds the third draft electoral law that the Shura Council had referred to a month and a half earlier, including the fact that prohibiting security forces from voting violated constitutional provisions guaranteeing equal political rights for all.[27] The Islamists' accusations that the SCC's decision was politically motivated were heightened by the fact that the court also issued a number of other important rulings: on the one hand, on 2 June 2013, the SCC ruled that the Shura Council had been elected on the basis of an unconstitutional electoral law, thus severely damaging its legitimacy; on the other, it ruled that the constituent assembly that was established in June 2012 was also unconstitutional, but specified that the 2012 constitution would remain in effect, given that it was approved in a popular referendum.

All in all, the endless debates on the Egyptian electoral law resulted in a delay of the second parliamentary elections of the post-Mubarak era. As observed by Nathan Brown, this had far-reaching consequences for the country's entire transition away from authoritarianism. Had parliamentary elections been successfully scheduled for the second quarter of 2013, it could have been expected that a significant amount of the opposition's energies would have gone into campaigning rather than a new sustained round of street protests (Brown 2013a: 50). Thus, the problem was not that elections came too early or too often, but rather that they were ill-timed. Following the removal of Mohammed Morsi, it was clear that the wheel of the whole electoral process – the electoral law and the scheduling of the elections – would have to be spun all over again, this time under the thrust of a completely different set of actors.

The July 2013 constitutional declaration issued by the newly appointed president, Adli Mansour, who came from the SCC, provided no indication as to how the electoral law would have to be drafted or even who would be responsible for overseeing the elections. Article 30 of the declaration stated that the electoral commission would be responsible for overseeing the referendum but no mention was made of the parliamentary or presidential elections. This appeared to be a major point of contention, in light of the amount of complexity and controversy that arose in the process of drafting the electoral law during 2012–2013. Little further guidance on how the electoral law would have to be drafted or whether there would be any mechanism to ensure that it would not be hijacked by one particular political force was provided in the new draft constitution released at the beginning of December 2013. According to the new constitution, the acting president was responsible for approving an electoral law which, according to article 102, had to take 'into account fair representation of population and governorates and equal representation of voters'. Regarding the voting system, the military and their political allies favoured individual seats, thereby discouraging the development of strong political parties and encouraging the election of well-to-do candidates who have connections to the state. Most other political forces, however, opposed the individual candidacy system on the ground that it had largely been responsible for electoral fraud, irregularities, vote-buying, and acts of coercion in previous elections (El-Adawy 2013). For these reasons, during negotiations over the summer 2013, most parties demanded a completely list-based proportional system, seen as the only bulwark against empowering the remnants of the old regime and weakening national party lists. A list-based proportional system with larger districts was regarded as more likely to produce a more diverse, pluralistic, and representative parliament. Nevertheless, in accordance with a strong jurisprudential tradition in Egyptian constitutional law the need arose that independents have the same opportunities to get elected as party members (Tavana 2012).

In conclusion, at the beginning of 2014 the jury was still out with regard to the rules regulating electoral politics in Egypt. Until that moment, the architects of Egypt's transition and those responsible for drafting the constitution had given little thought to the future of the country's electoral law. While seemingly more important issues, such as the role of religion in politics and the balance of power between the president and the parliament, have come to dominate the attention of decision-makers since 2011, the debate over these issues has developed at the expense of discussing inclusive laws regulating elections and the legitimate transfer of political power. As I have demonstrated, electoral laws have a profound impact on state institutions, such as political parties and their mutual relations, as well as on policies. Despite some manoeuvres, there has been little interest in the development of an equitable, consensus-driven electoral law that would empower Egyptian voters to take their decisions and ultimately determine the fate of electoral politics for the foreseeable future.

Tunisia: when legitimacy is not enough

Too much fragmentation?

The Tunisian elections for a National Constituent Assembly (NCA), held on 23 October 2011, were the first clear institutional test in the country's transition from authoritarian rule. The ten months that separated Ben Ali's flight from Tunisia on 14 January 2011, destined for exile in Saudi Arabia, and the elections were of fundamental importance to setting the country on the path of institutional transition and endowing it with a broadly agreed-upon set of rules. The cornerstone of such a roadmap was embodied by the broad consensus around the fact that the balance of power between the president and the parliament had to be renegotiated before new incumbents were elected. In other words, the choice was made to proceed with the drafting of a new constitution before holding new presidential and parliamentary elections. This 'decision to defer the decision', as Stepan (2012: 92) called it, was taken in a conscious manner to increase the incentives for party-building and to lower the prospects of prominent national figures running as non-party candidates in early presidential elections. This in turn was meant to strengthen the powers of the assembly and its room for manoeuvre in shaping the constitutional text, and to shelter it from too strong interference from a directly elected president (Interviewee 43). The following pages will assess the extent to which the Tunisian party system has undergone changes following the onset of the transition and the factors that can explain its transformation. Reference will be made to the electoral process and the results of the first free and fair elections held in the country since independence.

Further reflecting a certain ingrained tendency towards consensus and inclusion (Alexander 2010; Stepan 2012; Murphy 2013),[28] the elections for the NCA were preceded by the creation of the 'Supreme Organisation to Realise the Goals of the Revolution, Political Reform and Democratic Transition' (SORGR) – better known as the Higher Commission for Political Reform – under the supervision of Yadh

Ben Achour. The Commission, made up of 155, later 159, members from political parties, professional associations, and civil society organisations, was tasked with overseeing the overall process of transition, which included the drafting of a new electoral law in preparation for the elections. Stepan (2012: 92) has enthusiastically praised the Higher Commission for Political Reform as 'one of the most effective consensus-building bodies in the history of "crafted" democratic transitions'.[29]

The law that was adopted on 11 April 2011 was meant to regulate the elections of the NCA that would draft the new constitution, possess powers like those of a parliament, and select a government that would be responsible to the assembly. The legal framework for the elections provided that the 217 members of the NCA would be elected by closed-list proportional representation (PR) in 33 districts and the distribution of seats across lists within each district would be determined by an electoral formula widely known as the Hare Quota with Largest Remainders (HQ-LR).[30] After a number of decades of authoritarian rule involving manipulation of the electoral and party systems, the amended Tunisian electoral law was designed to prevent monopolistic control by any one party and to allow for the representation of multiple interests. The Higher Commission for Political Reform took the decision to adopt pure proportional representation, anticipating that this decision would have a crucial anti-majoritarian implication. The end result, which emerged clearly from the October 2011 elections, was that the system tended to produce distortions in favour of the small parties as well as the scarcely populated south and southwest constituencies.[31] As discussed by Carey (2013), the HQ-LR method awarded *Ennahda* 41 percent of the seats in the assembly, including its 4 percent bonus. But the bonuses of much smaller parties and alliances were as large or even larger than *Ennahda*'s in absolute terms, and thus many times larger in relative terms. The result stemming from the choice of the HQ-LR formula for converting votes into seats was that *Ennahda* fell well short of a majority of the seats in the constituent assembly. While inclusion was pivotal to ensuring the legitimacy of the institutions in the transition framework and the decision to provide incentives for proportional representation and negotiation among different political forces was thus largely regarded as a good one, in the medium-to-long term these electoral rules were seen as potentially hampering the development of the new Tunisian party system by jeopardising governability. Another mechanism that was put in place to run the electoral process was an independent electoral commission, the *Instance Supérieure Indépendantepour les Elections* (ISIE), replacing the Ministry of the Interior in overseeing the elections.[32] Initially independent from other administrative bodies and government agencies and enjoying financial autonomy, this electoral oversight body was gradually weakened and put under the control of the government. As a result, it was the government that acted as an intermediary between the ISIE and the administration. The reform of the ISIE, adopted in December 2012 during the boycott of the NCA by the MPs of some secular and leftist parties, created a controversial permanent institution against the backdrop of a number of interim institutions, including the governing ones.

A fundamental feature of the electoral process was the compressed timeframe in which it took place. Initially scheduled for 24 July 2011, it soon became clear that this deadline would have been difficult to meet in light of a number of difficulties in the decision-making process and the implementation thereof.[33] The different political forces that were preparing themselves to run in the elections were also divided about the possibility of postponing the elections, with the Islamists of *Ennahda* objecting to it while the smaller and less organised parties willing to gain time to establish themselves properly. In the end, the elections were postponed to 23 October. As a result of the little time available, the campaign saw a predominance of relatively unsophisticated discourses on television about the role of religion and how to deal with the anticipated victory of *Ennahda*, which in themselves were an indication of the mobilisation capacities and the interests of the main forces (Interviewees 40, 47).

Two principal explanations can be advanced with regard to the extreme fragmentation and absence of coalition-building of the Tunisian party system, particularly in its secular manifestations. The first has to do with the decades of authoritarian and patrimonial politics promoted by the previous regimes that created a fragmented party system and drove a wedge between the secular and Islamist groups, exacerbating their mutual mistrust (Haugbølle and Cavatorta 2011; Hibou 2011). This was a common practice (*'divide et impera'*) of Arab authoritarian regimes prior to the uprisings. A direct illustration of the extreme fragmentation of the party system in Tunisia after the uprisings is that around 1,600 lists were submitted, of which more than 1,500 were accepted. The total number of candidates was 11,200 (Murphy 2013: 239). This was the result of the mushrooming of political parties in the months after Ben Ali's departure, with more than 100 new legal parties established and many more that were denied legal status on various grounds. The second explanation concerns the lack of sound competition among these parties stemming from their scarce political differentiation on non-religious grounds. Following Ben Ali's selective liberalisation, an abundance of secular parties saw the light, but most of them tended to define their role solely in opposition to *Ennahda*. Their inability to build clearly differentiated platforms going beyond the secular vs. Islamist dichotomy and to articulate concrete proposals in terms of social and economic policies during the electoral campaign turned most of them into empty shells with no ability to aggregate interests.

In spite of the limited time available and the relative novelty for many Tunisians of the registration and vote procedures, the elections saw a quite unexpectedly high turnout rate (52 percent of the total population and 86 percent of those who had registered). The elections were widely viewed as fair, transparent, and well-organised (Ottaway 2013). In terms of results (Table 4.2), the elections produced a completely different scenario compared to the past for the Islamist party, *Ennahda*, and for its secular competitors, thus contributing to underlining the main fault-line in the Tunisian party system between 'religious' and 'secular' parties. *Ennahda* won soundly with 89 seats (41 percent) in the NCA, while the plethora of predominantly secular parties fared far worse. The *Congrès pour la République* (CPR) came second with 29 seats (13 percent of the total); the *Pétition Populaire pour la Liberté, la Justice et le Développement*, better known by its Arabic name *Aridha Chaabia* (Popular Petition), garnered 26 seats (12 percent); and the *Forum Démocratique pour le Travail et les Libertés* (FDTL) – or *Ettakatol* in Arabic – won 20 seats (9 percent).

Table 4.2 Distribution of seats in Tunisia's National Constituent Assembly (NCA)

Party/List	Number of seats	Percentage of seats
Ennahda	89	41.01
Congrès pour la République (CPR)	29	13.36
Aridha Chaabia	26	11.98
Ettakatol (FDTL)	20	9.22
Parti Démocrate Progressiste (PDP)	16	7.37
Al-Moubadara	5	2.31
Democratic Modernist Pole (Al-Qutb)	5	2.31
Afek Tounes	4	1.84
Tunisian Workers' Communist Party (Al-Badil al-Thawri)	3	1.38
Other	20	9.22
Total	**217**	**100**

Source: author's elaboration based on National Democratic Institute (NDI). 2011. *Final Report on the Tunisian National Constituent Assembly, October 23, 2011.* www.ndi.org/files/tunisia-final-election-report-021712_v2.pdf.

Polarising elections

Bearing in mind that the electoral law under which the NCA elections were held did not favour big parties, *Ennahda*'s victory appears even more remarkable. This has been explained in many ways (Murphy 2013: 240–241). First, the party was able to capitalise on its established organisational structure and grass-roots base to conduct an effective nationwide door-to-door campaign, hold rallies, and put up posters even in the remotest villages of the country. Second, following the legalisation of the party on 11 March 2011, it emerged as the true bulwark against a return to the past by touting its history of outright resistance to Ben Ali's authoritarianism. Many of its leaders had been jailed and had endured repression for years under the previous regime, something that enhanced their electoral credibility once the transition process began. Although the party was not at the forefront of the struggle against Ben Ali, it was soon recognised as the true and needed antithesis to the past. In terms of electoral campaign, the party offered a clear message of cultural (and moral) renovation and social development to be achieved through a relentless fight against corruption (Interviewees 37, 38). Finally, the campaign rules enacted by the ISIE, aimed at creating a level playing field for all political parties, ultimately tended to privilege those forces that already enjoyed widespread recognition and popular following like *Ennahda*. On the other side, the poor showing of most of the secular parties, including those that had a longer history of political activism, albeit constrained by widespread authoritarian practices, such as the CPR, was the result of this camp's extreme fragmentation and its leaders' inability to compromise with one another to reach a critical mass able to compete with *Ennahda*. Most parties' inexperience with the campaign rules and the very short period of electoral preparation further impacted on their ability to gain a meaningful result in the NCA elections. A string of internal conflicts and resignations plagued the secular parties following the elections. These also affected those forces that had gained a relatively good amount of support in the ballots.[34] According to some scholars this was due to the erosion of consensus after entering into coalition with *Ennahda* (Interviewee 38). This led to numerous reshuffles in the composition of the NCA and to the emergence of new political forces, the most significant of which was *Nidaa Tounes*.[35]

Lacking a majority, *Ennahda* had to form a ruling coalition (often called the 'Troika') with two secular parties, i.e., the CPR and *Ettakatol*, jointly controlling 138 seats out of a total of 217.[36] The ruling coalition was based on a power-sharing deal: the position of prime minister was assigned to Hamadi Jebali, Secretary General of *Ennahda* between June 1981 and February 2013; that of president of the republic to Moncef Marzouki, founder of the CPR and a veteran dissident against the Ben Ali regime; and that of president of the NCA to Mustapha Ben Jaafar, founder and leader of *Ettakatol*. According to many, the ruling coalition was plagued from the very beginning by internal divisions and inefficiencies that impacted on its performance (Interviewee 38). Not only were the alliance's problems seen as the sum of the problems of its constitutive parts, but it was also considered an alliance born of opportunism, and as such deeply unstable. For instance, the weak coordination among the members of the Troika with regard to the distribution of ministerial portfolios stemmed from the fact that the coalition was founded neither on a political pact nor on a common agenda. In addition, while some authors have praised the 'Tunisian model of transition' in light of its inclusiveness embodied by the alliance between moderate Islamists and moderate secularists (Ottaway 2013), others have pointed out that this narrative obscures more than it reveals, as the sharing of power was very unequal, with *Ennahda* pulling all the strings of the interim institutions (Hachemaoui 2013). This was the result of *Ennahda* controlling the formal institutions, on the one hand, as well as empowering the informal ones through the party structures, on the other.

At the level of formal institutions, the power-sharing deal struck in the initial phase of the transition period gave the president limited powers, while extending those of the prime minister. According to the interim ruling bargain, the president sets Tunisia's foreign policy in consultation with the prime minister; he is also commander-in-chief of the armed forces but can only appoint or fire senior officers in consultation with the prime minister. The so-called 'mini-constitution' – the Law on the Provisional Organization of the Public Powers, adopted on 16 December 2011 more than one month after the three coalition parties had reached an agreement on the distribution of powers among them – was instrumental in increasing *Ennahda*'s prerogatives in controlling the formal institutions (Interviewee 42). Turning to the pre-eminence of informal institutions, a sort of system parallel to the formal set of institutions, two examples can be mentioned. First, *Ennahda* has been accused of wanting to control, circumvent, and/or manipulate all the institutions of the state by exploiting its power structures and the resources available to it.[37] In this regard, it was less the prime minister than the party's president who governed, and it was less the NCA than the consultative council of *Ennahda* that deliberated, wielding extra-institutional veto power. Throughout his tenure, Prime Minister Jebali was constantly weakened from within his own party in accordance with plans to create the position of 'general coordinator of the government', which was supposed to be occupied by Ben Salem, Minister of Agriculture and one of the main hardliners of the party.

Second, in light of the extremely precarious security situation, spontaneous groups started to spring up immediately after the overthrow of Ben Ali with the goal of protecting neighbourhoods across Tunisia from vandalism and looting. In the weeks and months that followed, these groups of men and women formalised into local councils 'for the protection of the goals of the revolution'. The Leagues for the Protection of the Revolution, as they came to be called, have been strongly associated with *Ennahda*, particularly in the mainstream Tunisian media coverage often echoed by international media. Reports have variously referred to the Leagues as 'vigilantes', 'Islamists', 'militants', and, worst, as 'Islamist thugs'. Even though many assumed that the Leagues were composed of *Ennahda* lackeys, they actually had among their members people who had no party affiliation. Quite to the contrary, in fact, before the October 2011 elections, members from secular left-wing parties were a strong presence in the Leagues. Nevertheless, the NCA elections represented a watershed. After the victory of the Islamists of *Ennahda*, what was later to become the coalition of left-wing forces (Popular Front)[38] was quick to style the Leagues as *Ennahda*'s violent arm. This example attests to the extent to which *Ennahda* had gradually become a powerful force in what was born as a spontaneous set of organisations meant to protect the population from the security vacuum and to further the goals of the revolution in terms of fighting corruption and preventing elements from the former regime to come back.

Despite *Ennahda*'s monolithic appearance, internal coherence, and tight organisation, which largely contributed to its success in the first elections of the post-Ben Ali era, it was not immune from internal divisions. There have been tensions between pragmatism and principles, as the post-electoral circumstances demonstrated. The major split within *Ennahda* came as a direct consequence of the institutional crisis precipitated by the assassination of Chokri Belaid on 6 February 2013. In the convulsive weeks following this act of violence, which became the catalyst for much discontent with the slow progress of the constitution-making process and with what many perceived as *Ennahda*'s domination of Tunisian politics, the then prime minister, Jebali, called for the creation of a non-partisan government as the only means of easing political tensions and meeting the institutional conditions for actually holding the elections and for the success of the transition. As early as 28 January 2013, the prime minister's office had presented a document to the members of the NCA outlining a roadmap to prevent the country from plunging into a full-fledged institutional crisis and to restore the legitimacy of the NCA. The document, entitled 'Memorandum for a New Political Pact', insisted on the need to craft a new consensus around the architecture of the transition focusing, among others, on the following points: the guarantee of the civil character of the state, a non-partisan cabinet, the preservation of the state's monopoly on the legitimate use of force, and the prohibition of militias (Interviewee 42). The document and the political proposal it outlined were, however, rejected by the party leadership and in particular by its president, Rashid Ghannouchi, who claimed in an interview with *Ennahda*'s newspaper, *Al Fajr*, that:

> the ministerial reshuffle is neither a historical event nor a constituent operation [. . .]. In the absence of a final agreement on the reshuffle, the work will proceed with the current government and there is no need to solicit a vote of confidence from the National Constituent Assembly. The continuation of this government until the holding of elections will in no way create a crisis.[39]

Internal divisions between the two camps within *Ennahda* – the former coalescing around the then prime minister (and externally supported by the other forces of the ruling coalition) and the latter siding with Ghannouchi – went on for some weeks and turned into a zero-sum game that poisoned the political atmosphere in the first months of 2013 (Ottaway 2013: 4). Belaid's assassination further embittered the relations between the two camps, drawing the prime minister increasingly close to the positions of the other parties in the ruling coalition as well as those of other influential figures within Tunisia's institutions, such as General Rashid Ammar,[40] Chairman of the Joint Chiefs of Staff, the most powerful trade unions, the UGTT, and the influential employers' organisation, UTICA. In the end, however, the informal institutions mentioned above were once again responsible for tipping the balance of power in favour of *Ennahda*'s leadership. It was less the NCA than the party's Shura Council – the consultative body of the party – that had the power of deliberation and effectively pre-empted Jebali to ask for a vote of confidence on the project of a non-partisan government. Jebali reigned on 19 February 2013, following *Ennahda*'s refusal to commit to a new roadmap that would have stopped the deepening political polarisation in Tunisia. Instead, this refusal had the opposite effect of protracting the institutional stalemate and making the crisis more acute. The Larayedh government was formed on 11 March 2013. The divisions and contrasts within *Ennahda*, coupled with the substantial role played by the informal party institutions, had a constraining effect on the new government's ability to deliver, which in turn contributed to blocking the process of institutional change in the country. One telling example of this tense situation inside the party was the message that was notified to the new prime minister by the de facto general coordinator of the government stating that the party leadership would have pre-eminence over any plans or decisions taken by the government.

To counter the fragmentation of the secular party front and with the declared goal of having a greater chance to fare well in future elections, some coalition-building initiatives were undertaken (Interviewee 39). Beyond the creation of the Popular Front in October 2012 – comprising 12 left-wing parties; the Social Democratic Path, or *Al-Massar*, created in April 2012; the Republican Party (PR), also known as *Al-Jumhuri* (both of which would then join in the Union for Tunisia alliance created in February 2013); and the National Salvation Front, launched at the end of July 2013 – the most significant example of coalition-building in the period 2011–2013 was the creation of *Nidaa Tounes* by Beji Caid Essebsi, former prime minister between March 2011 and the NCA elections. The creation of this party, whose name derives from the call (*nidaa* in Arabic) on the members of the centrist, secular opposition to form a front to effectively counter *Ennahda*, represented the most important development in the Tunisian party system in the initial transition phase. Created from scratch in June 2012, the party, which could better be described as an 'alliance of different groups' (Ottaway 2013), quickly became a pole of attraction for a wide and diverse number of forces, ranging from former members of Habib Bourghiba's Republican Party (*Dustur*) and Ben Ali's *Rassemblement Constitutionnel Démocratique* (RCD) to a number of representatives of the UGTT and UTICA, out of the recognition that too many similar parties were vying for essentially the same constituency and that cooperation was the only strategy to create a viable alternative to *Ennahda*. In the initial phase, 11 members of the NCA joined the party by defecting from other forces, particularly the CPR and *Ettakatol*. Following the appearance on the Tunisian party scene of *Nidaa Tounes* and due to the internal conflicts and splits to which some secular parties have fallen prey, the party landscape and the nature of political alliances as represented within the NCA have changed dramatically since the October 2011 elections. For example, *Ettakatol* membership has dwindled from 20 to around six, while the CPR has undergone a split between the supporters of its president, and interim president of the Tunisian Republic, Moncef Marzouki, and those of its secretary general.

At the theoretical level, the literature insists that it is good for systems to disperse representation and foster inclusiveness at constitutional moments (Carey 2009). Although one round of elections is not sufficient to make a thorough assessment of the strengths and weaknesses of Tunisia's party system, it appears that its fragmentation is alarming even when compared to other party systems in transition countries characterised by high levels of fragmentation (Stepan 2012). Learning from these experiences, electoral law reform has gradually emerged in Tunisia as the number one priority to counter the highly fractured arrangement of party politics and coalition alliances, despite the fact that 'the constitution-making process has dominated politics since the January 2011 revolution' (Pickard 2013). In concrete terms, discussions have focused on the possibility of introducing a minimum threshold that would require each party to win at least a certain percentage of the votes nationwide to be eligible for a seat in the assembly. Some members of *Ennahda* have called for a threshold at the national level of 3 percent (Interviewees 37, 38). Most of the discussions regarding the new electoral law were framed within the context of the roadmap that unlocked the process of National Dialogue following the suspension of the meetings and deliberations of the NCA.[41] Linked to that, the timing and sequencing of the following elections was also an element of contention during the National Dialogue sessions in the attempt to reach a broad-based agreement regarding various issues pertaining to the institutional transition. Given the semi-presidential form of government of the Tunisian system, both parliamentary and presidential elections were to be scheduled to replace the existing transitional authorities. When they do, it was anticipated to make a lot of difference if both elections were held on the same day or close to each other, or if, on the other hand, the two dates were months apart (Pickard 2013). In the former case, the chance of one party winning both the parliamentary and the presidential elections increases. In the latter case, conversely, it is more likely that two different parties will gain control of the legislative and the highest executive powers. The prospect of a divided minority government in Tunisia during the transition phase and then the consolidation phase was a troubling one. As aptly demonstrated by Skach (2005), a divided minority government is the most susceptible to institutional conflict because, without a legislative majority, governments are unstable, and the president, faced with legislative immobility, has the maximum incentive to intervene by invoking his emergency powers.

Against this backdrop, the most powerful forces within the NCA have tried to shun any accusations related to the introduction of electoral rules that were meant to favour them in the next elections. Bearing in mind that the proportional system was introduced with a view to allowing for the inclusive participation of all political forces, the risk of not reaching clear and solid majorities in the next Tunisian assembly was anticipated. However, it was assumed that in the future the fragmentation of the party system would in all likelihood undergo a natural downward trend mainly as a result of two main, connected factors. First, the huge number of parties that contested the October 2011 elections, most of which fared badly, particularly within the secular camp, have undergone a process of rationalisation as a result of the electoral outcome. Second, if continued, the ability of some coalitions that emerged following the elections to create shared platforms would contribute to the development of these political parties individually and of the system as a whole. In conclusion, two contrasting dynamics have shaped the Tunisian party system in the initial phase of the country's transition from authoritarianism: on the one hand, the pull towards coalition-building to escape irrelevance, and, on the other, the electoral system's favourable treatment of smaller parties.

Notes

1. On electoral authoritarianism and its variants, see also Brumberg (2002); Levitsky and Way (2002); Pripstein Posusney (2002); Blaydes (2011) and Brownlee (2012).
2. The literature available on these issues is very rich. See Brooker (2000) and Morlino (2003) for two comprehensive points of view.
3. On framing in social movements theory, see McAdam, McCarthy and Zald (1996).
4. Under the parallel voting system used, two-thirds of the 498 total seats, meaning 332, were elected by means of party list proportional representation in 46 districts. The result was determined by the largest remainder method with a 0.5 percent threshold. The remaining 166 seats were distributed by bloc by means of the first-past-the-post voting method in 83 two-seat districts, with the possibility of a run off. These seats were open to candidates running as individuals, not affiliated to political parties. The first-past-the-post voting method is also known as 'winner-takes-all' or 'simple plurality'. First-past-the-post voting methods can be used for single and multiple member elections. In a single member election, the candidate with the highest number, not necessarily a majority, of votes is elected. In a multiple member first-past-the-post ballot

election, the candidates with the most votes, corresponding to the number of positions to be filled, are elected. See Eskander (2011).
5 Of the total 270 seats, 180 seats were assigned using the same two voting procedures as in the Lower House. The remaining 90 seats were to be appointed after the presidential elections.
6 Nathan Brown described the relation between the Muslim Brotherhood (MB) and the Freedom and Justice Party (FJP) in the following terms: as the MB acting as the 'helicopter parent' hovering close to its infant, the FJP, protecting it, and dictating its direction. A clear indicator of this tightly knit and dependent relation was the fact that the entire FJP leadership, including the future president Mohammed Morsi, came from the movement. See Brown (2011b).
7 The literature on the Muslim Brotherhood is abundant and multi-faceted. Some examples include various appraisals of the movement's trajectory in historical perspective (Harris 1964; Osman 2010) and geographical extension (Tadros 2008; Rubin 2010), as well as an articulation of the Muslim Brotherhood's relation with the manifold faces of the regime in the case of Egypt (Fahmy Menza 2013).
8 A number of authors attribute the civic forces' poor performance in the elections also to their continuous presence in and focus on the protests that took place throughout the autumn and winter 2011–2012, aimed at overthrowing the SCAF and ending the *de facto* military rule. On the contrary, the Muslim Brotherhood chose not to participate in the demonstrations against the SCAF. See Farag (2012: 225).
9 Conflicts with the Salafists emerged and escalated throughout 2012 over the formation of the government, a traditionally bureaucratic one, which in the end did not include any representative from *Al-Nour*. The Muslim Brotherhood-dominated government that was in power between 2012 and 2013 was led by Hisham Qandil, an independent, and partially consisted of figures from the previous Mubarak government.
10 On 14 April 2012, Khairat Al-Shater was disqualified from running by the Supreme Presidential Electoral Commission (SPEC), a body of judges appointed by the SCAF. The verdict was based on Al-Shater's having been accused of money laundering in 2006 and his belonging to a 'banned group'. See "Electoral commission upholds ban on 10 presidential candidates". *Ahramonline*. 17 April 2012. http://english.ahram.org.eg/NewsContent/36/122/39510/Presidential-elections-/Presidential-elections-news/Electoral-commission-upholds-ban-on–presidential-.aspx. In response to the SPEC's decision, the party's choice fell on Mohammed Morsi.
11 As a result of this move, Aboul Fotouh was expelled from the FJP in mid-June and he created his own party, the Strong Egypt Party, in July 2012.
12 One of the interviewees for this research emphasised that the Muslim Brotherhood had been trained to work as a non-governmental organisation (NGO) and to criticise the previous regime on the basis of *Sharia*, thus underscoring their lack of both expertise and specific competencies for decision-making (Interviewee 1).
13 Other authors ascribe the Muslim Brotherhood's reversal to the mistakes that were committed by the SCAF and its wanting to control the parliament (Abdul-Majid 2013: 19). However, these views tend to disregard the fact that the peak of the confrontation between the SCAF and the Islamists had not yet taken place in spring 2012.
14 Among the other signs of the organisation's internal fragility was the rift that occurred between the older and younger generations of the Muslim Brotherhood during the movement's Youth Conference in March 2011. Hundreds of young members of the Muslim Brotherhood demanded better representation in the movement's power structure and a more independent relationship between the nascent Freedom and Justice Party (FJP) and the Muslim Brotherhood. When none of these demands were acknowledged, a group of members, particularly young ones, broke away and formed their own political party, the Egyptian Current Party, in June 2011 (Interviewee 7).
15 "Morsi declared Egypt's first civilian president, but military remains in control". *Ahramonline*. 24 June 2012. http://english.ahram.org.eg/NewsContent/36/122/46061/

Presidential-elections-/Presidential-elections-news/Morsi-declared-Egypts-first-civilian-president,-bu.aspx.

16 A detailed account of the main political parties in the liberal and 'secular' camp created in the aftermath of the Egyptian uprising can be found in Abdalla (2013). The author also underscores the main challenges and obstacles confronting these political groups, including the lack of sustainable funding, generational rifts, structural weaknesses, internal struggles and currents, and lack of participation in formal politics.

17 Some constitutional experts have read this provision, despite its unclear wording, as stating that the electoral law should have been completed within two months of the constitution's entry into force, which is to say by February 2013. See al-Ali (2013a).

18 For a thorough account of Egypt's electoral laws until 2012, see Faris (2012). On the Shura Council, elected in early 2012 pursuant to the March 2011 constitutional declaration, see al-Ali (2013a). The Shura Council was elected by only around 8 percent of eligible voters mainly because it was granted only an advisory role. The results were heavily skewed in favour of Islamist parties. Finally, it is worth noting that the draft electoral laws that the Shura Council produced were merely amendments that left the general framework intact. The way in which these (indeed quite significant) changes were drawn up did not involve any negotiation among the country's main political forces, but rather reflected the view of a single group of forces aligned on one side of the political divide, i.e., the Islamists.

19 Ayman El-Dessouki. "Egypt's new elections law: too controversial and too biased". *Al Arabiya News*. 23 January 2013. http://english.alarabiya.net/views/2013/01/23/262003.html.

20 The National Salvation Front (NSF) was a political alliance of more than 35 Egyptian parties or party groups, formed in opposition to President Morsi's 22 November 2012 constitutional declaration. The NSF was one of the main forces that backed the military coup against Morsi on 3 July 2013. It subsequently split along different views on many issues, including the role of the military in the post-Morsi political system. Some observers have argued that the tenuous institutional connection between the NSF and its electoral base has prevented it from developing into a coherent political alternative, while at the same time this alliance has contributed to stopping the creation of new parties and political organisations. The result of this development has been two-fold: on the one hand, it has crystallised the old party system and the supremacy of traditional forces within it. On the other hand, it has failed to include some of the more militant 'revolutionary' forces that have eventually decided to go back to the streets (Interviewee 16). See also "Disputes in National Salvation Front emerge ahead of elections". *Ahramonline*. 18 July 2013. http://english.ahram.org.eg/NewsContent/1/64/76774/Egypt/Politics-/Disputes-in-National-Salvation-Front-emerge-ahead-.aspx.

21 On 26 February 2013, the NSF announced that it would boycott the elections and called for the dismissal of Prime Minister Qandil's government, the appointment of a national unity cabinet, and the creation of a committee to review the constitution. See "ElBaradei calls for boycott of parliamentary elections". *Ahramonline*. 23 February 2013. http://english.ahram.org.eg/NewsContent/1/64/65398/Egypt/Politics-/ElBaradei-calls-for-boycott-of-parliamentary-elect.aspx.

22 Article 177 contrasted with the already-mentioned article 229 that required that the procedures for the elections of the Lower House of parliament should begin within 60 days of the new constitution coming into effect.

23 Article 177 introduced what is often referred to as 'prior review' as opposed to 'subsequent review', whereby electoral laws are reviewed after they are approved by the executive. The nature and dynamics of prior review are entirely different from those of subsequent review. On the one hand, subsequent review can only take place after an appeal is made to the SCC. This means that even if a law is blatantly unconstitutional, the SCC cannot on its own initiative start a claim and invalidate the law. On the other hand, prior review is automatic, i.e., the court will in all cases be called upon to review the relevant law. See al-Ali (2013a).

24 For details on the specific provisions that were contested by the SCC, see Democracy Reporting International (2013) and "Draft electoral laws contradict Egypt's national charter: Constitutional Court". *Ahramonline.* 18 February 2013. http://english.ahram.org.eg/News/65090.aspx.
25 Views differed about whether the vagueness of the provision on the constitutionality of the electoral law was due to the need to prevent a lengthy procedure, also drawing from the precedent set by the presidential electoral law in 2012 drafted by the interim military rule without sending the amended version back to the court for a second review, or whether it was purposely done to entrust the Islamist-dominated Shura Council with the power to ignore one or several aspects of the SCC's decision without the possibility of judicial review. See al-Ali and Brown (2013).
26 Some of the criticisms voiced at the Shura Council in the following months were aimed at questioning its taking over the role of legislator in matters other than the electoral law, such a new NGO law, a protest law, and a judicial reform law. Egyptians who were opposed to the FJP's agenda argued that the council lacked the legitimacy to legislate on these issues, due to the fact that – among other things – only 8 percent of the population had participated in its elections. See "Inside Egypt's Shura Council, new NGO law brings controversy". *Ahramonline.* 26 March 2013. http://english.ahram.org.eg/NewsContent/1/64/67716/Egypt/Politics-/Inside-Egypts-Shura-Council,-new-NGO-law-brings-co.aspx and "New NGO draft law strikes fear in Egyptian civil society". *Ahramonline.* 24 May 2013. http://english.ahram.org.eg/NewsContent/1/64/71987/Egypt/Politics-/New-NGO-draft-law-strikes-fear-in-Egyptian-civil-s.aspx.
27 On this issue, arguably the most controversial aspect of the court's decision, the concern of the electoral law drafters was that, by allowing security forces to participate in the elections, they would most likely vote against the FJP's candidates in any upcoming election. Given their numbers (approximately 2 million), it was argued, they could easily sway the elections in favour of a particular outcome if they were indeed to vote as a single bloc. See al-Ali (2013a).
28 Many authors stress that some features of Tunisian society were responsible for a general climate that favoured moderation and consensus. Among the factors quoted are the relative homogeneity of the Tunisian population in terms of religious and ethnic affiliations – 98 percent are Muslim Arabs, most of whom belong to the Maliki school. The country also hosts well-integrated Berber (1 percent of the total population), Jewish, and European communities. Another factor that is often acknowledged as having had an impact on the country's modern and contemporary history, up to the 2011 revolution, is the population's relatively high level of education. Taking the Human Development Index (HDI), which captures three basic dimensions of human development, i.e., health, education, and income, between 1980 and 2012, one can see that Tunisia's HDI rose by 1.9 percent annually from 0.459 to 0.712, ranking the country 94th out of 187 countries. The HDI of the Arab states increased on average from 0.443 in 1980 to 0.652 in 2012, placing Tunisia above the regional average (Murphy 2013: 242; Zlitni 2012).
29 I will go back to the concept of 'crafted' transitions in the fifth chapter of this book. From Stepan's words, it is clear that Tunisia stands in stark contrast to the situation in Egypt described earlier.
30 Under this system, seats are effectively distributed in two steps. The first step is to set the quota or threshold of votes that each party must attain to win a seat. The vote for each party is then divided by the electoral quota. Subsequently, a seat is awarded to each party for each bloc of votes equal to the quota. In a second step, any remaining seats to be allocated are awarded on the basis of which party or parties have the highest number of votes remaining after the quotas have been used up. See Carey (2013). The PR system with the method of the largest remainder has usually been adopted in countries where inclusiveness in the parliament is considered a priority (Norris 1997).
31 These constituencies were traditionally neglected and marginalised by Ben Ali and his predecessor, Habib Bourghiba, who cultivated their power-bases in the urban coastal areas (Murphy 2013: 235).

116 *It all comes down to electoral politics*

32 For more information on the ISIE, its mission, and its composition, see www.isie.tn/Fr/accueil_46_3. A great number of international electoral observers, endowed with extensive monitoring prerogatives, were invited to monitor the first democratic Tunisian elections as well. See National Democratic Institute (2011a).
33 With regard to the slowness of decision-making, the extent to which the ISIE was responsible for the operational management of the elections is not clear. On the implementation side, some rules governing the electoral process were communicated to the candidates only a few days before the beginning of the campaigning period (Interviewee 48).
34 For more details on the internal competition and divisions in the CPR and *Ettakatol*, see Brody-Barre (2013: 218).
35 Details about this party will be discussed shortly.
36 *Ennahda* and the CPR had already worked together in the *18 October Collectif*, which also included the *Parti Démocrate Progressiste* (PDP). The partnership was remarkable both for its inclusivity – it was the first attempt at creating a coalition between secular forces and the Islamists – and its duration (from 2005 to the 2011 revolution). See Brody-Barre (2013).
37 President Marzouki was vocal in criticising what he described as '*Ennahda*'s policy of infiltrating the state machinery' on at least two occasions, in August and December 2012. See "Le président tunisien tire à boulets rouges sur ses alliés islamistes". *Le Monde*, 24 August 2012. www.lemonde.fr/tunisie/article/2012/08/24/le-president-tunisien-tire-a-boulets-rouges-sur-ses-allies-islamistes_1751279_1466522.html. See also Hachemaoui (2013: 11).
38 More information about the Popular Front will be provided shortly.
39 Quoted in Hachemaoui (2013: 16).
40 General Ammar resigned from the position of Chairman of the Joint Chiefs of Staff on 24 June 2013 maintaining that 'the assassination of Belaid mark[ed] the death of the Troika government', thus further stressing his support of Jebali's initiative for a non-partisan government. Video interview quoted in Hachemaoui (2013: 21).
41 See Chapter 3 for further details on the National Dialogue.

5 The deep state fights back

> I want to begin at the point where theories of failed revolution and failed democratic transition diverge: the institutions of the old order. Theorists of failed revolution tell us that too many of Egypt's old institutions and old elites survived the 2011 upheaval: the Armed Forces, the judiciary, the bureaucracy, and the old elites. Theorists of failed transition might seem to believe that not enough of the old institutions survived.
>
> from Ellis Goldberg. "Whatever Happened to Egypt's Democratic Transition?" *Jadaliyya*, 3 March 2013

From the standpoint of (democratic) transition theory, no transition from authoritarianism can be said to be accomplished unless full transparency and accountability are established over two important institutions, i.e., the military and the judiciary. Too close an association between these two institutions and the executive power, namely when the military plays an overtly political role or the judiciary is kept on a short leash by the executive power, is seen as a legacy of old authoritarian systems. The mechanisms for separating the military, the judiciary, and the executive are often dictated by the new constitutional provisions and are generally strongly debated by the political actors. Nevertheless, much of the military's and judiciary's autonomy and power *vis-à-vis* other institutions often springs from sources that lie outside the formal institutional framework.

During the transition, the critical thing to study is not so much the military itself, but the nature of civilian-military relations (Barany 2011; Cimbala 2012). While re-establishing civilian rule over the military is a precondition of democratic governance, transitions will likely prove too fragile unless the withdrawal of the armed forces from the process of decision-making is negotiated as well. Instating civilian control over the military essentially means three things: the military should be an apolitical servant of the government; defence policy should be under the control and direction of civilian authorities; and decisions regarding the use and deployment of the armed forces should also reside with the civilian leadership (Forster, Edmunds, and Cottey 2001). At the same time, the military are bound to remain an important actor during the transition process. There is much resistance to certain reforms within the military. Moreover, due to the low level of turnover in Arab army elites, leadership is often of a rigid and sometimes old-fashioned, conservative mindset. The army still believes it has a duty as guardian of the country, and the dilemma of civilian-military interdependence is likely to delay security sector reforms across the region. No understanding of the Egyptian transition would be possible, for example, without an appreciation of the role of the military both during the uprising and immediately afterward, seeping into the deepest remits of the struggle for power between the military and the (Muslim Brotherhood-dominated) civilian elites. The Tunisian case tells a similar story, even though it differs significantly from the Egyptian case in terms of the legacy of civilian-military relations and their impact on the transition.

Turning to the judiciary, this institution has occupied centre stage in the debate about institutional reforms in Arab transitions. In Egypt and Tunisia, both political and civil society groups have demanded constitutional changes aimed not only at increasing democratic control over government institutions, but also at securing the independence of justice sector institutions and the fair application of the rule of law. These were among the main grievances heard in Tahrir Square and elsewhere during the Arab uprisings. At the same time, demands for judicial reform in these countries have in most cases not simply been an outgrowth of the Arab uprisings. Quite the contrary, they were the object of furious debates and conflicts between state powers well ahead of the 2011 uprisings and the ensuing transitions. For example, Tunisian civil society and home-grown human rights organisations have established a strong record in the last few years in pushing for judicial reforms designed to increase the competence of judges, foster their independence from executive or legislative pressure, raise administrative and training standards, and improve the judiciary's efficiency (Interviewee 44).

When analysing the role of the judiciary in the Arab world, it is important to remember two basic facts. First of all, judicial bodies and judicial administration reflect the confluence of Islamic and civil law traditions (and some common law influence as well), set in the framework of largely authoritarian regimes. Second, in some limited but important respects the judiciary has effectively developed into a counter-majoritarian institution, able to control the executive and assert claims of constitutional interpretive power. This is clearly demonstrated by the fact that for a number of years before 2011, of the three branches of government, the courts were the one to which ordinary Egyptians resorted most frequently and with most success. The courts may be arbitrary, corrupt, and unresponsive, but they have proven to be more useful than the other branches. Attempts to change this situation by promoting greater accountability of the elected institutions as well as to review some of the prerogatives of the judiciary have resulted in an intra-institutional turf war. This chapter is devoted to exploring the dynamics of change and continuity within two of the most conservative and change-resilient institutions – the military and the judiciary – and the extent to which they have adapted to the imperatives of the transition. What emerges from the analysis carried out below in the cases of Egypt and Tunisia is that different patterns of conflict and adjustment have taken place in the two cases, mainly as a result of past legacies. In Egypt, one of the peculiarities of the period between 2011 and the beginning of 2014 is that the authority and legitimacy of the executive and the legislative branches of government diminished, while the authority of the judicial branch and the military (especially in the months after it relinquished power to President Morsi in July–August 2012) increased. The military became more autonomous, constitutionally and even practically, from the executive branch than at any other time in recent history and the judiciary intervened in politics with remarkable independence over the three years in question. This is not the case as far as Tunisia is concerned due to the different legacy of civilian-military relations, as well as to the choices made by some actors, e.g., *Ennahda* and the higher military apparatus in the case of Tunisia.

Egypt: boycotting change in the name of the 'revolution'

Institutional interests

A great deal of the literature on Egypt underscores the trajectory of the coercive apparatus as one of the most significant elements shaping the development of the Egyptian state, both politically and economically (Picard 1990; Albrecht and Bishara 2011; Kandil 2012). In light of its size and pervasiveness, the term 'coercive apparatus' needs to be unpacked first. Like other authoritarian regimes, Egypt's has relied on a panoply of different institutions to serve its security needs. These include the multiple branches of the military – the army, the navy, and the air force – the security/intelligence agencies, the police, and often a praetorian guard as well. The role of the military has been particularly pivotal in carrying out three primary missions. The first concerns the defence of the country from external aggressions. The second is to maintain security and order domestically. The third mission, which is overlooked in many analyses of the role of the military, has to do with the promotion of the military's institutional interests, including the protection of its internal cohesion, prestige, and legitimacy as a collective organisation, as well as the furthering of its economic interests, both institutionally and individually (Brooks 1999; Sayigh *et al.* 2011; Bellin 2012). Like any large complex organisation, the military has some institutional interests and prerogatives that its members seek to advance. These depend largely on the degree of institutionalisation of the military: the more institutionalised the military is, the more it has a sense of corporate identity. By contrast, a low degree of institutionalisation means that the military is organised along patrimonial lines, career advancement is governed by cronyism and political loyalty, and the distinction between the public and the private spheres and interests is blurred. Differentiating between high and low levels of institutionalisation is important in two respects. On the one hand, it determines the degree to which the military is tied to the regime's survival when popular pressure threatens the stability of the ruling apparatus, as in the case of the Arab uprisings (Bellin 2012: 132–133). On the other hand, the level of institutionalisation of the military is likely to have a deep impact on the transition from authoritarianism and the crafting of the new polity. Both factors are meaningful in the case of Egypt, given the existence of the so-called 'officers' republic', the self-perpetuating military network that permeates virtually all branches and levels of the state administration and of the state-owned sectors of the economy (Sayigh 2012).

Emerging following the overthrow of the monarchy by the Egyptian armed forces in 1952, the officers' republic grew steadily in the following decades thanks to its co-optation into the system of patronage revolving around the president. After some ebb and flow under Nasser and Sadat, it was during the Mubarak regime that an increasingly large number of senior officers was incorporated into the crony system created by the president and his clique, abstention from political engagement being repaid by the promise of benefits and bonuses upon retirement. This bargain contributed to the creation of an inflated caste of senior officers who could count on a sort of 'loyalty allowance' at the end of their career, usually consisting of the opportunity to continue it in the public sector and receive a second salary in addition to their military pensions and the associated bonuses and allowances (Sayigh 2012: 4). But, of the overall figure of 468,500 soldiers in active duty (in addition to 479,000 in the reserves and 397,000 in paramilitary forces) in 2010, only a minority within the upper ranks was able to reap the biggest rewards stemming from the military's incorporation into Mubarak's system.[1] Then, the major readjustment and privatisation measures launched by the Mubarak regime during the 1990s under pressure from the international financial institutions generated new opportunities for acquiring wealth and accumulating assets and gave access to significant parts of the Egyptian economy that remained state-owned (Cook 2007: 19–21) – opportunities that were granted in return for the loyalty, quiescence, and de-politicisation of a potentially challenging rival to the president's far-reaching powers.

The economic assets directly or indirectly – as in the case of the land that belongs to the military – controlled by the officers' republic are complex and vast. A detailed reconstruction of all the sources of income to date has not been possible due to the fact that data are difficult to collect and, more importantly, are not under the oversight of parliament or any other civilian body. An attempt at mapping the military enterprises can be found in Sayigh (2012), as well as in a number of articles published by the Egyptian scholar Zeinab Abul-Magd (2011 and 2012). As pointedly argued in one of her articles,

> Retired generals manage the vast enterprises owned by the military institution and produce goods and services for consumers rather than for military production. This includes chains of factories, service companies, farms, roads, gas stations, supermarkets, and much more. There are three major military bodies engaged in civilian production: the Ministry of Military Production, running eight factories; the Arab Organization for Industrialization, running 12 factories; and the National Service Products Organization, running 15 factories, companies, and farms. They produce a wide variety of goods, including luxury jeeps, infant incubators, butane gas cylinders, plastic tubes, canned food, meat, chicken, and more. They also provide services, like domestic cleaning and gas station management.
>
> (Abul-Magd 2012)

This already astonishingly long list of economic activities undertaken and directly controlled by the military would not be complete without mention of the fact that the military has in the last years become engaged in partnerships and joint ventures with local and foreign private sectors firms, thus fully behaving like a commercial actor (Marshall and Stacher 2012). Thanks to these policies, the economic enterprises owned and managed by the military amount to an estimated figure ranging between 25 and over 47 percent of the value of Egypt's economy.[2] Although a clear picture of the assets controlled by the military is difficult to obtain, most informed observers and analysts tend to agree that the economic empire directly controlled by the military makes them the most powerful institution in Egypt (Interviewee 1). To this must be added the exclusive control over the defence budget and the USD 1.3 billion in military aid annually earmarked and transferred by the United States to the Egyptian armed forces.

The embedding of former senior officers in the state apparatus and the involvement of military businesses in delivering public goods and consumer commodities has traditionally been justified by the higher military hierarchy with the pretext of having to defend national security interests. A more utilitarian type of explanation would be that the senior officers can 'get things done' as they are familiar with the bureaucratic and administrative system they themselves have created and penetrated with their networks. Furthermore, the military's rationale for its economic activity has stressed that it relieves the state of the burden of having to care for the military's needs, and in addition provides a lot of jobs and development opportunities for the country. Yet, it appears that many of the inputs critical to the military's economic activities are subsidised, which ultimately puts a strain on public resources while benefiting the powerful military apparatus (Cook 2007).

The military's penetration of civilian affairs under Mubarak caused the senior officer corps to become intertwined with the state apparatus, including public administration, infrastructure services, and local governments,[3] and with the country's political economy. Not only did this turn the military into a tool of regime maintenance, but made it one of the key players in the 'conflicting poliarchy' of various institutional and political actors (Sayigh 2012: 7). The substantial economic interests accumulated by the military, particularly the senior officers individually and as an institution, represent the most enduring legacy of its incorporation under Mubarak. These interests explain the behaviour of the military in the chain of events that triggered the Egyptian uprising and later shaped the transition. At the beginning of 2011, following the rise of Mubarak's son, Gamal, and his close ministerial and business associates, the military hierarchy was afraid that the neo-liberal policies promoted by this new Egyptian entrepreneurial class could endanger its crony-capitalist interests and privileges. As already discussed in Chapter 2, this was an important factor in the military's decision not to protect the Mubarak regime and instead to accelerate the pace of its demise under pressure from a significant number of largely peaceful protesters.[4] Following a similar script, the military intervened to bring down the first Islamist president in Egyptian history in early July 2013 by riding the discontent of allegedly millions of Egyptians who had signed the *Tamarrod* petition. Once again, the attempt to protect its extensive economic interests from the rapacious capitalist practices of the Muslim Brotherhood leadership was the main motive behind the military's move (Interviewee 23).

Despite their substantial grievances *vis-à-vis* the system of economic power created around Gamal Mubarak, the Egyptian military did not initiate the uprising and, during it, was more concerned with protecting the exceptional status and interests of the officers' republic, i.e., political prerogatives, material rewards, and social standing. By reinforcing and projecting its image as the guardian of Egypt's national interests, in this historical juncture done in the name of the 'revolution', the military exerted significant pressure during the transitional period, interfering with the constitution-making process and determining its sequence and overall timetable.[5] Following Mubarak's ouster, the military's pervasive powers, the 'state within the state' (Hellyer 2012), became more visible in the role played by the Supreme Council of the Armed Forces (SCAF), the commanding body of the Egyptian armed forces, which assumed full executive and legislative powers on 11 February 2011. Normally comprising 21 persons, including the chiefs of staff of the various military branches, the heads of military intelligence, and other armed forces services such as the Administrative Monitoring Authority (Sayigh 2012: 12–13), under the leadership of Field Marshall Tantawi, Minister of Defence since 1991, the SCAF took centre stage in Egypt's politics and sought to defend the privileged position of the military. To achieve this goal, during the 16 months in which it held power firmly in its hands, the SCAF failed to endorse, let alone initiate, any policy envisaging substantive reform or institutional change, which it regarded as inherently threatening to its core interests and power positions. According to some authors, the military's senior officers, particularly in the SCAF, found themselves in an uneasy position in the early stages of the Egyptian transition process and reacted by resorting to their traditional paternalistic, conservative, defensive, and, ultimately, authoritarian attitude (Sayigh 2012: 7–10).

The strategy pursued by the SCAF was to create a balance between meeting popular demands for change and keeping an eye on and advancing the military's interests. Manipulating civilian-military relations, which are in themselves already quite opaque and ambiguous as far as the horizontal distribution of powers between civilian and military agencies is concerned, in favour of the higher military hierarchy was one of the main instruments used to accomplish this. It is also the main reason why civilian-military relations tended to be at the centre of the process of institutional development kicked off by the uprising. Overall, it can be argued that the SCAF is disproportionately responsible for how the transition has been structured. The senior officers in this body, largely speaking with one voice, have used every opportunity to maximise their authority by underpinning it through both constitutional and extra-constitutional means. On the one hand, they have sought and successfully managed to entrench the military's power in Egypt's institutional framework by manipulating the constitution-making process. On the other, the SCAF has used extra-constitutional means to prop up its constitutionally recognised authority, as well as to extend its reach and erode civilian power by resorting to the military courts – an independent judicial system under the supervision of the Ministry of Defence – to try civilian protestors, by extending the emergency law, and by clamping down on independent media outlets.

From the earliest stages of the transition, several provisions in the constitutional declarations spelled out the means to protect and advance the military's interests. Most of them concerned the full institutional autonomy of the SCAF in managing all matters concerning the armed forces. In addition, they stated that the military budget would not be subject to civilian oversight and emphasised the role of the SCAF in domestic governance as it allegedly had been entrusted by the people with the task of 'defending the constitutional legitimacy' of the whole transition process, supervising the work of the constituent assembly and referring questions to the Supreme Constitutional Court (SCC) for a binding judgement in the event of disagreement between the SCAF and the constitution-drafting body.[6] For example, not only was the March 2011 constitutional declaration overwhelmingly silent about any steps that would get the officers out of politics as quickly as possible, but it also established a National Defence Council that was 'tasked with evaluating affairs concerned with means of securing the country and its safety' (art. 54). This body, whose antecedent had been set up under Nasser and then formally established in the 1971 constitution as an instrument of presidential power but had been moribund until that moment, was to be headed by the president. However, the National Defence Council came to be de facto controlled by the military due to the predominance of military over civilian representatives among its members.

Reference to the National Defence Council was also made in the 2012 constitution. Its significance in the context of civilian-military relations was heightened as the constitutional text provided for two different bodies with very similar names and compositions but different tasks. Article 197 spelled out the structure and mandate of the National Defence Council as opposed to the National Security Council, whose composition, mission, and competencies were outlined in article 193. A tangible indicator of the powers and autonomy granted to the military establishment was the mandate of the National Defence Council, making it 'responsible for matters pertaining to the methods of ensuring the safety and security of the country [and] for discussing the armed forces' budget'. In addition, according to the same article 197, 'its opinion [ought to] be sought in relation to draft laws on the armed forces'. However, the National Security Council was broadly speaking the body responsible for ensuring the security of the country by addressing disasters and crises of all kinds. These provisions further contributed to distinguishing clearly between the arena in which the military establishment had full control, above and beyond civilian power, to determine important aspects of the state's functions and the arena in which a more shared civilian-military power would be exercised.

The June 2012 constitutional declaration also contained other, more far-reaching provisions regulating civilian-military relations: it established the military as a self-governing authority, free to operate without any form of external oversight, including by the state's civilian and elected authorities. As already discussed in Chapter 3, it also allocated important legislative powers and some of the president's powers to the SCAF itself until a new parliament was elected. This set of provisions significantly expanded the military's powers and attempted to fill a partial legal vacuum. Indeed, the issue of the military's status had remained essentially dormant from the beginning of the transition in early 2011 until the June 2012 constitutional declaration was published, if one excludes the aborted Selmi document. In filling this gap, article 53 bis provided that the SCAF would be 'responsible for deciding on all issues related to the armed forces'. On the one hand, this provision was vague enough so as not to explicitly mention the significant amount of economic activity the military engaged in, which did not strictly speaking qualify as a military issue. On the other hand, the expression 'related to the armed forces' was sufficiently broad to include all matters even tangentially related to the military, thus suggesting that the SCAF's intent was to have all of the military's economic affairs under its decision-making authority alone. This effectively undermined any form of civilian oversight over the military and also prevented any civilian authorities – including the newly and directly elected president – from intervening in forming the military's policy.

The provision was clearly in breach of one of the main tenets of democratic governance, i.e., the principle of civilian control over the military. As underscored by a number of authors, it also substantially departed from the 1971 Egyptian constitution, under which the military was formally subject to civilian control and the authority of the president (al-Ali, Roberts, and Toh 2012). Since Egyptian presidents historically rose to power through the ranks of the military, however, the division between military and civilian authorities became distorted from the 1950s onward, de facto rendering civilian oversight over the military meaningless. Another interpretation of civilian-military relations prior to 2011 sees them as much more than a transactional relationship, a bargain, between two separate forms of institutional power. The military's crucial and intimate association with the president, with whom the military apparatus shared substantial interests, worldviews, and fortunes, ensured the continuity of the Egyptian political system. Both formal and informal institutions were critical in this regard. An example of informal institutions relating to the power of the military establishment was the much discussed issue of presidential succession before 2011. In the wake of the Egyptian uprising, and in particular after the summer of 2011, the SCAF sought to formalise the military's autonomy from the state's civilian institutions, possibly motivated by the prospect that Egyptians could elect the first president who had not risen through the ranks of the military – something which eventually happened when Morsi became Egypt's first civilian president in June 2012.

Finally, forming an important part of the December 2012 Egyptian constitution were the provisions related to the military, its powers, and its relations with the civilian establishment. It can be argued that the power of the military emerged unscathed and was even reinforced in the final draft of the constitution approved in the popular referendum. In total disregard of some of the most pressing demands of the 'revolutionary' forces in Tahrir Square, such as putting an end to military trial of civilians, the final text of the constitution did not include such a provision and instead explicitly stated that civilians could be tried by military courts for crimes that 'harm the armed forces' (art. 198). Once more, the exact meaning of that term was left to be defined by subsequent legislation. The novelty, however, lies in the fact that the practice of military trials of civilians was elevated to a constitutional principle that cannot be easily overturned by new legislation.

As discussed in the previous paragraphs, in 2011 the SCAF sought to control the constitution-making process by enshrining the protection of its vested interests in constitutional declarations and other documents outlining the principles that would guide the transition. One such principle was the notion that the military's budget would remain secret and outside of the scope of civilian oversight. In the months of the SCAF's rule following the fall of Mubarak, the military's attempt to monopolise the constitution-making process and to over-stretch the principle of maintaining the military's autonomy led to massive protests in the country, which eventually resulted in dozens of deaths and thousands of wounded.[7] Although the SCAF dropped this initiative as a result of popular opposition, that particular provision made a comeback during the constitution-making process. Once again, the terms of the provision were fairly vague and open to interpretation. While an early draft explicitly maintained that the military's budget would appear as a single figure in the annual state budget law without a breakdown, this was somewhat watered down in the final draft, which provided that discussing the military's budget was the responsibility of the National Defence Council, composed of eight military members and seven civilians, as already recalled. The fact that the reference to a 'single figure' had been removed and that there was no indication that the council was exclusively competent for discussing the matter does not detract from the fact that the Egyptian military establishment was granted enormous prerogatives and (financial) autonomy, which its counterparts in other countries do not enjoy (International Crisis Group 2012).

Deep or wide... it's the state!

Some reflections are in order here with regard to what these factors pertaining to civilian-military relations tell us about the relationship between the SCAF and the Muslim Brotherhood. The SCAF's behaviour in the framework of the constitution-making process, acting discretionarily and dictating the rules of political transition to suit its core interests, contributed to fuelling uncertainty. Because of its substantial powers over the transition process, the military apparatus was forced to redefine its relationship with the Egyptian state and with the other political actors, in particular with the emerging Islamist parties, towards which it adopted an increasingly paternalistic attitude. As demonstrated in Chapter 3, in the first months of the transition, a substantial, temporary convergence of interests appeared between the top of the military hierarchy and the Muslim Brotherhood's leadership, which was sealed by the Islamists' approval of and vote for the SCAF's transition plan put to referendum in March 2011. This convergence, which took place despite the deep distrust the Muslim Brotherhood had always inspired in some (powerful) Egyptian institutions, including the coercive apparatus and the judiciary, was motivated by the contingent, mutual need to find (strong) partners with which to ally in pursuit of their goals. As far as the Muslim Brotherhood was concerned, the convergence with the military was dictated by their desire to normalise relations with one of the institutions with which they had long been in conflict, and to share the burden of governing the country. As for the military, the engagement with the Islamists was dictated by the need to provide a civilian face to its military rule while preventing any opposition group from gaining enough control of the institutions to pave the way for a fundamental shift in civilian-military relations.[8]

This initial convergence of interests was, however, not sufficient to prevent the increasing power grab on the part of the military, as we have seen, to which the newly elected Islamists authorities responded with the sudden removal, on 12 August 2012, of the top military leaders of the SCAF, Field Marshall Tantawi, Chief of Staff Lieutenant General Sami Anan, and other senior military leaders, replacing them with considerably younger officers. On the same occasion, Morsi declared the June 2012 constitutional declaration null and void and assumed the presidential powers that the military had grabbed for itself. This move was welcomed from various parts, with some underlining the ability of the leadership of the newly elected Muslim Brotherhood to roll back the powers acquired by the military (El Fegiery 2012). In contrast, other views tended to underscore the fact that this important change at the top of the military apparatus was the result of internal dynamics within the military itself (Hellyer 2012). These views clearly pointed to a much more complex situation and to the existence of a previous backdoor agreement between President Morsi and a number of military leaders, including General Al-Sisi, representing a new guard within the higher military hierarchy (Interviewee 28). This new generation of military officers seemed to have had an interest in removing the old guard both for personal reasons, linked to their possibility to fully share in the status-related and economic benefits of belonging to the military apparatus, and for motives connected to the need to remedy the damaged legitimacy, popularity, and professionalism of the armed forces.

SCAF's exercise of discretionary and autonomous powers during the initial phase of the Egyptian transition had made the military both more powerful and more vulnerable. From this stemmed the need to cut down the military's involvement in political affairs as long as this would not threaten the military's core interests. In other words, the new guard clearly wanted to return to the position the military apparatus had maintained prior to February 2011 as a means of recovering the military's popularity. Furthermore, years if not decades of the military's infiltrating the state apparatus and economy had arguably weakened the professionalism of the military as an institution and its ability to ensure public security, as demonstrated, among other things, by the string of terrorist attacks against the military that took place in the Sinai peninsula after the beginning of the transition and that had strongly embarrassed Tantawi's SCAF leadership.[9] All in all, it can be argued that the August 2012 move was not the military submitting to civilian control, but rather a 'coup *within* the military establishment as senior officers were forced out by ambitious others' (Hellyer 2012, emphasis in the original). Another motive behind the military's decision to distance itself from the daily management of politics was the need to protect the institution from being blamed for having failed to address the socio-economic grievances of the Egyptian population one and a half years after the 'revolution' (Interviewee 7). The logical consequence of this view is that Morsi did not play the key role; he was simply instrumental in allowing some echelons of the military to implement their, arguably mutually beneficial, plan. Finally, this particular circumstance in the relationship between the Muslim Brotherhood and the military apparatus ultimately contributes to explaining the motives behind the many provisions favouring the military as an institution in the Muslim Brotherhood-dictated 2012 Egyptian constitution. By calling the shots in the removal of Tantawi and his clique, the new military leadership renegotiated the 'deal' with the Islamists on new bases and obtained a sort of 'military immunity' and the assurance that their substantial economic interests would be protected. At the same time, the Muslim Brotherhood's leadership was drawn into believing that they had successfully obtained the military's neutrality in the transition.

These changes in the higher military hierarchy notwithstanding, the constitutional declarations and texts that followed President Morsi's ouster did not alter the provisions in favour of the military set out in the documents drafted by the Muslim Brotherhood-dominated bodies, but rather reinforced them. The SCAF's strategy to protect its core interests while balancing them with popular demands for change came full circle in the months following the military coup, when the officers' republic struck back with full force, not only against the Muslim Brotherhood but also against the forces for change that had been unleashed by the 2011 uprising. One goal of the SCAF's strategy had been achieved, that of holding elections in parallel with the constitution-making process, which – as demonstrated in Chapter 4 – contributed to increasing the polarisation among the political actors and, in the officers' view, to successfully avoiding energies that could be turned against their managed transition plan and threaten their power (Frisch 2013: 189). The gulf between the Islamists and civic forces had become wider and wider and the military could, in that way, stand between the battling forces and assume, more than ever, the role of defender of national security and, ultimately, the status quo.

From the institutional point of view, the enormous power enjoyed by the Egyptian military has once again been formally codified in the new constitution, the draft of which was presented to the nation at the beginning of December 2013. The constitution enshrined autonomy for the military and no longer treated it as part of the executive branch of government but rather as a branch in itself. This provision has wide-ranging implications and was accompanied by the requirement that the military approve the Minister of Defence for the subsequent two presidential terms, starting from the date on which the constitution comes into effect (art. 234). While the principle whereby the Minister of Defence would be drawn from the officer class was already codified in the 2012 constitution, the new provision served to strengthen the military's reach and privileges. Another very important change concerns the broad jurisdiction over civilians attributed to military courts. Contrary to the 1971 and 2012 constitutions, which failed to specify the scope of jurisdiction of military trials over civilians, thus leaving it open to further legislation, the draft constitution passed in 2013 significantly restricted it to specific cases (art. 204). However, the combination of vague and broad language with the extensive penetration of civilian affairs by the military establishment meant that military courts were likely to have potentially unrestrained jurisdiction whenever they wish.[10] In addition to consolidating the power of the military, the new constitution also granted substantial sway to the wider security and intelligence agencies, including the police. According to the new constitutional text, a Supreme Police Council – composed of its most senior officers – had to be consulted on any law affecting the police, effectively ensuring that the much needed security sector reform would run through existing police institutions.[11] Furthermore, general intelligence officers were subject to military courts, not to civilian justice (art. 204), which de facto provided them with immunity from civilian oversight or prosecution.

As the detailed illustration of the previous pages has shown, civilian-military relations have always defined the interplay between important state institutions. Not only has the pivotal role of the Egyptian military in both economic and political terms contributed to holding back the development of accountable and transparent civilian-military relations, but it has also steered the whole transition in the direction of strong continuity with the past. This is in keeping with its interests as a status quo-oriented institution. Some people have used the expression 'deep state' to point to the existence of a 'state within the state' type of entity that has the potential to obstruct institutional changes and reforms, also significantly undermining the performance and legitimacy of elected civilian authorities.[12] This expression was coined to describe a group of influential anti-democratic coalitions within the Turkish political system, composed of high-level elements within the intelligence services (domestic and foreign), the military, the security apparatuses, and the judiciary during the 1970s, but has since then penetrated the discourse on Middle Eastern politics and has been most recently and widely used to refer to the comeback of the military and other institutions in Egypt.[13] Other usages of the term refute the reduction of the deep state to one or more powerful interest networks and instead define it as a type of resilience of a set of informal institutions and logics that enable the coercive apparatus and the judiciary to disrupt formal democratic institutions (Söyler 2013). In this light, the deep state is not necessarily something strong and powerful, but rather something that is able to obstruct change through the persistence of certain behaviours and codes of conduct.[14]

Both understandings of 'deep state' can be applied to the Egyptian case to illuminate the interplay between changes and continuities in institutional development. In addition to the struggle for power among formal institutions, some of which have clearly tried to resist change, what can explain the strong institutional continuities is the persistence of old patterns of behaviour within certain institutions. The power of informal institutions and logics explains the fact that, in the words of an Egyptian academic, 'the way politics is handled has remained the same: the same technocrats pursue the same actions with the same results' (Interviewee 1). Thus, certain institutions and powers have opposed change simply by continuing to apply old logics and procedures. These not-so-confined pockets of resistance within the Egyptian state, generally harbouring a very strong hostility towards the Muslim Brotherhood, can be found not only in the coercive apparatus but also in the judiciary and the vast unreformed bureaucracy, comprising around 8 million people or 10 percent of the population, which actually runs Egypt on a day-to-day basis and has ensured the continuation of the state (Interviewees 18, 25).

The Muslim Brotherhood-dominated cabinet that was formally in power between August 2012 and July 2013 was confronted with the resistance of various other institutions as it sought to get Egypt's state apparatus back to work. Civil servants and the mammoth state bureaucracy might not have been politically or ideologically opposed to Egypt's new authorities, but a certain degree of resistance to any type of change characterised these institutions and this resulted in ambivalence, go-slow tactics, and passive non-cooperation with government directives. The domains in which these practices of resistance to change were most evident were the enforcement of security and the provision of basic goods and services by public authorities. The Ministry of the Interior, in particular, emerged as a principal holdout against the Muslim Brotherhood's presidency and government, while various security agencies arguably adopted an attitude of inaction in performing their normal functions and passive hostility towards the transition process, thus contributing to fuelling anarchy, crime, and the rampant growth of the informal sector, all of which heightened the people's revolutionary mood.[15] This point contradicts one of the arguments advanced by Morsi's detractors, i.e., the idea that the Muslim Brotherhood successfully proceeded during the few months it was in power to '*Ikhwanise*' the state. Quite to the contrary, the Islamist party failed to penetrate state institutions thoroughly and was swept away very quickly when push came to shove. In addition to the inertia of powerful state institutions, this is explained by the fact that the Muslim Brotherhood did not have the ability nor willingness to overhaul state institutions. It was more concerned with maintaining the status quo through the restructuring of the institutional order than with the revolution (Interviewee 35).

Turf wars

One of the institutions that represented the most insurmountable barrier to the Muslim Brotherhood's alleged penetration of the state was the judiciary, as already mentioned, the leading conservative force in the country's institutional framework (Interviewees 12, 41). Just as civilian-military relations have provided the arena for intense power struggles, so the relation between the judiciary and other powers, particularly the executive, has always been complex. Over the past few decades, the judiciary has managed to forge an indisputable reputation for integrity and relative independence from the political regime, mainly thanks to the legalistic character of Egyptian authoritarianism as well as some specific provisions in the 1971 constitution. Following its harsh confrontation with Nasser, who accused it of being too powerful, these constitutional provisions were meant to guarantee the principle of the independence of the judiciary (art. 65

and art. 165), the irrevocability of judges (art. 166), and the non-interference of the executive in trials, although all this was operationalised 'in accordance with the law' (Brown 2012a).[16] This does not detract from the fact that the judiciary's personnel, working methods, and relationship to other state institutions have been shaped by decades of authoritarianism and by the executive's repeated heavy-handed attempts to interfere with the judges' work. These have involved different forms of co-optation, both economic and political, widespread corruption, the courts' lack of budgetary autonomy, the president's prerogative to name the General Prosecutor and the president of the SCC, and, most importantly, the numerous attempts to skirt the courts, ignore their rulings, or simply not execute them (Kienle 2001: 117–131; Bernard-Maugiron 2008).[17]

The Egyptian judiciary, which has always been very politicised, was severely tested in the wake of the 2011 uprisings as it was inundated by a plethora of cases related to political and economic corruption, the misappropriation of public funds, not to mention the killing of demonstrators and the brutal suppression of peaceful unrest. Its inability or unwillingness to uphold the rule of law in some of these cases greatly contributed to eroding the social capital the judiciary enjoyed among the Egyptian society.[18] In the period between 2011 and the beginning of 2014, the judiciary acted as a force in favour of the status quo, despite the existence of some reformist figures within its ranks, and significantly interfered with the course of sought-after political change. On the one hand, there were hardly any attempts to reform the judicial system. In 2011, the judiciary itself advanced two bills for a reform of the judicial system, one by the 'Judges' Club' – the most powerful professional association related to the judiciary in Egypt – and the other by the Supreme Council – the body that is responsible for overseeing the functioning of the entire judicial sector, including its administrative affairs, appointments, and promotions for the regular courts (Brown 2012b). However, both proposals remained dead letters due to the disbandment of parliament in June 2012. On the other hand, the judiciary's role in the transition has been the object of intense and often antagonistic debates in the highly polarised Egyptian political scene. Whereas in the view of certain sectors of the public opinion, opposed to the Muslim Brotherhood's non-inclusive handling of power, the judiciary represented a bastion of legality against the newcomers' abuses and particularly their attempt to take over state institutions, according to other views the judiciary suffered from substantial continuity with the authoritarian system in place under Mubarak and in this light the Muslim Brotherhood's relentless attempts to overhaul it were justified. In this regard, the FJP presented a bill in the Upper House of parliament in April 2013 proposing a radical restructuring of the judiciary and forcing all judges over 60 years of age into retirement. This would have meant the reshuffling of some 3,000 high magistrates, potentially those most compromised with the regime, and their replacement by younger judges or new recruits.[19] Furthermore, during its year in power, the Muslim Brotherhood's leadership grew increasingly frustrated with the manner in which legal cases were used by the courts to challenge its authority. In particular, the SCC's rulings on the constitutionality of the electoral law laid the ground for an escalation of tension, if not open hostility, between the Islamist party and one of the judiciary's most important components. If challenging the constitutionality of the electoral law was not in itself seen as an indicator of the judiciary's doggedness against the Muslim Brotherhood, the highly charged political environment in which it took place heightened the suspicion among the Muslim Brotherhood's sympathisers that the timing and content of the move were politically motivated. As already recalled in Chapter 4, the court's rulings came as a result of article 177 of the 2012 constitution, which required that electoral laws have to be reviewed by the SCC before they can be sent to the executive for signature. At around the same time, on 2 June 2013, the SCC went one step further and ruled that the Shura Council itself had been elected on the basis of an unconstitutional electoral law. This effectively disqualified the entire Muslim Brotherhood-dominated parliament, given that the SCC had already issued a ruling on exactly the same basis in relation to the Lower House of parliament in June 2012, and further weakened the Islamist party.

While the 2012 constitution did introduce some new legal mechanisms and institutional changes related to the judiciary, it retained many of the provisions of the previous text, including its flaws. While the independence of the judiciary was protected (art. 168 and art. 170) and a clear mechanism was provided for the appointment of the General Prosecutor that safeguarded his independence (art. 173), no details were provided on how judges were to be appointed or dismissed, nor was any information given as to how their salaries were to be determined (al-Ali 2013a).[20] In the constitutional amendments issued on 8 July 2013 and the changes proposed by the ten-member technical committee, no further attempt was made to reform the judiciary. Indeed, the technical committee's proposed amendments suggested that any legislation on judicial reform opposed by the judiciary ought to be approved by a two-thirds majority in parliament, effectively granting the judiciary a veto on the matter (art. 158).[21] This trend towards granting the judiciary immunity from change has turned out to be even stronger in the constitution drafted in 2013. The judiciary, which arguably supported the military's takeover from the Muslim Brotherhood, has gained substantial autonomy in the new text. An example of this is the fact that judicial bodies were granted the power to administer their own affairs, including their own budget, which is incorporated in the state budget as a single figure (art. 185). As far as the SCC is concerned, it was the object of some specific provisions (art. 191–195) that, among others, granted it the right to appoint its own president.

This account of civilian-military relations and the status and powers of the judiciary in Egypt reveals the extent to which years of authoritarian practices have deeply woven into the Egyptian state institutions, laws, and patterns of political behaviour that are hard to remove. Over the course of decades, the Egyptian state has grown both in depth and, even more importantly, in scope. Not only have a number of formal and informal institutions become so entrenched and some behaviours and logics so pervasive, but critical state institutions have also developed a significant amount of internal autonomy if not outright independence. The different branches of the coercive apparatus, the judiciary, and the bureaucracy were all allowed to grow exponentially and to take root in the Egyptian political fabric under the constant supervision of the president, who ultimately held the reins of power of the whole state apparatus and could intervene to manage it by appointing or co-opting individuals to key positions and by fostering institutional duplication. The result was a strong sense of corporate identity within specific institutions, i.e., the military, the judiciary, and the bureaucracy, as well as the expansion of the Egyptian state in many directions. Nathan Brown has used the metaphor 'Balkanisation' to describe the widening of the Egyptian state – as opposed to its deepening. The 'Balkanisation' of the state is the process whereby 'each part of these assemblages of states-within-the State [i.e., the military, the judiciary, and the bureaucracy] developed its own (often ossified) leadership, doling out benefits within its part of the State in order to cement ties of loyalty' (Brown 2013b). At the same time, and partially by virtue of their role as representing some of the most strategic interests of the state or the welfare of the people, all these institutions tend to see themselves as above politics and endowed with a superior level of professionalism and integrity as opposed to the actors that crowd the political realm and from time to time try to assert their control upon them.

The impact of the process of Balkanisation of the state upon the Egyptian transition has been two-fold. On the one hand, the struggle over these institutions' autonomy or even independence has ended with the victory of the status quo-oriented forces who have managed to secure legal and institutional changes (or lack thereof) that could make them virtually self-perpetuating bodies. On the other hand, a very important development, which has not been emphasised enough in the literature on the Egyptian transition, has been the emergence of conflicts within each of these institutions, as younger or reform-minded members have pushed against a senior leadership often closely associated with the old regime. Instances of such trends have been the internal reshuffle within the military in August 2012 and the creation of the *Tayyar Al-Istiqlal*, the independence movement within the judiciary, which was partially penetrated by the Islamists (Interviewee 26). Overall, the Balkanisation of the Egyptian states appears to have been a very powerful instrument for limiting change and ultimately preventing the Muslim Brotherhood from becoming a forceful presence through its allegedly pervasive *Ikhwanisation* of the state. Despite some attempts by the Islamist-dominated Lower House of parliament, the Morsi presidency, and, to some extent, the Upper House of parliament to rein in the powers and autonomy of some state institutions, e.g., the judiciary, while working to placate or negotiate with others, e.g., the military, three years after Mubarak's forced departure it seemed that the process of remoulding these institutions had been fully blunted and many of the envisioned changes reversed. As mentioned above, some old institutions and logics have obtained even more autonomy under the new legal and institutional framework, thus bringing to the surface the strong continuities existing with the past institutional framework, its promoters, and their vested interests.

Tunisia: delaying change to cope with uncertainty

Political or apolitical . . . it's still legitimate!

Tunisia offers a completely different set of challenges and opportunities as far as the role in the transition of the more or less powerful and structured coercive and judicial institutions is concerned. At the same time, according to a number of authors, already in 2011 Tunisia stood the best chances of developing greater transparency, accountability, and democratic control over the country's security sector, provided a number of shortcomings are addressed (Hanlon 2012; Lutterbeck 2012). This is best explained by the intertwining, virtuous dynamics created by some of the characteristics of the Tunisian military itself and by the level of inclusiveness and consensus displayed by the Tunisian transition, as illustrated in the previous chapters. These virtuous dynamics have been largely self-reinforcing in nature. Civilian-military relations in Tunisia developed according to a totally different script compared to Egypt and the military itself has never represented the powerful 'deus ex machina' as in Egypt (Interviewee 38). A number of contextual factors related to the inherent architecture and functioning of the Tunisian authoritarian regime are important in accounting for the situation of relative de-politicisation as well as the professionalism of the country's armed forces. These factors have substantially influenced the attitude and behaviour of the military institution both during the uprising and in the first three years of the transition.

Important among the contextual political factors that have contributed to the distinctive features of the Tunisian military and have set it off from the experience of other countries in the Arab world is the legacy of the first post-independence leader, President Habib Bourghiba, in terms of his training and profession as well as the cultural milieu in which he developed. First of all, Bourghiba was a lawyer, contrary to most Arab leaders of the time who came from the military. Second, he was a convinced Francophile and thus adopted the French republican principle, meaning a clear separation between political and military power, as a blueprint for the Tunisian army (Ware 1985: 37). Last, Bourghiba was equally concerned about the potential emergence of a centre of power that might compete with him and his ruling party, the *Neo-Dustur*. As a result of these factors, one of the most striking differences between Tunisia and the majority of other Arab countries when it comes to the role of the military has always been the latter's relatively apolitical nature and limited political influence. Unlike in many other countries in the region, for example Egypt, the Tunisian military was deliberately and consistently marginalised by the country's leadership and removed from the centre of political power. This was accomplished through the prohibition of any sort of political activity or individual enrichment or status by the members of the armed forces as well as regular purges of officers suspected of harbouring political ambitions and plans (Camau and Geisser 2003). The same policy of keeping the military away from politics was followed by Bourghiba's successor, Ben Ali, even though he had a military background (Murphy 1999: 164–165). The military's non-interference in political and public affairs also contributed to keeping its size small and the country's military spending low, at least compared to regional standards.[22] According to the figures quoted in the *Military Balance*, the Tunisian armed forces were the smallest in North Africa, with the number of their personnel oscillating between 35,000 and 45,000 up to 2010 (Hackett 2010: 274–275; Kallander 2011). Similarly, defence spending – hovering around 1.5 percent of the gross domestic product (GDP) – has always been very low compared to the other countries in the region. All in all, and thanks to these features, the Tunisian armed forces were able to develop a rather strong corporate, institutional ethos, despite their limited numbers, based on their inherently 'republican' role as defenders of the integrity of the country, rather than on some vested political or economic interests of the 'military caste'.

This element, i.e., the military's sense of identity as the institution in charge of ensuring the defence of the country beyond its own, largely absent, partisan influence, played a pivotal role in shaping the military's attitude towards the Ben Ali regime after the beginning of the popular mobilisation that eventually led to the latter's collapse. When the Tunisian military was called upon to confront the rapidly swelling, largely peaceful demonstrations, it refused to do so and practically sided with the demonstrators against the regime. Even more significantly, on 13 January 2011, the army withdrew its forces from the Tunisian capital, where it had been deployed by Ben Ali only the previous day as a last-ditch attempt to stop the popular mobilisation, only returning to the streets of Tunis upon the president's departure from the country on 14 January.[23] Paradoxically, the geographical, political, and economic marginalisation of the military under Ben Ali limited the stake its leadership had in sustaining the incumbent regime in January 2011.[24] The military's decision not to use force against the demonstrators was indeed the result of a cost assessment by the higher-ranking officers that was largely shaped by their apolitical nature. Some authors claim that the term 'apolitical' is not the correct one to describe the military's decision to forgo using force to actively suppress the demonstrations as this act was in itself deeply political and reflected political calculations (Brooks 2013: 205–208). The military indeed estimated that the costs it would have incurred in violently suppressing the uprising were significantly higher than the gains it could have obtained, either organisationally or individually, by intervening in defence of the regime. On that occasion, the military acted as the de facto key veto power in the country by steering the situation in one particular direction. It appears that the nature of civilian-military relations is crucial to understanding the armed forces' behaviour when confronted with the dilemma of whether or not maintaining a regime in power best serves their interests.

As a result of its role in putting an end to the Ben Ali regime, the Tunisian military emerged during the transition period as one of the institutions enjoying the greatest degree of legitimacy among the population. The military leadership, however, chose not to exploit this additional capital and the instability in which the country was thrown during the first months of the transition to meddle in politics.[25] Despite some fears that it might be tempted to take on a stronger role in domestic politics, the army has voluntarily and officially stayed in the background and left the task of redesigning the country's future order largely to the civilian bureaucracy, the nascent political parties, and the civil society groups. To dispel any doubts, General Rashid Ammar, Chairman of the Joint Chiefs of Staff, appeared in a rare public address on 24 January 2011, only ten days after Ben Ali's departure, and stated that 'the army [would] protect the revolution', which most people interpreted as the military's willingness to eschew any overtly political role.[26]

With regard to the legal and institutional framework, the fact that the Tunisian military did not play any political role under Ben Ali does not mean that it lay beyond the reach of political power. Due to the unrivalled degree of power concentrated in the hands of the president in Tunisia, the armed forces were one of those sectors of policy-making in which this power could express itself. Quite to the contrary, the parliament, like others in the region dominated by the president's party, in this case the *Rassemblement Constitutionnel Démocratique* (RCD), did not exercise any significant influence over the military even though articles 28 and 30 of the 1959 Tunisian constitution clearly foresaw a role for parliament in approving the military budget and in exercising oversight over military issues. With respect to the government, Tunisia has represented an exception to the largely military-dominated apparatuses within the Ministries of Defence in the region, as the minister himself and the higher officials in the ministry have always been civilians. All in all, it can be argued that even under Ben Ali (and his predecessor), the Tunisian military was subject to a form of civilian control, albeit clearly not a democratic one.

During the process of revision of the constitution, the role of the military has undergone very little transformation. This is in line with its relatively uncontroversial and apolitical nature. In particular, its mandate was clearly enshrined in article 17 of the new draft constitution issued on 1 June 2013, which stated:

> the national army is a disciplinary-based armed military force that is composed and structurally organized in accordance with the law. The army must defend the nation, its independence and the integrity of its territory. It must remain politically impartial. The national army supports the civil authorities in accordance with the provisions set out by law.

The spelling out of the political impartiality of the military has been called upon by the armed forces themselves to prevent the military's instrumentalisation by political actors (Interviewee 45). An initial proposal providing for a more prominent consultative role for the armed forces' leadership on military and national defence issues seems not to have been taken into account in the final draft of the new Tunisian constitution (Hanlon 2012: 5). Finally, in terms of military hierarchy, no significant reshuffling has taken place since the departure of Ben Ali, while an effort has been made to raise the number of conscripts by offering higher wages with a view to increasing the size of the military apparatus.[27]

Bastions of conservatism

What emerges from this account is that the Tunisian military has undergone only limited changes during the transition, but at the same it has posed no resistance to them whatsoever. This does not mean that other institutions in Tunisia have not resisted change or acted beyond the reach of accountable, civilian bodies. The police, the security apparatuses, and the judiciary fall into the category of those institutions whose opacity and autonomy has been difficult to rein in. As in the other Arab countries, the Tunisian authoritarian regime substantially resorted to oppressive, unaccountable, and corrupt security and intelligent apparatuses as its instrument for exercising extensive control over the population and suppressing internal dissent. While the dual police system – comprising the National Police (*Police* or *Sûreté Nationale*), which operated mainly in larger cities, and the paramilitary National Guard (*Garde Nationale*), which was responsible for rural areas – and the intelligence apparatuses were under the formal control of the Ministry of the Interior, some militias were accountable directly to the palace. This was the case, for example, of the Presidential Guard, including between 5,000 and 6,000 men entrusted with the task of protecting the regime – a job they tried to fulfil to the bitter end by engaging in looting and violence and sowing chaos in January 2011.

Beginning in the 1990s, the size of the police and the security forces grew substantially – by some accounts quadrupling – while the legal framework regulating them remained poor (Murphy 1999). In fact, Tunisia had come to be seen as one of the most heavily policed states in the world, with estimates of the total number of policemen ranging between 130,000 and 200,000 (Lutterbeck 2012: 9).[28] The climate of arbitrariness and impunity that bred the intimate relationship between the police, on the one hand, and the Ben Ali regime, on the other, was buttressed by the existence of an instrumentalised and non-autonomous judiciary. Under Ben Ali, the judicial system fell squarely under the control of the executive power, in particular the president and the Ministry of Justice. The president himself had sweeping powers over the judiciary by controlling the Supreme Council of Magistrates (*Conseil Supérieur de la Magistrature*), which was the highest supervisory body responsible for appointing, promoting, and sanctioning judges. The council was presided by Ben Ali and the majority of its members were either from the government or nominated by it (Lutterbeck 2012: 12). As such, the judiciary was widely perceived as another pillar of Ben Ali's authoritarian regime as it served the double purpose of neutralising political opponents and rewarding the president's cronies and corrupt circle (Hibou 2011: 116–123).

Therefore, reform of the security apparatuses and of the corrupt but apolitical judicial system has emerged as one of the most pressing priorities during the Tunisian transition. Yet, this has been a difficult challenge to tackle due to strong resistance to change within these institutions.[29] Apart from the dismissal of some high-ranking officials and the publication of a white book on police reform entitled 'Security and Development: Towards Security at the Service of Democracy' (*Sécurité et développement: vers une sécurité au service de la démocratie*), both of which occurred during the first year of the transition, no other major overhaul of the country's internal security forces has taken place. As a result, several of Ben Ali's cronies have remained in important positions within the Ministry of the Interior (Hanlon 2012: 7). There are a number of reasons for this shortcoming. First, the general context of uncertainty associated with the political transition and the struggle for power among the main political actors during the drafting of the constitution have largely diverted attention from the need for reform of the security apparatuses. Second, as lack of security has constantly featured as one of the major concerns of the population, undertaking a too deep and wide-ranging restructuring of the security sector has been commonly perceived as a risk for the stability of the country. Finally, some representatives of civil society blamed the situation on *Ennahda*'s inability to completely sever ties with some remnants of the old regime in the Ministry of the Interior. According to them, this is part of an accommodation strategy that brings advantages to both parties: the *Ennahda* government benefits from the security machinery that has been kept intact, while old regime figures maintain their privileges (Interviewees 44, 47).

Whatever the explanation, it is fair to argue that the first three years of the transition have seen only very modest structural reforms, both within the security apparatuses and the judiciary. In the latter's case, despite the acknowledgement that only by loosening the executive's grip on the judiciary will it be possible to ensure respect of the rule of law, the only measures that have been taken are indiscriminate purges of judges and the publication in 2012 of a detailed and promising roadmap covering various aspects of judicial reform for the following four years.[30] The only significant step towards ensuring the judiciary's independence from the executive has been the creation of a new Constitutional Court (*Cour Constitutionnelle*) in the new constitution (art. 115–121), something that did not exist previously.

In conclusion, the most prominent institutions in Tunisia that have displayed an inherent resistance to reform have been the Ministries of the Interior and Justice. Not only have both been concerned most with retaining their privileges and the possibility to act arbitrarily, but their ability to hijack the transition process and steer it in some directions has also been limited by a number of watchdogs both among Tunisia's political actors and in civil society. Human rights organisations, such as the National Council for Liberties in Tunisia (*Conseil National pour les Libertés en Tunisie*) and the Tunisian League of Human Rights (*Ligue Tunisienne des Droits de l'Homme*), are prominent cases in point (Interviewee 47).

Notes

1 The figures on the size of the military are taken from Hackett (2010: 248–251). See also Picard (1990), who argued that, since the 1980s, significant cuts were made to military budgets throughout the Arab world, including in Egypt, which led to a search by the military for alternative income through neo-patrimonial activities in the market place.

2 Due to the opacity of the information available on the military's economic assets, it is no surprise that views on this issue display quite sizable divergences, both in terms of actual figures and of the implications of the military's control of a substantial part of the Egyptian economy (Interviewees 1, 8, 28, 32).

3 The majority of Egypt's governors have been senior-ranking military and police officers.

4 Hillel Frisch has put forth the argument that one of the reasons why the higher military hierarchy was unwilling to send troops in massive numbers to confront civilians, especially the Islamists, had to do with their fears of testing the loyalty of the middle command and exposing the growing cracks in the unity of the armed forces and in the chain of command linking the senior to the lower rungs of the officers' class and,

further down, to the rank and file. This and similar arguments emphasising fractures within the military, mostly along generational lines, also help explain the developments that took place in August 2012 when Morsi 'ousted' the upper echelons of the military apparatus. See Frisch (2013: 193).
5 The military's unmistakably political role was made evident on 11 December 2012 when the Minister of Defence, Al-Sisi, invited Morsi, other ministers, and a wide spectrum of political parties and forces and public figures to what he called a 'social dialogue'. This move underscored the military's status as an autonomous institutional actor with a prominent political role within the post-Mubarak Egyptian political system. The meeting was later cancelled as Morsi declined Al-Sisi's invitation. See "Egypt's defence minister calls for 'dialogue meeting' Wednesday". *Ahramonline*. 11 December 2012. http://english.ahram.org.eg/NewsContent/1/64/60316/Egypt/Politics-/Egypts-defence-minister-calls-for-dialogue-meeting.aspx.
6 This was the expression used in the so-called 'Selmi document', the document drafted between June and November 2011, circulated and then withdrawn by Deputy Prime Minister Ali Al-Selmi in November 2011, that sought to define 'supra-constitutional principles' to guide the constitution-making process. See "Political parties and powers to approve El-Selmi document, on condition it is amended". *Ahramonline*. 16 November 2011. http://english.ahram.org.eg/NewsContent/1/64/26754/Egypt/Politics-/Political-parties-and-powers-to-approve-ElSelmi-do.aspx.
7 The bloodiest incidents between the military and the demonstrators took place at the Maspero building, the state broadcasting centre, on the Nile Corniche on 9 October 2011 and in and around Mohamed Mahmoud Street between 19 and 24 November 2011. During the first incident, the military crushed a demonstration by Copts, leaving 28 demonstrators dead and 212 others injured. Between 19 and 24 November 2011, 45 demonstrators demanding an end to military rule and the formation of a civilian government were killed by the military. See "Reconstructing Maspero's bloody Sunday: An Ahram Online investigation". *Ahramonline*. 1 November 2011. http://english.ahram.org.eg/NewsContent/1/64/25521/Egypt/Politics-/Reconstructing-Masperos-Bloody-Sunday-Ahram-Online.aspx and "Million-strong protests in Egypt demand end of military rule, Tantawi accepts Cabinet resignation, battle continues". *Ahramonline*. 22 November 2011. http://english.ahram.org.eg/NewsContentP/1/27243/Egypt/Live-Updates-Tens-of-thousands-pour-into-Tahrir-to.aspx.
8 According to some views, immediately after Mubarak's fall, the military initially floated the idea of seeking an alliance with the youth groups, such as the 6 April Movement, that had participated in the uprisings. However, they soon realised that the best actor they could ally with was the Muslim Brotherhood due to the fact that it was, as it then amply demonstrated during the elections, the most organised and deeply-rooted organisation on the Egyptian political scene (Interviewees 6, 26).
9 "Sinai on the brink: Arms trafficking and the rise of Egypt's Jihadist groups". *Ahramonline*. 7 August 2012. http://english.ahram.org.eg/News/49807.aspx. It is worth specifying that developments that took place under Mubarak had already weakened the military establishment in that the president had significantly enhanced the power of the police and the security agencies at the expense of the military, thus turning Egypt not so much into a garrison but rather a police state (Kechichian and Nazimek 1997; Harb 2003; Hashim 2011). The rise of the 'security state' under Mubarak, particularly since the 1990s, and the intensification of the struggle against the Islamists, were signalled by the growth of the security services to an estimated 1.4 million in early 2011, corresponding to 1.5 times the combined size of military personnel and their reserves. Also, in terms of budget, the figure annually allocated to the Ministry of the Interior rose at three times the rate of the defence budget during the same period. On the growth of the security services under Mubarak and related figures, see Sayigh (2012: 15–16) and International Crisis Group (2012: 10). Also quite telling are the words with which Henry Clement and Robert Springborg described the military inefficiency:

> [The military] is bloated and its officer core is indulged, having been fattened on Mubarak's patronage. Its training is desultory, maintenance of its equipment is profoundly inadequate, and it is dependent on the United States for funding and logistical support. [...] The *raison d'être* of the military was always to support the Mubarak regime, not defend the nation.

See Clement and Springborg (2011).

10 Article 204 on the military judiciary of the 2013 draft constitution reads as follows:

> The military judiciary is an independent judiciary that adjudicates exclusively in all crimes related to the armed forces, its officers, personnel, and their equals, and in the crimes committed by general intelligence personnel during and because of the service. Civilians cannot stand trial before military courts except for crimes that represent a direct assault against military facilities, military barracks, or whatever falls under their authority; stipulated military or border zones; its equipment, vehicles, weapons, ammunition, documents, military secrets, public funds or military factories; crimes related to conscription; or crimes that represent a direct assault against its officers or personnel because of the performance of their duties.

11 Going beyond the scope of this work, it is worth recalling the importance of security sector reform (SSR) as the most important operational concept for promoting change of security institutions in the direction of greater accountability, transparency, and effectiveness. A relatively recent concept, SSR posits that security institutions should not only be effective and efficient in providing security for the country's citizens, but should also be controlled by and accountable to democratically elected civilian authorities and should act in respect of the rule of law. As such, the changes pursued by SSR represent less a technical issue than a very political challenge. On the topic of SSR in the Arab world and in Egypt in particular, see the thematic papers compiled for the Arab Reform Initiative by Sayigh (2007) and Aclimandos (2012), and Luethold (2004) and Brumberg and Sallam (2012).

12 The concept of 'deep state' bears some resemblance to that of 'shadow state', although the two differ in one main respect, namely the fact that a shadow state is usually regarded as working in parallel to the formal institutions of the state and is more visible than the deep state (Interviewee 40).

13 Turkish Prime Minister Erdoğan has spoken of the 'deep state' in the following terms as recently as 2012:

> every state has its own deep state; it is like a virus; it reappears when conditions are suitable. We continue fighting these structures. We cannot of course argue that we have completely eliminated and destroyed it because as a politician, I do not believe that any state in the world has been able to do this completely.

Quoted in "What is deep state?". *Today's Zaman*. 26 December 2012. www.todayszaman.com/columnists/markar-esayan_302319-what-is-deep-state.html.

14 Some experts interviewed for this work have actually suggested that the state in Egypt is weak and ineffective in terms of its ability to deliver. This stems from the fact that all its institutions have been tarnished and depleted by many years of authoritarian practice, thus leading to a deterioration of state capacity. Clearly this explanation only partially fits the Egyptian military, which has always been perceived as a 'strong' institution in Egypt's history, but this does not necessarily imply, however, that it is efficient (Interviewees 5, 6, 41). See also Migdal (1988).

15 "Egypt govt struggles with ongoing diesel fuel shortages". *Ahramonline*. 12 February 2013. http://english.ahram.org.eg/News/64625.aspx and Ben Hubbard and David D. Kirkpatrick. "Sudden improvements in Egypt suggest a campaign to undermine Morsi". *The New York Times*. 11 July 2013. www.nytimes.com/2013/07/11/world/middleeast/improvements-in-egypt-suggest-a-campaign-thatundermined-morsi.html.

It is worth stressing the fact that both of Morsi's two Ministers of the Interior as well as their aides were key figures under the Mubarak regime and in particular under Habib El-Adly, the former Minister of the Interior who was sentenced to life in prison for corruption and conspiring to kill demonstrators during the January 2011 unrest. Ahmed Gamal El-Din was the former director of the public security authority and occupied the position of Minister of the Interior between August 2012 and January 2013; Mohammed Ibrahim Moustafa took office in January 2013 and was one of the few ministers who kept his cabinet place after the July 2013 coup.

16 On the so-called 'massacre of the judiciary', see Brown (1997: 89–91).
17 The General Prosecutor is an essential figure in the Egyptian judicial system since he has the right to supervise all penal proceedings and therefore determines those that are zealously prosecuted and those that are overlooked. The choice of a loyal Prosecutor was one of the ways in which the old regime was able to exercise its control over the judiciary. Independent according to the constitution but operating in an authoritarian political system, the SCC has always been a bastion of the old regime in that it has often been referred to as full of Mubarak's appointees. In terms of the laws governing the SCC, including the appointment of its president, in the summer of 2011 the SCAF changed them by decree allowing the court to select its own president from among the three most senior judges instead of having the president name him. See Brown (2012b).
18 Chronic deficiencies stemming from the lack of competence and efficiency have always impinged on the quality of the Egyptian judiciary. According to some estimates, more than 200,000 cases stood before the Court of Cassation in early 2013 (Interviewee 21).
19 Civic forces saw that as unacceptable interference on the part of the executive in the judiciary's internal affairs. Indeed, a wide majority of judges reacted against the law by suspending work and organising demonstrations, and the former Minister of Justice, Ahmed Mekki, a reformist judge named by Morsi, also resigned in April 2013 to protest against the bill. See "Egypt justice minister demands guarantees over judicial independence". *Ahramonline*. 23 April 2013. http://english.ahram.org.eg/News/69940.aspx.
20 The 2012 constitution again entrusted the president with the power to appoint the General Prosecutor, 'based on the selection of the Supreme Judicial Council from among the Deputies to the President of the Court of Cassation, the Presidents of the Court of Appeals and Assistant Prosecutor Generals, for a period of four years'.
21 The unofficial translation of the proposed amendments to the constitution by the ten-member technical committee can be found at the following link: www.constitutionnet.org/vl/item/egypt-proposed-amendments-constitution-2012.
22 The Tunisian military has often been named *'la grande muette'* (the big silent one) in light of its being distant from politics. See Lutterbeck (2012: 6).
23 The fact that Ben Ali chose to deploy the military to police the capital was a significant development in itself as the military was not used to playing such a role of safeguarding internal security. Resorting to the security institution that enjoyed the greatest legitimacy in the eyes of the Tunisian population can itself be interpreted as a last, frantic attempt by Ben Ali to quell the protests (Interviewee 45).
24 Senior members of the armed forces have openly admitted that in Ben Ali's hierarchy of security institutions, they were at the bottom. In terms of geographical marginalisation, military personnel used to be deployed to less populated or geographically peripheral areas of the country to do public works projects, as well as to undertake peacekeeping missions in Africa. See Hanlon (2012: 4).
25 During the first months of the transition, the visibility of the military greatly increased as they were called upon to provide security in the streets, protect key infrastructures, and restore law and order following the defection of the police across the country. They also had to deal with the refugee crisis from neighbouring Libya and ensure public security during the elections of October 2011.

26 See David D. Kirkpatrick. "Chief of Tunisian army pledges his support for the revolution". *New York Times*. 25 January 2011. www.nytimes.com/2011/01/25/world/africa/25tunis.html?_r=0.
27 "Tunisia's army: Is it still up to the task?". *Tunisialive*. 7 June 2013. www.tunisia-live.net/2013/06/07/tunisias-army-is-it-still-up-to-the-task/.
28 Immediately after the Tunisian uprising, it emerged that these estimates were greatly inflated and that the real number of policemen in Tunisia was much lower, around 50,000. However, it has always been difficult to establish the exact size of the security apparatuses due to the lack of officially published statistics. See Hanlon (2012: 5–6) and Lutterbeck (2012: 18).
29 "To build trust, Tunisia's security forces must be reformed". *Tunisialive*. 17 August 2013. www.tunisia-live.net/2013/08/17/to-build-trust-tunisias-secuirty-forces-must-be-reformed/.
30 Ministère de la Justice. *Programme d'Action, 2012–2016*. www.e-justice.tn/fileadmin/fichiers_site_francais/actualites/Programme_d_action_2012-2016.pdf.

6 Forward looking

> Without a deep understanding of time, you will be lousy political scientists because time is the dimension in which ideas and institutions and beliefs evolve.
>
> from Douglass C. North. 1999. "In Anticipation of the Marriage of Political and Economic Theory". In *Competition and Cooperation: Conversations with Nobelists about Economics and Political Science*, edited by James E. Alt, Margaret Levi, and Elinor Ostrom, 316. New York: Russell Sage Foundation

Introduction – Egypt and Tunisia at the beginning of 2014: a new point of arrival

The Arab uprisings and the ensuing transition processes triggered new hopes and expectations that countries such as Egypt and Tunisia could attain democracy. Seen from the perspective of the forces that participated in the so-called Arab revolutions, the destruction of the old institutional order would leave space for new political systems able to bring dignity, rights, freedom, and justice, accompanied by socio-economic development. The extent to which these high expectations have been translated into actual political outcomes is the object of this chapter. To accomplish this goal, not only does it provide new empirical facts about the Arab transitions and their outcomes, but it also brings together the threads of this research and assesses the relation between the constitutive elements of institutional development discussed in detail in the previous chapters and political development. As such, this chapter looks at a specific point in time – the beginning of 2014 – as the 'new point of arrival' of the transition processes, while acknowledging the fact that the overall timeframe adopted in this work covers only a small fraction of much longer and complex processes whose end points lie well beyond the scope of this research. It thus takes a snapshot of the political development of Egypt and Tunisia at a particular moment in time, coherently with the middle range approach that underpins this book, and discusses it by letting empirical evidence establish a constant dialogue with theory.

A definite timeframe has to be circumscribed in order to have a clear standpoint from which to assess and compare the performance of the two case studies with regard to the factors of political development identified and discussed in Chapters 1 and 2, i.e., legitimacy, accountability, and responsiveness. More importantly, by treating the Arab transitions as closed-ended processes, it is possible to formulate reflections about the link existing between the processes of change and continuity at the institutional level discussed in detail in the previous chapters and some indicators of democracy derived from the literature. The first aim of this chapter is thus to tender an explanation of the different paths of political development and outcomes in the two countries in the short-to-medium term. Another aim of the chapter is to explicitly test the following hypothesis about the impact of temporal factors on transition processes: *the timing and sequencing of the turning points are fundamental factors in explaining different outcomes in the short-to-medium term political development of the countries undergoing transition processes.* Consistently with the theoretical approach outlined in Chapter 1, what I mean by 'turning points' is those crucial moments in the transition in which institutional development takes one direction instead of another as a result of the interplay between structural constraints and agency. Examples of such moments are the founding elections, the adoption of a new constitution, which is not always accompanied by the shaping of an agreement over the basic rules of the game, and other significant events linked to the development of specific institutions and to their mutual relations, e.g., the conflict between the president and the judiciary in Egypt. While there is no need to further stress the importance of institutional dynamics as determinants of political development, particularly in the case of states undergoing transition processes, the following pages are largely devoted to exploring the incidence of temporal factors over political development. In other words, the timing and sequencing of the turning points are essential factors to be taken into account in the analysis of transition processes and of their outcomes. This stems from the fact that, as demonstrated in the previous chapters, institutional development processes are imbued by and placed within temporal dynamics. On the one hand, the changes and continuities undergone by institutions during the transition do not follow a fixed script and the variations in terms of the solutions and their timing in the different cases are fundamental for differentiating among alternative political outcomes. On the other hand, transitions often represent self-reinforcing processes that are overwhelmingly influenced by the sequence of events. This is in line with one of the strongest theoretical points made by the historical institutional literature, namely the existence of path-dependence dynamics that make it possible to appreciate the interplay of distinct social processes. At the same time, this does not mean that certain political outcomes are necessarily locked in once the transition is set on a given path – thus allowing space for contingency. Nevertheless, it is fair to expect that the timing and sequencing of the events during the early years of the transitions will influence their long-term courses. All in all, the importance of time, timing, and sequencing will be tackled more precisely in the last section of this chapter, as these factors represent the lens through which the Egyptian and Tunisian transitions will be gauged from a comparative perspective.

By fulfilling these two aims, i.e., assessing the relations between the constitutive elements of institutional development and political development, and appraising the salience of temporal factors, the ultimate goal of this chapter, and of the whole research endeavour presented in this book, is to provide theoretically relevant insights into the factors and processes – both structural, temporal, and agency-related – that have shaped the Arab transition processes. This means providing an answer to the overarching question that has guided this research, namely what factors have most significantly influenced the transition processes in the Arab countries. This chapter is structured as follows. The first part compares and contrasts the political outcomes in Egypt and Tunisia by focusing on the short-to-medium term timeframe. This part moves from the concept of democratic installation already introduced in Chapter 1 and assesses the extent to which it can be argued that the two countries are more democratic, i.e., the state institutions are more legitimate, more accountable, and more responsive, at the beginning of 2014 than at the time when the transitions started. The second part goes back and forth between empirical data and theory to demonstrate the crucial importance of inclusive institutions for the attainment of democracy. Finally, the concluding section thoroughly discusses the role of temporal factors in shaping the quality of institutions.

Explaining the different short-term outcomes of the Arab transitions

Democratic installation

As stated above, this final chapter looks at the Arab transitions as closed-ended processes, focusing in particular on the impact of the institutional changes and continuities assessed in the previous pages on the broader political development of Egypt and Tunisia in the short-to-medium term. The literature on democratic installation provides a useful point of departure for assessing the extent to which the two countries have successfully accomplished their 'transition to democracy' and what kind of influence factors related to institutional development have had on this process in the period between 2011 and the beginning of 2014 (Di Palma 1990; Huntington 1991). Before delving into the issue of democratic attainment and the indicators that have been used to 'measure it', it is worth recalling the difference between 'transition' and 'installation', not so much from the point of view of the temporal, chronological order, but rather in light of these concepts' different conceptual meanings.

While the concept of transition refers to, and has been used in this work to mean, the movement from an authoritarian regime to an unspecified something else entailing the restructuring or confirmation of the country's institutional framework, the meaning of installation coincides with the fulfilment of a number of conditions for the successful transition to democracy, understood as the final point of arrival. While, on the one hand, transition entails a lot of uncertainty with regard both to the process itself, as this is associated with a great number of false-starts, steps backward, or paralyses, and to its 'final outcome'; on the other hand, installation does not lend itself to uncertainties or ambiguities in that the concept clearly specifies what the conditions for the attainment of democracy are. As already specified in Chapter 1, these two processes or phases are distinct but closely linked to one another. As much as institutional uncertainty tends to characterise the transition phase, it is not possible to talk about democratic installation without a minimum degree of certainty about the new institutional framework and a modicum of agreement among the actors. During installation, particular attention is in fact devoted to the role of actors and their actions in crafting the agreements that will regulate their mutual interaction within the boundaries created by the (new) institutional framework. Linking transition to installation, the institutional indeterminacy that characterises the former in terms of the core procedures that are necessary for producing democracy may result in the postponement of the latter.

Introducing a clear standard of what is actually necessary for a completed transition to democracy makes it easier to compare Egypt and Tunisia in their political development trajectories. In simple terms, the transition to democracy can be said to be complete when the first signs of democracy becoming 'the only game in town' are evident (Di Palma 1990; Valenzuela 1992). This notion entails both procedural and substantive elements. Regarding the first set of factors, it is appropriate to map out the criteria that establish how far any given country has gone towards completing its transition to democracy successfully, i.e., the instauration of a democratic polity, as follows. First, at least a minimum level of agreement and consensus needs to be reached among the actors regarding the political procedures that are necessary to ensure the creation of an elected government. Second, and linked to the first, political competition among the actors in the framework of a free and popular vote is needed to bring about the government. Third and finally, the elected government has to enjoy de facto powers and has to be able to exercise them without interference from other bodies. These conditions enshrine the factors that are both necessary and sufficient to be able to use the word 'democratic' from a purely procedural perspective. Ultimately, democracy means the creation of an elected government on the basis of an agreement among political actors, as well as its ability to exercise its authority within certain limits defined by the law and without interference from other forms of power.

The emphasis on the need to reach an agreement on the specific institutional arrangement required to produce a democratic government is key to my understanding of 'democratic installation' and shifts our attention to issues concerning decision-making, conflict, and consensus among the actors. In line with this reasoning, other authors argue that democracy is about '[t]he development of a pattern, and ultimately a culture, of moderation, accommodation, cooperation, and bargaining among political elites' (Diamond 1999: 166; Rustow 1970). It is therefore important to look at those factors that promote the development of such a culture. As much as a 'democratic culture' facilitates the emergence of a sound institutional framework thanks to consensus and bargaining, it is directly and ultimately shaped by the institutional development process undergone during the transition. This is why it is so important to look at the institutions, their changes, and their continuities to assess the level of democratic installation reached by any given country. Most of these institutional factors concern constitutional arrangements, as well as political and administrative institutions, such as political parties, bureaucracies, the judiciary, and the coercive apparatus that need to be transparent, independent, and effective. Complementing the analysis of institutional changes and continuities in the Arab transitions carried out in the previous chapters, and in the spirit of illuminating the conditions for producing a democratic government, it is argued that constitutionalism is a fundamental factor and, as such, it is discussed at greater length later in this chapter. Not only should the process of writing a constitution be a relatively wide-ranging exercise to forge inclusion and consensus going far beyond majoritarianism, but it most importantly entails a commitment to self-binding procedures of governance and a clear hierarchy of laws.

Nevertheless, procedural aspects alone are not sufficient to speak of a successfully completed transition to democracy. A host of substantive 'democratic qualities' need to be present as well. This corresponds to the definition of democracy as the final outcome of transition processes as it is set out in this chapter. Recalling the theoretical insights developed in Chapter 1, three factors are underscored there, namely legitimacy, accountability, and responsiveness. Although these three factors are usually discussed in the literature on democratisation as procedural qualities of democracy, they possess a rather strong substance-related content in that they are tightly related to the citizens' enjoyment of certain rights (Morlino 2011). Legitimacy is indeed a reflexive quality linked to the people's perception of the government's ability to guarantee their enjoyment of basic rights and liberties, in particular civil rights such as freedom of expression and of association. The respect of these basic rights, which has to be sanctioned first of all by the constitution and other legislative texts, is a fundamental factor shaping the relationship between the rulers and the ruled and is the result of the actions and reactions of a number of bodies and institutions, among which the judiciary and the security apparatuses play an important role. Accountability is linked to the enjoyment of political rights, with a special emphasis on participation in the (democratic) processes that allow people to select their representatives and to hold them accountable through subsequent electoral rounds. In addition to being guaranteed by the law, the possibility to express one's political preferences has to be ensured and accompanied by a number of other rights, such as the respect of the rule of law and, on the more practical side, the right to campaign. Finally, responsiveness captures the distance between the rulers' policies and the citizens' needs and preferences. As in the case of legitimacy, this quality of democracy is expressed by the people's perception with regard to the state authorities' ability to answer their needs in terms of material well-being, employment, and access to basic services. Responsiveness is thus strictly related to the enjoyment of basic social rights.

The direct reference to civil, political, and social rights further gives substance to the meaning of the qualities of democracy that are used here to assess the success of a democratic transition process. These qualities, i.e., legitimacy, accountability, and responsiveness, are indeed the same factors that were missing or severely undermined before 2011, thus triggering the outbreak of the Arab uprisings. By focusing on legitimacy, accountability, and responsiveness, the assessment of the Arab uprisings and of transition processes thus comes full circle. There is a further political and intellectual advantage to examining substantive factors as the basis of democratic governance. When looking disproportionately at procedural factors, one runs the risk of overestimating the significance of these factors and considering them as sufficient conditions of democracy, while in reality they are at best necessary conditions. This is, for example, the case of those analyses that attribute too central a role to elections and other procedural aspects as a basis for classifying a regime as democratic or non-democratic. As aptly illuminated by the literature on electoral authoritarianism, one has to beware of the manifold forms the 'electoralist fallacy' may assume (Schedler 2006; Brownlee 2007).

Comparing the transition outcomes

Writing in August 2011, Nathan Brown underscored the striking common elements in the transition processes in Egypt and Tunisia, highlighting the following features:

> The basic political structures of the state have remained intact despite political upheaval; the transition process is fairly rapid; the political scene is rapidly becoming populated with a wide variety of political forces; those forces have gravitated between a consensual approach and sharp competition; a political gulf between Islamist and non-Islamist forces has emerged; and the process, for all its problems and occasional bouts of violence, has remained relatively peaceful.
>
> (Brown 2011c: 5)

At the beginning of 2014, instead, it seemed that most (if not all) of these common features had simply disappeared and the two countries were projected on two completely different, if not outright opposing, paths. One can thus venture to answer the following question: is the Egyptian regime of early 2014 mainly a transformed – updated – version of that of 2010, or has the old regime really collapsed in the course of a revolutionary process, giving rise to a new one bearing no resemblance to the previous system? The same question can be asked for Tunisia. To answer this question from a comparative perspective, one needs to refer to legitimacy, accountability, and responsiveness to assess political development in the short-to-medium term. In the Egyptian case, the period between 2011 and the beginning of 2014 has seen the country plunge further into uncertainty and chaos, which is reflected in the people's perceptions of the authorities' ability to cater for their basic needs and to respect their rights. The obsession with elections and popular consultations, through which the constantly reshuffling leadership has sought to obtain popular endorsement, often accompanied by a distorted reference to the goals and expectations of the January 2011 'revolution', has failed to provide a basis for accountability. Quite to the contrary, and in addition to the profound impact of elections on the heightening social and political polarisation discussed in Chapter 4, there has been a steady erosion of the authorities' accountability, particularly in their resort to referenda as an instrument for sanctioning a particular point of view. This trend manifested itself to its full capacity in the aftermath of the military coup, which took place in July 2013 and was accompanied by a harsh wave of political repression, and in the calculated, full-bore, and state-led mobilisation campaign against any form of dissent and opposition in the run-up to the constitutional referendum of January 2014. Not only has the military coup established the precedent that it can step in if it does not approve of the direction that politics is taking, but it has also strongly compromised civilian oversight over the coercive apparatus. The military and the other security services – a vast empire of monitoring, policing, and intelligence services – have been made less accountable and more powerful, giving these politicised institutions even greater license to tailor the rules of the game to their political preferences and to act with impunity against anybody who crosses the red lines they themselves have established. In addition, the resort to repressive and dictatorial practices by the coercive apparatus represents a blow to the legitimacy of the (self-appointed) state authorities, which can be said to have established a renewed version of the military-led authoritarian regime in place until early 2011. A number of similarities notwithstanding, it appears that the coercive apparatus plays a much more significant political role at the beginning of 2014 than three years earlier. The resort to the well-known mechanisms of arrest and persecution of political opponents, the invalidation of basic freedoms and rights in the name of national security, and the 'war on terror' may sound legitimate for some strata of the population, but they are in reality against some of the most basic norms for the protection of such rights that can be found in the new constitution. This raises the risk of cyclical instability in the country, even though it should be stressed that the level of violence directed by the Muslim Brotherhood's sympathisers at their opponents during the summer 2013 could have been much worse had they not effectively resorted to self-restraint (Interviewee 37).

The fact that virtually anyone who dissents from the current regime is at risk is connected to a second by-product of the flawed institutional development process described in the previous chapters. It concerns the lack of predictability through stable, legitimate rules. Democratic politics rests upon the guarantee that all sides understand and agree on the rules of the game, as well as on the possibility of having them enforced on everyone. Without such predictability, which is largely the result of the deplorable state of the judiciary in Egypt, i.e., its lack of competence and effectiveness, citizens' rights are under constant risk of being obliterated in the name of other institutional interests. The judiciary, in particular, is likely to remain the institution most to blame for the lack of respect of basic civil and political rights in Egypt due to its overwhelming interest in protecting its own prerogatives, often in a vindictive way, after having escaped the attempted assault on its independence by President Morsi in 2013. To complete this picture, it goes without saying that the responsiveness of the Egyptian state authorities to the needs of the population has been extremely low in the period between 2011 and the beginning of 2014. Whether out of neglect and sheer lack of competence resulting in the failure to enforce coherent policies, as in the case of the Islamist leadership between 2012 and 2013, or as a result of ideological short-sightedness as far as the interim authorities – mainly composed of technocrats – are concerned, it is a fact that the socio-economic grievances of the Egyptian population have largely remained unaddressed. While some of the problems are chronic, such as pollution, chaos in the streets, youth unemployment, and housing issues, others have undergone a marked deterioration. This is the case, for example, of the already recalled lack of security and the rise in crime, as well as the plummeting of tourism with huge repercussions on the balance of payments. The mismatch between the authorities' policies and actions and the people's concrete needs and high expectations has widened between 2011 and 2013. Overall, it can be argued that Egypt appeared to be teetering on the edge of authoritarian instability at the beginning of 2014, while the pathologies of uncertainty, unaccountability, and unresponsiveness continued to afflict the country's politics. This is directly related to the Balkanisation of the state discussed in Chapter 5 and to the persistence of old or seemingly restructured institutions and institutional logics. All in all, it appears that re-fashioned competitive authoritarianism under strong military tutelage has been the mid-term outcome of the Egyptian uprising.

Tunisia is often described as the sole bright spot in the Arab region's transitions towards greater democracy. In fact, two out of the three dimensions of political development displayed a more positive outlook in the case of Tunisia compared to Egypt at the beginning of 2014. In particular, one of the main goals of the Tunisian transition has been to preserve the legitimacy of the process, something the Islamist party *Ennahda* and all the other institutional actors have strictly complied with throughout the transition. Beyond all the shortcomings stemming from major substantial and procedural disagreements, the Tunisian authorities have been able to steer the transition process in the direction of ever greater legitimacy and accountability (Murphy 2011). Three years after Ben Ali's departure, not only has this process ended by endowing the small North African country with a constitutional text that represents a clear break with the past, but the interim authorities have also succeeded in creating a carefully crafted series of institutions that provide the backbone for a more inclusive, transparent, and democratic polity in which basic rights and freedoms are respected. In this light, it can be argued that the sequence of events that have taken place in Tunisia represented a true revolution and that the country has accomplished all the steps for democratic installation, including reaching a consensus on the political procedures for an interim government and subsequently an elected one, and enshrining in the constitution clear guarantees for the protection of the executive, legislative, and judicial powers from the interference of other institutions. The apolitical and marginal role of the military amounts to one of such guarantees.

This is in stark contrast to the Egyptian situation, in which Mubarak's fall did not in itself represent a revolution as the fundamental framework of the state, based on the officers' republic created in 1952, has remained in place. By attacking the headquarters of Mubarak's National Democratic Party (NDP) in 2011, the Egyptian demonstrators destroyed the regime's façade and not its core. The military had been the sole source of political power in Egypt since 1952 (Roberts 2013). Only under Mubarak was the higher military apparatus sidelined from the day-to-day control of government. This, however, did not mean that it was displaced by an alternative source of power. By the beginning of 2014, one can say that the military had reclaimed and reasserted its historical political primacy over the country's institutional framework. Quite to the contrary, the significant differences in the military's role notwithstanding, the abolition of the *Rassemblement Constitutionnel Démocratique* (RCD) has actually meant the fall of the central source of power and principal instrument by which the state exercised its hegemony over Tunisian society. The RCD was a genuine ruling party, or a *parti-état*. Its dislodging has been accompanied by uncertainty and the need to rebuild the link between the state and society on new bases, but no alternative power centres have tried to control the transition process in Tunisia.

Debating inclusiveness

Procedural and substantive views

The comparison of Egypt and Tunisia at the beginning of 2014 showed that political development followed different paths in the two cases. I now turn to explaining the variance observed by introducing the concept of inclusiveness. The ways in which the various versions of the constitution have been drafted, scrapped, and revised have laid the ground for the core institutional and political problems besetting Egypt at the beginning of 2014. The main problem of the Egyptian transition has been the lack of consensus among the elites. Deep, polarising political divisions have been exacerbated by the actors' tendency to tighten their positions instead of loosening them in search for common ground. The events following the military coup in July 2013 and the level of brutal and even de-humanising propaganda that has been turned against the Muslim Brotherhood could not illustrate this situation better. In the previous years of the transition, the Islamist party had adopted a similar behaviour, although arguably not anywhere near as violent, towards its political opponents. Mutual suspicion, coupled with the Muslim Brotherhood's inability or unwillingness to share power and downplay its purely majoritarian understanding of government prerogatives, is the most significant reason for the Muslim Brotherhood's failure to be accepted by the other political actors, i.e., the civic political forces and groups, and by the existing institutional structure – the military and the judiciary. During 2012–2013, the Islamist president and the Muslim Brotherhood's leadership did not use the one-year window of opportunity effectively to consolidate their power by reinforcing the 'alliance' with the military and by reaching out to those political and social forces that had participated in the uprising but had then not been able to channel their instances towards meaningful political action. The Islamist government's failure to take into account and mediate between the interests of the state and those of other resourceful veto powers, such as the military and the judiciary, and to alleviate the population's socio-economic grievances, as well as the sense of isolation of the civic forces in particular, was responsible for the collapse of the first experiment of Islamist politics in the country that has always represented a model for the Arab world. This is very well illustrated by the constitution-making process. Instead of searching for a broad agreement and thus forging a consensus around the 2012 constitution, the Muslim Brotherhood's leadership engaged in a power grab and narrow, majoritarian domination, eventually forcing the document through without the consent of significant portions of the state and society. Put differently, the Islamist government was not able to provide enough guarantees to those who were protected by the previous authoritarian regime (and to the rest of society) through the crafting of inclusive institutions, a concept that is explored at greater length later in this chapter.

With regard to inclusion and consensus building, the Tunisian experience has been remarkably different from the Egyptian one. Albeit still fragile and far from democratic consolidation, the Tunisian transition appeared to be set on the course of incremental progress towards democracy. At the beginning of 2014, Tunisia marked its successful democratic installation by passing a new constitution that has been described as a progressive document and a milestone for the country. This long-awaited document was the result of a participatory process and of the consensus reached among a broad majority of political actors in the midst of an intense political struggle, at times fraught with violence.[1] A protracted period of confidence building helped in the negotiation of a number of pacts and agreements that have provided some guarantees for the respect of the rules of the democratic game. The basic content of these pacts and agreements corresponds to the very core meaning of democratic practice, specifically an implicit quid pro quo among contending groups, according to which each political party or group agrees to protect the others' rights in exchange for recognition of its entitlement to govern should it win an election. Instrumental in hammering out these agreements was the role played by the Islamist party, *Ennahda*, which was able to use its position of pre-eminence to create a situation conducive to consensus by accepting to compromise on a number of issues. As described in Chapter 3, the party compromised, for example, on the form of government in favour of a semi-presidential system and accepted to give up on the reference to *Sharia* in the final text of the constitution. On the one hand, this behaviour facilitated reaching an agreement with the other political forces on the substance and the procedures for passing the new constitution and, on the other, it led to the party's own moderation. The moderation hypothesis is consistent with the behaviour of other (more radical) Islamist movements that have found themselves in conditions similar to those of Tunisia (Schwedler 2007; Cavatorta and Merone 2013). This hypothesis is formalised in the 'moderation through inclusion' nexus, whose relevance is stressed here in the Tunisian case although it goes beyond the scope of this research. Critical in this respect is to reflect on the conditions that favour inclusion and acceptance into the existing institutional structures and the boundaries of the political discourse. First, for veritable inclusion to take place, institutions need to be fully inclusive. This may sound like a tautological argument, but in reality the inclusive character of the institutions is simply a necessary but not sufficient condition for inclusion to lead to moderation. Second, for actors to undergo moderation through inclusion, they must be prepared to give something up and to subject themselves to constraints. The example of the *Sharia* in the Tunisian case is a very telling one.

From the discussion of the Egyptian and Tunisian cases, it is apparent that, while it is natural to expect mutual distrust and animosity under circumstances of intense uncertainty, there are a number of factors that can facilitate the emergence of understandings and ultimately the accumulation of trust. In addition to the presence of a political culture of tolerance, restraint, and respect for democratic norms, the most important factor explaining the success of democratic installation, and hence the diverging Egyptian and Tunisian paths, is the quality of institutions. The quality of institutions involves an array of factors broadly coinciding with the constitutive elements of institutional development discussed in the previous chapters. It is indeed important to look at institutional development as the mechanism that crafts varying degrees of inclusive institutions. In this framework, both substantive and procedural issues need to be addressed with a view to developing a comprehensive, inclusive institutional framework. The most important substantive issues that belong to the category of institutional quality include horizontal accountability and the respect of the rule of law; vertical distribution of power including the ways in which electoral preferences are turned into power positions; devolution of power and autonomy from the central to the local government; and constitutional design at large with an emphasis on clarity and coherence of the constitutional text.

Procedurally, the following are some guiding questions for assessing the constitution-making process in particular: Should constitutions be drafted by elected, broadly representative constituent assemblies or by appointed, highly specialised bodies? Should the transitional parliament have the dual task of drafting and legislating in the interim period? How large should the drafting body be and of what sort of people should it be composed of (politicians, legal experts, civil society activists)? What parts of the drafting and bargaining are hammered out better in private settings and what deliberations are more appropriately held in public? What level of engagement and participation by the people in the drafting process should be foreseen? Should the population be allowed time and scope to revise the draft after it has been completed, providing it with an opportunity for something other than a yes-or-no vote? Through what kind of mechanisms? What is the added value of having a list of basic principles negotiated and approved before the actual text is drafted? What should the role of existing organised political forces be? How should minority groups be given a voice in a majoritarian process? What kind of ratification rules should there be for approving the final document?

Designing the 'most appropriate' political institutions is a tricky business. In fact, there is no 'constitutional formula' that is right for all national and historical situations, as its constitutive factors – the form of government, the provisions about elections, the role and power of the military, and the articulation of the judiciary – necessarily need to fit each country's needs and circumstances. Nevertheless, the different institutional trajectories highlighted in the two cases analysed in this book broadly begin from similar, or at least comparable, starting points, namely the overconcentration of authority in the hands of the executive, one of the key political complaints of the uprisings in both Egypt and Tunisia. More specifically, the need to change the state institutions and to make them more legitimate, accountable, and responsive originated from a feeling that power was centralised and unaccountable, that decision-making was monopolised by a small circle around the president, and that the dominant political and economic elites had little concern for public well-being, were completely disconnected from public opinion, and could rule without any meaningful oversight from anybody. This situation was made even worse by the weakness of parliaments, the unenforceability of human rights protection, and, more broadly, the absence of the rule of law.

When assessing the point of arrival of the constitution-making processes in Egypt and Tunisia one is struck by the high degree of variation displayed by the two cases presented in Chapters 3 and 5. One point stands out clearly, namely the extent to which the content and structure of the new constitutions distance themselves from the previous texts. Both the 2012 and the 2014 Egyptian constitutions are in strong continuity with previous experiences of constitution making. They resemble the 1971 text to a surprising degree, with many provisions from the previous constitution maintained. Many had hoped for a more radical shift, given that a popular uprising had taken place. Instead, the majority of the basic principles have only been modified slightly. In practice, however, even minor changes can have a major impact on the way in which legal principles are interpreted and applied. Other factors therefore come into play; it matters, for example, that both the 2012 and the 2014 constitutions were drafted in a hasty manner – not more than six months as far as the 2012 constitution is concerned – which is exceedingly short in comparison to other countries, and that many changes were introduced in the last few hours before the process was completed. Inversely, constitution making in the Tunisian case started with a blank page as the 1959 constitution was initially set aside and then totally overhauled during the transition.

Moving from this initial general assessment and taking into account that the focus of this research is on dynamic issues, it is important to consider that the substance of institutions is subject to change over time. When addressing institutional development, one needs to be aware of a range of fundamental concerns. I will discuss two of them in particular, namely a) the implications of widespread unanticipated consequences on institutional development, and b) the capacity of learning processes to generate institutional development. First, specific institutional arrangements tend to have multiple effects, some of which cannot be anticipated by the actors engaged in the transition process. This argument casts doubt on the validity of the 'logic of appropriateness' behaviour that assumes that institutional designers are fully aware of the outcomes of their actions. This is indeed not the case, due to a series of limitations, including temporal limitations. The question of the actors' time horizons constitutes a central issue in assessing institutional development processes. When political decision-makers, one of the most important categories within the elites, have short time horizons, then long-term institutional outcomes can be seen more as by-products than as the goals of the institutional designers (Pierson 2004: 112–115). The long delays that often divide short-term intentions and preferences from the actual outcomes, which manifest themselves in the long run, are particularly salient during periods of transition, in which crucial new rules are put in place in contexts of general de-institutionalisation and overall uncertainty and volatility (Elster, Offe, and Preuss 1998). This heightens the effects of unintended consequences. Indeed, as argued by Pierson, 'unintended consequences may be particularly likely in the domain of institutional design, precisely because it typically involves bargained outcomes among competing interests in contexts where multiple issues are simultaneously at stake' (Pierson 2004: 117). Furthermore, it is appropriate to expect that changes at the level of formal institutions take place quicker than those at the level of informal institutions and logics, which are often slow-moving processes. The presence of unanticipated institutional effects in transition processes is a difficult challenge for social scientists, as much as the unintended consequences of the authoritarian resilience measures adopted by the Arab regimes until 2011 confused some observers and analysts and led to their failure to anticipate the uprisings.

At this point, the question arises if the actors can anticipate such unintended institutional effects, acknowledging that institutional development is a process that unfolds over time, and thus factor them in while taking their initial actions. This second concern in addressing institutional development involves the issue of learning and the extent to which actors are able to take the necessary corrective steps to design institutions that are more in line with their preferences both in the short and in the long-term. In Chapter 2, two symmetrical learning processes, the former facilitating the rise and spread of the uprisings from one country to another, and the latter ensuring the resilience of authoritarian regimes through repression, elite co-optation, or ideology manipulation, have been discussed (Heydemann and Leenders 2011). Turning to institutional development it seems that learning does not represent a significant reliable tool to close the gap between intensions and preferences, on the one hand, and outcomes, on the other (North 1990). In addition to this, the timeframe adopted (2011 to the beginning of 2014) in this book does not make it possible to address this issue properly.

Nevertheless, the important thing to point out is that the essential ingredient is to construct an inclusive and participatory process to draft the new constitution and thus ensure that the new institutional architecture makes sense and represents as broad a consensus as possible in society. In other words, what could steer the political development of a country undergoing transition in one direction instead of another in the short-to-medium term is the possibility of crafting an inclusive political pact. Against this backdrop and going back to our case studies, it is appropriate to argue that, from the beginning, there seemed to be a fundamental difference in the two constitution-making processes. Three criteria stand out clearly in this regard. The first one is whether there was a shared and inclusive vision to constitution making preceding the actual drafting of the text. In Tunisia, an effort was made to develop a consensual and inclusive approach to constitution making. The formation of the 'Supreme Organisation to Realise the Goals of the Revolution, Political Reform and Democratic Transition' (SORGR) immediately after Ben Ali's ouster allowed many significant political players, even some long excluded from political life, to have a say in the transition. In a sense, the fact that the Tunisian leadership was able to initiate an open and broadly participatory process even in the absence of a clearly defined set of rules helped provide the whole constitution-making process with sufficient legitimacy to overcome conflicts and disagreements. In Egypt, by contrast, the Supreme Council of the Armed Forces (SCAF) failed to form a similar body, simply carrying out consultations in either ritualistic or opaque manners, as well as taking decisions that were outside of its authority. This initial failure to craft an inclusive constitution-making process had serious costs, especially as controversies mounted and various constituencies felt excluded and without any means other than demonstrations to make their voices heard.

A second difference between Egypt and Tunisia with respect to the quality of institutions is the nature of the constitution-drafting body. In Tunisia, that the body was directly elected and tasked with exercising full legislative as well as drafting functions explains the fact that its members were naturally inclined to reach out to their constituencies and take their views into account. While this was an element of weakness or at least disturbance in the early stages of the transition process, its advantage became apparent once the constitutional text was approved. It has helped foster consensus and reinforce the view that the new Tunisian constitution is everyone's constitution. In Egypt, the fact that the body was smaller, more specialised, and not directly selected by the people clarifies why its members had less inclination to reach out to the people during the constitution-making process. Only limited consultations took place between the constituent assemblies (in their plural form) and the majority of the population throughout the different constitution-making stages.

Third and finally, it is important to consider the interplay between the constitution-making and the electoral processes, as the sequence of these steps tends to have an important effect on the short-to-medium term political development of a country in transition. Anticipating what will be discussed at greater length in the next section, i.e., the importance of temporal factors in institutional development processes, it can be argued that Egypt and Tunisia rushed into writing the new constitutions, albeit to different degrees and with even more incomparable end results. This is not to say that the constitution-making process should have been delayed, but it should have been sequenced better with the other steps in the transition, particularly the electoral process. The case of Egypt is quite telling in this respect in light of the strong political polarisation that has characterised the transition. According to the constitutional amendments approved in the national referendum of March 2011, the new constitu was to be drafted by a 100-member constituent assembly selected by the two houses of the parliament, upon invitation of the president. This implied that parliamentary and presidential elections should have occurred before the drafting of the new constitution. However, article 60 of the constitutional declaration of 30 March 2011 changed the wording of the provision as it stood in the referendum, substituting 'Supreme Council of the Armed Forces' for 'president'. Not only did the change in wording contradict the framework approved by voters, but it also appeared to set in motion an extremely rushed constitution-making process. Egypt's Minister of Parliamentary Affairs, Mohamed Attiya, confirmed in January 2012 that the presidential election would take place only after the new constitution was drafted and approved in a national referendum, despite having moved the presidential election forward to June 2012.[2] This scenario provided a very short window for drafting the new constitution – perhaps as little as two months – and placed the SCAF in a strong position to exert formal and informal pressure on the shape of the new text. Furthermore, the prospect of an accelerated timeline increased the friction between the Muslim Brotherhood's Freedom and Justice Party (FJP) and most other political forces. Seeing its golden opportunity to shape the new constitution, the Muslim Brotherhood insisted that there should be no deviation from the wording of the constitutional declaration of March 2011, leaving the civic forces increasingly convinced of a backroom deal between the SCAF and the FJP, and heightening mutual distrust. As demonstrated in Chapter 3, the timing and sequencing of the constitution-making process, on the one hand, and of the presidential elections, on the other, was changed again in spring 2012 due to the difficulties and delays in nominating the second constituent assembly and the increasingly stark confrontation between the Muslim Brotherhood and the judiciary. While the ramifications of this deeply flawed sequencing of transition steps need not be further emphasised, it is clear that this particular course of action was influenced by some choices made at the very beginning of the transition, thus implying a path-dependence dynamic.

In the Tunisian case, the way in which the transition was engineered had the unintended beneficial consequence of allowing enough time for consensus building among the actors, which contributed to easing their mutual mistrust and favouring the negotiation of inclusive institutions. This was made possible by building on the legitimacy of the elections for the National Constituent Assembly (NCA). Nevertheless, one of the downsides of this approach was that over the summer of 2013, while Egypt was going through the initial phase of the restoration of the old institutional order, the main Tunisian players seemed to have lost sight of the broader roadmap of the transition and were drawn into a zero-sum game over identity and values in the constitutional bargaining. This risked jeopardising the whole transition process, but eventually led to the emergence of a legitimate and accountable framework of consensus, of which the constitution represents the focal point.

In conclusion, it appears from the theoretical background and the empirical insights presented above that developing inclusive institutions, both from the substantive and procedural points of view, is a very important condition for political development. A similar argument has been thoroughly and convincingly explored in Acemoglu and Robinson's *Why Nations Fail* (2012). The authors have proposed a simple theory that, in their view, can be used to explain the main features of economic and political development in various areas of the world and across different times. This theory argues that a country's level of prosperity rests upon political foundations. More specifically, the explanation points to the distinction between 'inclusive' and 'extractive' political institutions as a way of accounting for different paths of political and economic development. While the scope of the argument proposed by Acemoglu and Robinson is far wider than the one made in this book, as they are primarily concerned with economic development and issues of poverty and prosperity, the gist of it is very similar. When adopting a closed-ended definition of transition, the quality of institutions that see the light as a result of these processes, often entailing both changes and continuities, is strongly correlated to political development and democracy. By 'quality of institutions', as it should be clear by now, I mean both procedural and substantive inclusiveness in the institutional development informing the distribution and administration of power. In political science, the concept of inclusion is linked to that of participation and ultimately to the possibility for the citizens of a given state to enjoy civic, political, and social rights, i.e., full citizenship. Alternatively, if a set of institutions fail to tick the box of inclusiveness, it is because they enable the elites to serve their own interests, which tend to collide with or prevail over those of the mass of the population. This situation of overwhelmingly extractive institutions is likely to foster illegitimacy, unaccountability, and unresponsiveness. All in all, the institutional framework of a given country, its trajectory of development within historical processes, and its inclusiveness, both substantively and procedurally, provide incentives that explain that country's political development. In the presence of cases that share other important geographical, temporal, socio-economic, cultural, and religious variables, the inclusive vs. extractive feature of an institution makes it possible to differentiate among different political development trajectories in the short-to-medium term.

One of the points that was emphasised in the critical reviews of *Why Nations Fail* was the allegedly overly deterministic approach to institutional development espoused by the book. They claimed that these institutions, be they inclusive or extractive, are treated in the book as hardly changeable. In other words, path-dependence processes of institutional formation and development dominate. While this book has not adopted such an overly deterministic approach due to the important role played by agency and contingency in influencing institutional development, it is still true that path-dependence dynamics at multiple levels have to be duly accounted for in assessing political development, as has been demonstrated in the empirically grounded analysis presented in the previous chapters. To grasp these dynamics the temporal dimension and its impact on the development of inclusive institutions is key. Time, timing, and sequencing should indeed be treated as a third key factor, next to structure and agency, in explaining the Arab transitions and their political outcomes in the short-to-medium term.

Why time matters

The previous section has argued that inclusive institutions are important for legitimacy, accountability, and responsiveness. The correlation established between the quality of institutions and political development opens the way for further investigation of the conditions that facilitate the creation of inclusive institutions. This means going back to the issue of institutional development – the central theme of this book – in keeping with the dynamic approach to institutions discussed at some length in Chapter 1. By summarising the empirical analysis as much as possible, it can be argued that Egypt presents some features of a transition with strong continuities with the past and ultimately the restoration of some elements of the 'deep state', while the Tunisian case resembles a 'pacted transition'. How can such institutional differences be explained given the relatively comparable situations in terms of the main drivers of the transition in the two countries? The empirical analysis carried out in the previous chapters has rightly underlined the decisive importance of structural factors, including the legacy of the previous institutional architecture, and agency. However, these are not the only forces driving institutional development, although they certainly do account to a large extent for the quality of institutions, which in turn influences the short-to-medium term political development of a given country. Another important set of context variables is represented by temporal factors: time, timing, and sequencing.

According to the historical institutional approach that permeates this book, temporal factors provide considerable leverage in explaining institutional development. More than time in itself, i.e., the fact that the transition process or some segments of it span a longer or shorter timeframe, what matters is timing and sequencing (Bartolini 1993; Pierson 2004). Technically, the fact that the new Egyptian constitution was brought out quicker than the Tunisian one is not enough to call these types of explanations temporally sensitive analyses. One has to go beyond the typically Braudelian focus on the *longue durée* and consider two additional factors constituting the temporal dimension, i.e., timing and sequencing. To say that timing matters implies linking together quite separate social processes, i.e., considering the impact of something *relative to something else*. The example of the interplay between the constitution-making process and the elections sheds light on the powerful explicative power of timing when referring to two or more processes that are distinct but not disconnected. With regard to sequencing, the concept of path-dependence is based on the assumption that the order of events or processes is likely to have a crucial impact on outcomes because the event or process that occurs first will trigger positive feedback, thus consolidating particular arrangements established at a turning point/critical juncture. Going back to the example of the constitution-making process and the elections, it makes sense to argue that the relative sequence of these two important processes shapes the transition because positive feedback from one may decisively affect the other when it occurs later. As pointed out by Mahoney and Reuschemeyer (2003), an event taking place at a particular point in time may trigger a chain of causally linked events that, once set in motion, occurs independently of the event or process that initially triggered it. Moving from this, it is clear that different temporal orderings of the same events or processes are likely to produce different outcomes. This, however, does not amount to a claim about perpetual self-reinforcement, i.e., the idea that, once selected, a particular path will persist indefinitely. Quite to the contrary, any particular path, once initiated, sets the stage for a particular kind of reaction in some other direction. The final outcome – in our case, the final quality of the institutions – results from a host of pull and push factors connected to the interplay between structure, i.e., the existing institutional framework and other elements of the social context, and agency, i.e., the actors' preferred outcomes and strategies, and contingency, unfolding through time. Unsurprisingly, when and in what sequence an event or process takes place matters a great deal, as does how the institutionalisation process interacts with more fluid elements of the broader socio-economic context (Jervis 2000).

The critical importance of timing and sequencing is best captured when one compares the impact of temporal factors on different transition processes. Only through synchronic comparison of the different transition experiences at different points in time is it possible to substantiate the claim that events at a turning point induce path-dependence dynamics, which ultimately lead to strikingly divergent outcomes, even when the starting points were initially similar. The empirical evidence presented in Chapters 3 to 5 demonstrates that only an accurate reconstruction of timing and sequencing in comparative perspective can gauge the possible sources of institutional development, including those sources of resilience that are likely to accumulate with the passage of time. A further point concerns the possibility of calling into question the idea of 'clustering' in institutional outcomes. Synchronic comparison of the Arab transition processes at different points in time shows that there is much that escapes the concept of temporal and functional clustering, i.e., the idea that given similar initial conditions and given the actors' inherent tendency to adopt optional institutions – a point that is made particularly by rational choice accounts – there is then the tendency to produce similar institutions. This idea, which is not backed by the empirical evidence collected on the Arab transitions, disregards other fundamental factors that pertain to the social context.

Notes

1 "After two years of compromises, Assembly celebrates new Constitution". *Tunisialive*. 27 January 2014. www.tunisia-live.net/2014/01/27/after-two-years-of-compromises-assembly-celebrates-new-constitution/.
2 "Confusion overshadows decision to elect Egypt's President before Constitution". *Ahramonline*. 3 January 2012. http://english.ahram.org.eg/News/30851.aspx.

Conclusions

The uprisings of 2011 and the ensuing transition processes have triggered an unprecedented amount of interest in the political dynamics of the Arab world among scholars and policy-makers alike. These events and processes were welcomed as a novelty in the landscape of the region, and expectations, fears, enthusiasm, and disillusionment were among the most heightened feelings they gave rise to. I was one of those people who looked at what was taking place in Egypt and Tunisia and elsewhere with a mixture of joy and anxiety; I was glued to the television screen when the live scenes of Avenue Bourghiba or Tahrir Square sent vibes throughout the entire region; I talked to lots of people during my numerous travels to these countries, listened to their aspirations, assessed the progress (or lack thereof) of the transition processes, and interviewed all kinds of people about the future of the Arab region. In all of this, I always felt I was being drawn into the whirl of information, statistics, and journalistic accounts that were cramming our newspapers and magazines and those from the region. Still, this incredible amount of information did not make me feel less thirsty for knowledge and answers that would allow me to make sense of what was happening on the ground. I thus decided, almost naturally, to turn my attention towards some of the questions swirling around me and to try and provide some explanations for the developments taking place in the Arab world. Despite the temporal vicinity, I was struck by the lack of sound academic reflection on the Arab uprisings, with the exception of a few path-breaking analyses (Bellin 2012; Achcar 2013; Tripp 2013; Laremont 2014; Gerges 2015; Chalcraft 2016). As I was coming from the policy-oriented research community, the paucity of academic works on the topic was perhaps even more deafening. I therefore decided to start my own journey and that is what has brought me to write this book.

This work on the Arab uprisings has investigated the factors that influence the political development of countries moving away from authoritarianism in the short-to-medium term. The broad question this book has attempted to answer is: *what are the most important factors that have influenced the transition processes in the Arab countries?* Moving from this question, the book has dug into the available literature to identify the most adequate theoretical and methodological tools to address the issues raised. On the one hand, studies of (democratic) transition provided the almost indispensable starting point for analysis. However, when considering the literature focused on Southern European transitions to democracy in the early 1970s and on other changes of regime in the subsequent decades, it appears that a theory of democratisation does not exist (Morlino 2011). This is powerfully summed up in one of the most authoritative statements made in this regard by O'Donnell, Schmitter, and Whitehead: 'We did not have at the beginning, nor do we have at the end [...] a "theory" to test or to apply to the case studies' (O'Donnell *et al.* 1986: 3). At best, what we have is a set of theoretical insights that are temporally and regionally bound. These include, for instance, the relevance of pacts and agreements to the unmaking of the authoritarian regimes and the possibility of achieving democratic installation, understood as a distinct process from both transition and consolidation (Higley and Gunther 1992).

On the other hand, area studies – and in particular the analysis of political development in the Arab world – have provided other pieces useful for appreciating the processes triggered by the Arab uprisings. Most of these studies have explored the factors that constrained the attainment of democracy in the region up to 2011. While this literature failed, on the whole, to provide us with the tools to predict the Arab uprisings and focused mainly on case studies from which insights were derived that cannot easily be generalised, it has nevertheless left us with a significant amount of information on the role of 'Arab presidents for life', civilian-military relations, political-economic dynamics favouring rents and co-optation, and the importance of neo-authoritarian restructuring resulting from both domestic and external drivers (Brown 1997; Kienle 2001; Guazzone and Pioppi 2009; Owen 2012). But like the literature on democratic transitions, area studies have also offered a paucity of theorisation. Indeed, some of their insights have been partially called into question as a result of the processes underway in the Arab countries between 2011 and the beginning of 2014. This point will be elaborated further shortly.

Given the absence of a clear, self-contained body of theories to be applied to the analysis of the Arab transitions, this book has adopted an inductive approach leading to the development of theoretically relevant insights during the interpretation of the empirical material derived from the case studies. However, four hypotheses have guided the research. They have been drawn from neo-institutional analyses that have, over the last few decades, produced a great deal of theorisation not matched by an adequate amount of theory testing in comparative politics (Pierson 2004). Among the key concepts borrowed from the neo-institutional approaches and utilised in this book to assess and investigate the Arab transitions and their impact on the short-to-medium term political development of the countries in the region are 'institutions', 'institutional development', 'agency', 'timing', and 'sequencing'. All of them were specified in Chapter 1, providing the theoretical backbone for this research and later on used as the pillars of 'my own theory' of institutional development in the Arab transitions. Scholars and analysts working from a variety of theoretical perspectives, i.e., both rational choice models and historical institutional analyses, have produced compelling work emphasising and assessing the tremendous significance of institutional arrangements for political and social outcomes (Hall and Taylor 1996). By contrast, far less progress has been made in exploring the sources of institutional development across different geographical and temporal settings. Two basic questions that largely remain opaque and that this book has tried to address are: a) what determines the choice of a particular institution in different contexts? and b) what determines how institutions, once created, change over time? This research has attempted to fill this gap by undertaking an empirically grounded assessment of particular contextual driving forces of institutional development in the framework of the Arab transitions. These processes have been investigated as they unfold over time.

First of all, this work has identified and discussed at great length the four sets of constitutive elements of institutional development in the context of the Egyptian and Tunisian transitions. These elements, presented in Chapter 1 and then thoroughly considered in the central chapters of this book (Chapters 3, 4, and 5), are the constitution-making process, electoral dynamics, civilian-military relations, and the status and role of the judiciary within the institutional architecture. The book has demonstrated that the meaning and functioning of these institutions, as well as their mutual relations, tend to undergo significant change during the initial phase of the transition. Indeed, processes of institutional engineering represent the core of transition processes as the restructuring of the rules of the game is perceived as a fundamental step to setting the country firmly on the path of transition from authoritarianism. It is thus no coincidence that both Egypt and Tunisia have been predominantly engaged with the constitution-making process and the shaping of the new party system. Drawing from the empirical evidence presented in the previous chapters, the first finding of this book is that it is possible to talk about the existence of transition processes when institutional development, understood as changes and continuities in the basic institutional framework of a given country, take place.

Nevertheless, it is not enough to state that institutional development is what shapes the initial phase of transition processes. It is also important to provide an explanation for the pace, direction, and content of the changes (or lack thereof). Chapters 3 and 4 demonstrated that, although moving from comparable conditions, i.e., an entrenched authoritarian system, limited powers attributed to parliament, and widely felt socio-economic grievances, institutional development in Egypt and Tunisia in the period between 2011 and the beginning of 2014 took two very different paths, both in procedural and substantive terms. This puzzle led me to investigate the factors that have had an impact on institutional development and that I have broadly identified as the interplay between structural constraints, on the one hand, and agency and contingency, on the other. The former illuminates the path-dependence dynamics that are always involved when dealing with institutional development. It regards the 'stickiness' of the previous institutional structures and logics, i.e., the institutional legacy of the authoritarian system. Chapter 5 presented the analysis of often invisible dynamics of resilience to change in the context of the Arab transitions. Resourceful veto powers, such as the Egyptian military, have constrained change and in some cases derailed the attempts to move away from authoritarian power structures and logics. The latter factors, agency and contingency, point to the interaction among actors that takes place through conflicts, pacts, temporary convergence, and agreements, and is one of the main drivers of institutional development. The empirical evidence discussed in Chapters 3 to 5, for example, raises questions about the different behaviours, preferences, and strategies of the Islamist parties in Egypt and Tunisia. The Egyptian Muslim Brotherhood's failure to make itself accepted by the existing institutional structure, despite – or because of – its repeated attempts to change it, and by the other political forces was mainly the result of its inability to compromise, to seek consensus beyond a purely majoritarian understanding of its electoral victory, and, ultimately, to moderate its stances. Once again, this contrasts with the Tunisian experience in which not only the Islamist party, *Ennahda*, but also the majority of the other political and social forces worked arduously to foster an inclusive, legitimate, and, ultimately, more successful transition. In light of the above, two additional findings can be stated: institutional change and continuity co-exist in the Arab transitions due to the strength and pervasiveness of the authoritarian legacy, while the mutual behaviours, strategies, and choices of the actors, particularly the elites – and not the horizontally articulated, leaderless youth movements described in Chapter 2 – moving within the boundaries of existing institutions, are among the most important factors shaping institutional development.

The second goal of this book has been to shed light on the ways in which different paths of institutional development have influenced political outcomes in the short-to-medium term. This has meant assessing the relations between the constitutive elements of institutional development and political development. In particular, legitimacy, accountability, and responsiveness were singled out as the factors whose absence or severe deterioration triggered the Arab uprisings in 2011. It thus makes sense to discuss them as the potential point of arrival of this research and to analyse the extent to which Egypt and Tunisia tick these boxes. While it is not possible to do justice here to the host of theoretical and empirical inter-linkages advanced in Chapter 6 to account for the different political outcomes observed in the short-to-medium term in the two cases, it is nevertheless important to stress one of the most far-reaching findings emerging from this research. This finding pertains to the quality of institutions, mainly understood in terms of inclusiveness and identified as the single overarching factor explaining democratic success or failure in Egypt and Tunisia in the short-to-medium term. In addition to structure and agency, the existence of inclusive institutions is directly linked to temporal factors, in particular timing and sequencing, and their impact on institutional development. The focus on timing and sequencing in the context of the Arab transitions is one of the main contributions offered by this research to the historical institutional debate.

Implications for the literature and the way forward

This book is an exploratory work that has aimed at showing the potential of some lines of enquiry derived from (democratic) transition studies and historical institutional approaches for the appreciation of the political events and processes triggered by the Arab uprisings in 2011. Although the exploratory nature of this book makes further research necessary for confirmatory results to be achieved, some of its findings and conclusions already have wider implications. This book indeed offers important contributions, both empirically and theoretically. Empirically, it sheds light on the complex processes that have taken place in the Arab world in the period between 2011 and the beginning of 2014. In particular, it provides new insights into transition phenomena by contextualising the comparative analysis of a select number of Arab countries into the broader narrative about transitions and democratisation developed in different geographical and historical contexts. In spite of a number of evident and relevant differences, the transformations that struck the Arab world in the second decade of the third millennium have been compared to the profound changes that took place in Eastern and Central Europe in 1989–1991 (Masoud 2011; Springborg 2011a; Way 2011). This work thus engages the literature analysing such processes with a view to highlighting similarities and differences.

The evidence provided by this book is also relevant in terms of theory refinement and development. Two theoretical contributions, in particular, are offered by this work. First, it contributes to establishing a productive dialogue across disciplines, namely between area studies and democratisation studies, deepening our understanding of the political evolution of the Arab countries and enriching the literature on (democratic) transitions with new cases. These two branches of the literature have so far had only limited chances of interaction due to the sheer absence of democratic experiences in the Arab world prior to 2011. The second theoretical contribution offered by this book derives from the fact that it engages with some of the most state-of-the-art insights developed by the historical institutional literature. As discussed at great length in Chapter 1, this literature provides both the intellectual boundaries and the methodological tools to appreciate the impact of institutional development on political outcomes. Issues of timing and sequencing, path-dependence, and process tracing, which derive from the historical institutional literature, are used in this middle range work to refine our knowledge of general patterns of political history and the ways in which they interact with contingent features of political development, with particular emphasis on agency, conflict, and choice. Last but not least, the relevance of this research lies also in its composite, multidimensional nature, whereby it is well placed to contribute to both the academic and the practitioners' debates on the Arab transitions. While this book is meant primarily to contribute to enhancing the academic reflection on these issues, its potential contribution to shaping the policy-oriented debate and informing policy-makers' decisions on contemporary political issues should not be underestimated.

In this part of the conclusions, it is important to go back to the theoretical point from which this research started in order to glean some insights that go beyond the set of cases considered. Navigating through the Arab transitions makes it easier to illuminate the strengths and weaknesses of the main theoretical frameworks that have been applied to the study of Arab politics till now. While during the 1990s the democratic transition paradigm prominently advanced explanations to events taking place in the region by referring to a linear path from authoritarianism towards democracy, this was replaced during the following decade by the paradigm of authoritarian resilience. The primary contribution of the 'persistence of authoritarianism' literature, as emphasised in Chapter 2, has been to explain the survival of authoritarian regimes in the region, some lasting as long as 30, 40, or even more years (Bellin 2012). Following the Arab uprisings, both theoretical frameworks have arguably come under scrutiny and area studies experts have found themselves grappling with the dilemma of developing more nuanced explanatory models to account for the events of 2011–2013 (Pace and Cavatorta 2012; Sadiki 2015).

On the one hand, the democratic transition paradigm has been revitalised and given a new lease on life by the comparative assessment of the Arab transition processes through the lens of similar processes that have taken place in other temporal or geographical contexts (Kaldor 2011). This newfound enthusiasm should, however, be tempered by the recognition that the processes through which democracy takes hold are extremely complex and have so far failed in almost all the countries in the Arab region that have undergone unrest and turmoil. On the other hand – notwithstanding the fact that the falls of Ben Ali and Mubarak, to name but two examples, have cast some doubt on the validity of the paradigm of authoritarian resilience, calling into question its ability to explain the unintended consequences that any form of limited change or authoritarian upgrading brings with it – some of the mechanisms through which ruling elites were seemingly able to reconfigure authoritarian power have been at play in the aftermath of the Arab uprisings too. Controlled liberalisation, '*divide et impera*' strategies, and selected repression have indeed featured prominently in some of the new regimes' toolbox. While it is fair to claim that a certain overemphasis on the roles of the state, ruling elites, coercive apparatus, and traditional political actors, to the detriment of the transformation and changes taking place within the wider society, has been one of the main features of the 'persistence of authoritarianism' literature, it is also worth stressing that the concept of 'sustainability', which has been used in Chapter 2 to account for the structural conditions that led to the outbreak of the Arab uprisings in 2011, is an indirect product of this paradigm.

All this has important consequences for the soul-searching exercise of areas studies scholars and practitioners: both theoretical paradigms have been challenged and reconfirmed by the transition processes unleashed by the Arab uprisings. While these theoretical frameworks have long been regarded as mutually exclusive, or at best in competition, the research presented in this book arguably calls for combining some elements of both paradigms with a view to accounting more effectively for complex and dynamic processes of political change and continuity in the Arab world. While democracy cannot be regarded as the linear, pre-determined outcome of the Arab transition processes, since strong continuities exist between some pre-2011 authoritarian institutional frameworks and their restructured versions at the beginning of 2014, important forces for change have nevertheless been 'unexpectedly' unleashed by the very authoritarian mechanisms that were meant to prevent change. Today, these forces are the carriers of new voices, new demands, and new ways of doing politics. Only the complex interplay between changes and continuities, structure and agency unfolding through time and in specific sequences of events can account for the political development of the Arab world towards greater democracy or authoritarian persistence.

Finally, four plus one potential lines of research are proposed here to continue, expand, and refine the findings and conclusions advanced in this book. First, our understanding of transition dynamics in Egypt and Tunisia would be greatly enhanced by a thorough investigation of the impact of external actors and the external environment on these processes. In some cases, like in Egypt, it is apparent that external pressures and incentives have played a not so negligible role in facilitating the uprising and in shaping the ensuing transition. In other cases, like in Tunisia, the impact of the external environment has only manifested itself indirectly. The need to take into account the web of international relations in which the Arab countries find themselves is also linked to a second aspect: the attention to economic facts and policies. This book has treated socio-economic dynamics mainly as contextual factors that have not had a direct impact on the political processes underway during the transition. It has to be acknowledged that this is an undue simplification of a much more complex set of interactions and mutual influences between political and socio-economic dynamics and processes. Thus, scholars should be encouraged to focus their attention on significant longer-term socio-economic changes and their influence on political development (Springborg 2011b; Achcar 2013: 263–293). This means, for example, looking into the socio-economic policies promoted by the Islamist parties throughout the region, which have substantially been in continuity with the free enterprise economic credo of the previous governments' economic programmes. This would provide insight into the Herculean socio-economic challenges confronting the Arab countries and standing in the way of political development and stability. It would also mean shedding light on the deep crisis of the western, neo-liberal economic model and the set of policies that the American and European partners have proposed and concretely implemented in cooperation with the new authorities in the region.

Third, it would be interesting to investigate further the crucial difference that emerged in Chapter 6 between the behaviour, strategies, and goals of the Tunisian and the Egyptian Islamists, against the backdrop of the inclusion-moderation nexus (Schwedler 2007; Schwedler 2011). At the same time, the transition processes unleashed by the Arab uprisings have shed light on the increasing heterogeneity within the Islamist camp. The often conflictual dynamics between the Egyptian Muslim Brotherhood and the Salafists are worth underscoring in this regard. An important moment shaping the relationship between the two forces was the chain of events that, during the summer of 2013, led to the ousting and violent repression of the Muslim Brotherhood leadership and its sympathisers by the new self-appointed military-led regime. The fact that the Salafists went back to their traditional quietist approach and did not side with the Muslim Brotherhood, thus escaping the wave of military violent repression, needs to be further explored and its underlying motivations made clear. Some questions that could be addressed in this regard are the following: To what extent (if any) do Islamist parties differ from other political forces? What determines their strategies and actions *vis-à-vis* other institutional actors and structures? What makes them prone to compromise? What role does *Sharia* play in the Islamist parties' ability and willingness to strike compromises?

Finally, since power is largely absent from the analyses of (democratic) transitions, this issue deserves further investigation, and fruitful ways to cross-fertilise the theoretical contribution offered by this book with the literature articulated around power dynamics could be found. One meticulous attempt to discuss power and hegemonic relations in the context of the Egyptian 'revolution' has been made by Chalcraft (2014). Nevertheless, in most analyses, the issue of power features only indirectly as one of the resources whose relative distribution across the spectrum of actors influences their behaviours, preferences, and choices. To overcome this gap, the manifold forms of institutional, economic, and social power could be looked into not as a residual category that indirectly influences the transition but as one of its main constitutive driving forces. Last but not least, although some might feel that it goes without saying, the theoretical framework developed and adopted in this book could be applied to other cases of transition from authoritarianism in the Arab world, thus confirming its explanatory potential or invalidating it with the arrival of new empirical material.

Appendix
List of interviews

Interviewee no.	Role	Place	Date
1	Professor of political science at Cairo University	Cairo	13 October 2012; 19 May 2013
2	Member of the Egyptian Constituent Assembly	Cairo	13 October 2012
3	Professor of economics and Minister of Finance under the July 2013 Interim Government	Cairo	14 October 2012; 21 May 2013
4	Young Muslim Brotherhood's sympathiser	Cairo	14 October 2012
5	Professor of political science at the American University in Cairo	Cairo	15 October 2012; 23 May 2013
6	Egyptian researcher	Cairo	16 October 2012; 20 May 2013
7	Egyptian researcher	Cairo and Cambridge	16 October 2012 (Cairo); 23 May 2013 (Cairo); 3 July 2013 (Cambridge)
8	Member of *Kifaya!* and later member of the parliament (until the disbandment of the Lower House)	Cairo	16 October 2012
9	Professor of economics at Cairo University	Cairo	17 October 2012
10	Member of the Egyptian Constituent Assembly	Cairo	17 October 2012
11	Egyptian researcher	Cairo	17 October 2012; 20 May 2013
12	Former editor of *Ikhwan Online*	Cairo	17 October 2012
13	Professor of political science at the American University in Cairo	Cairo	18 October 2012; 21 May 2013
14	Foreign correspondent	Cairo	18 October 2012
15	Presidential candidate (June 2012) and leader of the Strong Egypt Party	Cairo	18 October 2012; 21 May 2013
16	Egyptian researcher	Cairo	18 October 2012; 20 May 2013

17	Professor of political science at Cairo University and member of the committee of legal experts named by the SCAF to revise the 1971 constitution	Cairo	19 October 2012; 21 May 2013
18	Human rights activist	Cairo	20 October 2012
19	Researcher on Tunisia	Bologna	7 February 2013; 11 November 2013 (Skype interview)
20	Professor of political science and constitutional law at University Cadi Ayyad, Marrakesh	Bologna	8 February 2013
21	Chair of the department of history at the American University in Cairo	Bologna	8 February 2013
22	Member of the National Salvation Front (NSF)	Cairo	18 May 2013
23	Researcher on Egypt	Cairo	18 May 2013
24	Professor of political science at the American University in Cairo	Cairo	19 May 2013
25	Egyptian journalist	Cairo	19 May 2013
26	Egyptian researcher	Cairo	20 May 2013
27	Member of the Shura Council	Cairo	20 May 2013
28	Professor at the American University in Cairo and expert on civilian-military relations	Cairo	20 May 2013
29	Former ambassador and member of the Egyptian Council for Foreign Relations	Cairo	21 May 2013
30	Constitutional expert	Cairo and Rome	21 May 2013 (Cairo); 1 July 2013 (Rome)
31	Egyptian journalist	Cairo	22 May 2013
32	Egyptian researcher on civilian-military relations	Cairo	23 May 2013
33	Leading figure of the Egyptian Muslim Brotherhood	Rome	30 May 2013
34	Professor of political science at George Washington University	Washington, DC	21 October 2013
35	Professor of political science at Georgetown University, Doha Campus	Washington, DC	21 October 2013
36	Representative of the State Department	Washington, DC	21 October 2013
37	Researcher on Egypt	Washington, DC	22 October 2013; 21 November 2013
38	Researcher on Tunisia	Washington, DC	23 October 2013
39	Researcher on Tunisia	Washington, DC	4 November 2013 (Skype interview); 22 November 2013
40	Professor of political science at the London School of Economics	London	6 November 2013

(*Continued*)

(Continued)

Interviewee no.	Role	Place	Date
41	Egyptian researcher		15 November 2013 (Skype interview)
42	Member of the National Constituent Assembly (NCA)	Tunis	18 November 2013
43	Member of the Higher Commission for Political Reform	Tunis	18 November 2013
44	Non-governmental organisation (NGO) representative	Tunis	18 November 2013
45	Former Tunisian military officer	Tunis	18 November 2013
46	Member of the Tunisian opposition	Tunis	18 November 2013
47	Non-governmental organisation (NGO) representative	Tunis	19 November 2013
48	Member of the *Instance Supérieure Indépendante pour les Elections* (ISIE)	Tunis	19 November 2013
49	Member of *Nidaa Tounes*	Tunis	19 November 2013
50	Tunisian researcher	Tunis	19 November 2013
51	Member of *Ennahda*'s Political Bureau	Tunis	19 November 2013
52	Member of *Ennahda*'s Political Bureau	Tunis	19 November 2013
53	Member of the *Parti Démocrate Progressiste* (PDP)	Tunis	20 November 2013
54	Tunisian researcher	Tunis	20 November 2013
55	Non-governmental organisation (NGO) representative	Tunis	20 November 2013
56	Spokesperson of the *Congrès pour la République* (CPR)	Tunis	20 November 2013
57	Tunisian researcher	Washington, DC	22 November 2013
58	Professor of political science at the London School of Economics	London	11 December 2013

Bibliography

Abdalla, Nadine. 2013. "Egypt's Revolutionary Youth. From Street Politics to Party Politics". *SWP Comments* 11. www.swp-berlin.org/en/publications/swp-comments-en/swp-aktuelle-details/article/egypts_youth_from_street_politics_to_party_politics.html.

Abdulbaki, Louay. 2008. "Democracy and the Re-Consolidation of Authoritarian Rule in Egypt". *Contemporary Arab Affairs* 1 (3): 445–463.

Abdul-Majid, Wahid. 2013. "Egypt at the Crossroads. Egypt's Future: Three Scenarios". *Contemporary Arab Affairs* 6 (1): 17–27.

Abu Dhabi Gallup Center. 2011. "Egypt From Tahrir to Transition". June 2011. www.gallup.com/poll/148133/egypt-tahrir-transition.aspx.

Abul-Magd, Zeinab. 2011. "The Army and the Economy in Egypt". *Jadaliyya*, 23 December 2011. www.jadaliyya.com/pages/index/3732/the-army-and-the-economy-in-egypt.

Abul-Magd, Zeinab. 2012. "The Egyptian Republic of Retired Generals". *Foreign Policy*, 16 May 2012. http://mideastafrica.foreignpolicy.com/posts/2012/05/08/the_egyptian_republic_of_retired_generals#sthash.TMMP9iFb.dpbs.

Acemoglu, Daron, and James A. Robinson. 2012. *Why Nations Fail: The Origins of Power, Prosperity, and Poverty*. New York, NY: Crown Business.

Achcar, Gilbert. 2013. *The People Want: A Radical Exploration of the Arab Uprising*. London: Saqi Books.

Aclimandos, Tewfick. 2012. "'Healing Without Amputating?': Security Reform in Egypt". *Arab Reform Initiative*. www.arab-reform.net/%E2%80%9Chealing-without-amputating%E2%80%9D-security-reform-egypt.

Afsah, Ebrahim. 2012. "Constitution-Making in Islamic Countries – A Theoretical Framework". In *Constitutionalism in Islamic Countries: Between Upheavals and Continuity*, edited by Rainer Grote and Tilmann J. Groeter, 475–511. Oxford: Oxford University Press.

al-Ali, Zaid. 2012. "The New Egyptian Constitution: An Initial Assessment of its Merits and Flaws". *OpenDemocracy*, 26 December 2012. www.opendemocracy.net/zaid-al-ali/new-egyptian-constitution-initial-assessment-of-its-merits-and-flaws.

al-Ali, Zaid. 2013a. "The Constitutional Court's Mark on Egypt's Elections". *Foreign Policy*, 13 June 2013. http://mideastafrica.foreignpolicy.com/posts/2013/06/06/the_constitutional_court_s_mark_on_egypt_s_elections#sthash.GEpcJjsE.dpbs.

al-Ali, Zaid. 2013b. "Another Egyptian Constitutional Declaration". *Foreign Policy*, 15 July 2013. http://mideastafrica.foreignpolicy.com/posts/2013/07/09/another_egyptian_constitutional_declaration#sthash.NkJLOlzR.dpbs.

al-Ali, Zaid, and Nathan J. Brown. 2013. "Egypt's Constitution Swings into Action". *Foreign Policy*, 5 April 2013. http://mideastafrica.foreignpolicy.com/posts/2013/03/27/egypt_s_constitution_swings_into_action#sthash.2cfR6ye0.dpbs.

Bibliography

al-Ali, Zaid, Christopher Roberts, and Amos Toh. 2012. "The Egyptian Constitutional Declaration Dated 17 June 2012 – A Commentary". *International IDEA*. www.constitutionnet.org/files/commentary_to_june_2012_constitutional_declaration_final.pdf.

Alberts, Susan, Chris Warshaw, and Barry R. Weingast. 2012. "Democratization and Countermajoritarian Institutions". In *Comparative Constitutional Design*, edited by Tom Ginsburg, 69–100. Cambridge: Cambridge University Press.

Albrecht, Holger. 2012. *Racing Against the Machine: Political Opposition Under Authoritarianism in Egypt*. Syracuse, NY: Syracuse University Press.

Albrecht, Holger, and Dina Bishara. 2011. "Back on Horseback: The Military and Political Transformation in Egypt". *Middle East Law and Governance* 3: 13–23.

Albrecht, Holger, and Oliver Schlumberger. 2004. "Waiting for Godot: Regime Change Without Democratization". *International Political Science Review* 25 (4): 371–392.

Albrecht, Holger, and Eva Wegner. 2006. "Autocrats and Islamists: Contenders and Containment in Egypt and Morocco". *The Journal of North African Studies* 11 (2): 123–141.

Al-Din Arafat, Alaa. 2009. *The Mubarak Leadership and Future of Democracy in Egypt*. New York: Palgrave Macmillan.

Alexander, Christopher. 1997. "Authoritarianism and Civil Society in Tunisia". *Middle East Report* 205. www.merip.org/mer/mer205/authoritarianism-civil-society-tunisia.

Alexander, Christopher. 2010. *Tunisia: Stability and Reform in the Modern Maghreb*. London: Routledge.

Alexander, Christopher. 2011. "Tunisia's Protest Wave: Where It Comes From and What It Means". *Foreign Policy*, 3 January 2011. http://mideast.foreignpolicy.com/posts/2011/01/02/tunisia_s_protest_wave_where_it_comes_from_and_what_it_means_for_ben_ali.

Allal, Amin. 2010. "Réformes Néolibérales, Clientélismes et Protestations en Situation Autoritaire: les Mouvements Contestataires dans le Bassin Minier de Gafsa en Tunisie (2008)". *Politique Africaine* 117: 107–126.

Allani, Alaya. 2009. "The Islamists in Tunisia Between Confrontation and Participation: 1980–2008". *The Journal of North African Studies* 14 (2): 257–272.

Allani, Alaya. 2013. "The Post-revolution Tunisian Constituent Assembly: Controversy Over Powers and Prerogatives". *The Journal of North African Studies* 18 (1): 131–140.

Almond, Gabriel A., and Sidney Verba. 1963. *The Civic Culture: Political Attitudes and Democracy in Five Nations*. Princeton, NJ: Princeton University Press.

Amnesty International. 2009. "Behind Tunisia's 'Economic Miracle': Inequality and Criminalization of Protest". *Amnesty International*. www.amnesty.org/en/library/info/MDE30/003/2009.

Anderson, Lisa. 2006. "Searching Where the Light Shines: Studying Democratization in the Middle East". *Annual Review of Political Science* 9 (1): 189–214.

Assaad, Ragui. 2007. "Labor Supply, Employment and Unemployment in the Egyptian Economy, 1988–2006". *Economic Research Forum Paper* 701. Cairo: Egyptian Centre for Economic Studies.

Ayubi, Nazih M. 1995. *Over-stating the Arab State: Politics and Society in the Middle*. London/New York: I.B. Tauris.

Banting, Keith G., and Richard Simeon, eds. 1985. *Redesigning the State: The Politics of Constitutional Change*. Toronto: University of Toronto Press.

Barany, Zoltan. 2011. "The Role of the Military". *Journal of Democracy* 22 (4): 24–35.

Barraclough, Steven. 1998. "Al-Azhar: Between the Government and the Islamists". *The Middle East Journal* 52 (2): 236–249.

Bartolini, Stefano. 1993. "On Time and Comparative Research". *Journal of Theoretical Politics* 5 (2): 131–167.

Bayat, Asef. 2006. "The Political Economy of Social Policy in Egypt". In *Social Policy in the Middle East: Political, Economic and Gender Dynamics*, edited by Valentine M. Moghadam and Massoud Karshenas, 135–155. Basingstoke: Palgrave Macmillan.

Bayat, Asef. 2009. *Life as Politics: How Ordinary People Change the Middle East*. Stanford: Stanford University Press.

Beblawi, Hazem, and Luciani, Giacomo, eds. 1987. *The Rentier State*. London/New York/Sydney: Croom Helm.

Beinin, Joel. 2009. "Neo-Liberal Structural Adjustment, Political Demobilization, and Neo-Authoritarianism in Egypt". In *The Arab State and Neo-Liberal Globalisation: The Restructuring of State Power in the Middle East*, edited by Laura Guazzone and Daniela Pioppi, 19–46. London: Ithaca Press.

Beinin, Joel, and Zachary Lockman. 1987. *Workers on the Nile: Nationalism, Communism, Islam and the Egyptian Working Class, 1882–1954*. Princeton, NJ: Princeton University Press.

Beinin, Joel, and Frédéric Vairel, eds. 2011. *Social Movements, Mobilization, and Contestation in the Middle East and North Africa*. Stanford: Stanford University Press.

Beissinger, Mark R. 2007. "Structure and Example in Modular Political Phenomena: The Diffusion of the Bulldozer/Rose/Orange/Tulip Revolutions". *Perspectives on Politics*, June 2007: 259–276.

Beissinger, Mark R. 2009. *Nationalist Mobilization and the Collapse of the Soviet State*. Cambridge: Cambridge University Press.

Bellamy, Richard, ed. 1996. *Constitutionalism, Democracy and Sovereignty: American and European Perspectives*. Aldershot: Avebury.

Bellin, Eva. 2004. "The Robustness of Authoritarianism in the Middle East: Exceptionalism in Comparative Perspective". *Comparative Politics* 36 (2): 139–157.

Bellin, Eva. 2005. "Coercive Institutions and Coercive Leaders". In *Authoritarianism in the Middle East: Regimes and Resistance*, edited by Marsha Pripstein Posusney and Michele Penner Angrist, 21–42. Boulder, CO/London: Lynner Rienner.

Bellin, Eva. 2011. "Lessons From the Jasmine and Nile Revolutions: Possibilities of Political Transformation in the Middle East?". *Middle East Brief* 50: 1–8.

Bellin, Eva. 2012. "Reconsidering the Robustness of Authoritarianism in the Middle East". *Comparative Politics* 44 (2): 127–149.

Bennett, Andrew. 2010. "Process Tracing and Causal Inference". In *Rethinking Social Enquiry*, edited by Henry E. Brady and David Collier, 207–219. Lanham, MA: Rowman & Littlefield Publishers.

Ben Romdhane, Mohamed. 2006. "Social Policy and Development in Tunisia Since Independence. A Political Perspective". In *Social Policy in the Middle East: Political, Economic and Gender Dynamics*, edited by Valentine M. Moghadam and Massoud Karshenas, 31–77. Basingstoke: Palgrave Macmillan.

Bermeo, Nancy. 1997. "Myths of Moderation: Confrontation and Conflict During Democratic Transitions". *Comparative Politics* 29: 305–322.

Bernard-Maugiron, Nathalie, ed. 2008. *Judges and Political Reform in Egypt*. Cairo: American University in Cairo Press.

Berry, Jeffrey M. 2002. "Validity and Reliability Issues in Elite Interviews". *PS: Political Science and Politics* 35 (4): 679–682.

Blaydes, Lisa. 2011. *Elections and Distributive Politics in Mubarak's Egypt*. Cambridge: Cambridge University Press.

Blount, Justin, Zachary Elkins, and Tom Ginsburg. 2012. "Does the Process of Constitution-Making Matter?". In *Comparative Constitutional Design*, edited by Tom Ginsburg, 31–66. Cambridge: Cambridge University Press.

Borowiak, Craig T. 2011. *Accountability and Democracy: The Pitfalls and Promise of Popular Control*. New York, NY: Oxford University Press.

Boubekeur, Amel. 2009. "The Tunisian Elections: International Community Must Insist on Moving Beyond Façade Democracy". *Carnegie Endowment for International Peace*. www.carnegieendowment.org/2009/10/23/tunisian-elections-international-community-must-insist-on-moving-beyond-fa%C3%A7ade-democracy/bn3j.

Bourdieu, Pierre. 1984. *Distinction: A Social Critique of the Judgment of Taste*. London: Routledge.

Braudel, Fernand. 1958. "Histoire et Sciences sociales: La longue durée". *Annales. Économies, Sociétés, Civilisations* 13 (4): 725–753.

Brody-Barre, Andrea G. 2013. "The Impact of Political Parties and Coalition Building on Tunisia's Democratic Future". *The Journal of North African Studies* 18 (2): 211–230.

Brooker, Paul. 2000. *Non-Democratic Regimes: Theory, Government, and Politics*. New York: St. Martin's.

Brooks, Risa. 1999. *Political-Military Relations and the Stability of Arab Regimes*. London: Routledge.

Brooks, Risa. 2013. "Abandoned at the Palace: Why the Tunisian Military Defected From the Ben Ali Regime in January 2011". *Journal of Strategic Studies* 36 (2): 205–220.

Brown, Nathan J. 1997. *The Rule of Law in the Arab World: Courts in Egypt and the Gulf*. Cambridge: Cambridge University Press.

Brown, Nathan J. 2002. *Constitutions in a Non-Constitutional World: Arab Basic Laws and the Prospects for Accountable Government*. Albany, NY: State University of New York Press.

Brown, Nathan J. 2011a. "Egypt's Constitutional Ghosts". *Foreign Affairs*, 15 February 2011. www.foreignaffairs.com/articles/67453/nathan-j-brown/egypts-constitutional-ghosts.

Brown, Nathan J. 2011b. "The Muslim Brotherhood as Helicopter Parent". *Foreign Policy*, 27 May 2011. http://mideastafrica.foreignpolicy.com/posts/2011/05/27/the_muslim_brotherhood_as_helicopter_parent#sthash.VXavdwRu.dpbs.

Brown, Nathan J. 2011c. "Constitutional Rebirth. Tunisia and Egypt Reconstructing Themselves". *United Nations Development Program*. www.constitutionnet.org/vl/item/constitutional-rebirth-tunisia-and-egypt-reconstruct-themselves-study.

Brown, Nathan J. 2012a. "Egypt's Judges in a Revolutionary Age". *Carnegie Endowment for International Peace*. http://carnegieendowment.org/2012/02/22/egypt-s-judges-in-revolutionary-age.

Brown, Nathan J. 2012b. "A Guide Through the Egyptian Maze of Justice". *Carnegie Endowment for International Peace*. http://carnegieendowment.org/2012/06/06/guide-through-egyptian-maze-of-justice/b68l.

Brown, Nathan J. 2013a. "Egypt's Failed Transition". *Journal of Democracy* 24 (4): 45–58.

Brown, Nathan J. 2013b. "Egypt's Wide State Reassembles Itself". *Foreign Policy*, 17 July 2013. http://mideastafrica.foreignpolicy.com/posts/2013/07/17/egypt_s_wide_state_reassembles_itself#.UeglFku_RwA.twitter.

Brown, Nathan J., and Michele Dunne. 2013. "Egypt's Draft Constitution Rewards the Military and Judiciary". *Carnegie Endowment for International Peace*. http://carnegieendowment.org/2013/12/04/egypt-s-draft-constitution-rewards-military-and-judiciary/gvc8.

Brown, Nathan J., Michele Dunne, and Amr Hamzawy. 2007. "Egypt's Controversial Constitutional Amendments". *Carnegie Endowment for International Peace*. www.carnegieendowment.org/files/egypt_constitution_webcommentary01.pdf.

Brownlee, Jason. 2007. *Authoritarianism in an Age of Democratization*. Cambridge: Cambridge University Press.

Brownlee, Jason. 2012. "Executive Elections in the Arab World: When and How do they Matter?". *Comparative Political Studies* 44 (7): 807–828.

Brownlee, Jason, and Joshua Stacher. 2011. "Change of Leader, Continuity of System: Nascent Liberalization in Post-Mubarak Egypt". *Comparative Democratization* 9 (2): 1–9.

Brumberg, Daniel. 2002. "The Trap of Liberalized Autocracy". *Journal of Democracy* 13 (4): 56–68.

Brumberg, Daniel, and Hesham Sallam. 2012. "The Politics of Security Sector Reform in Egypt". *Special Report* 318, United States Institute of Peace. www.usip.org/publications/the-politics-security-sector-reform-in-egypt.

Brynen, Rex, Bahgat Korany, and Paul Noble, eds. 1998. *Political Liberalization and Democratization in the Arab World*. Boulder, CO: Lynne Rienner.

Bunce, Valerie J., David Patel, and Sharon Wichick. 2014. "Diffusion and Demonstration". In *The Arab Uprisings Explained: New Contentious Politics in the Middle East*, edited by Marc Lynch, 57–74. New York: Columbia University Press.

Buzan, Barry, Ole Waever, and Jaap de Wilde. 1997. *Security: A New Framework for Analysis*. Boulder, CO: Lynne Rienner.

Camau, Michel, and Vincent Geisser. 2003. *Le syndrome autoritaire. Politique en Tunisie de Bourghiba à Ben Ali*. Paris: Presses de Sciences Politiques.

Capoccia, Giovanni, and R. Daniel Kelemen. 2007. "The Study of Critical Junctures. Theory, Narrative, and Counterfactuals in Historical Institutionalism". *World Politics* 59: 341–369.

Carey, John M. 2009. "Does It Matter How a Constitution Is Created?". In *Is Democracy Exportable?*, edited by Zoltan Barany and Robert G. Moser, 155–177. Cambridge: Cambridge University Press.

Carey, John M. 2013. "Electoral Formula and the Tunisian Constituent Assembly". Dartmouth College, 9 May 2013.

Caridi, Paola. 2012. "Civil Society, Youth, and the Internet". In Silvia Colombo *et al.*, *New Socio-Political Actors in North Africa: A Transatlantic Perspective*. Mediterranean Papers Series, 1–8. Washington, DC: German Marshall Fund of the United States.

Carothers, Thomas. 2002. "The End of the Transition Paradigm". *Journal of Democracy* 13 (1): 5–21.

Carothers, Thomas. 2006. *Confronting the Weakest Link: Aiding Political Parties in New Democracies*. Washington, DC: Carnegie Endowment for International Peace.

Cavatorta, Francesco, and Fabio Merone. 2013. "Moderation Through Exclusion? The Journey of the Tunisian Ennahda From Fundamentalist to Conservative Party". *Democratization* 20 (5): 857–875.

Chalcraft, John. 2014. "Egypt's 25 January Uprising, Hegemonic Contestation, and the Explosion of the Poor". In *The New Middle East: Protest and Revolution in the Arab World*, edited by Fawaz Gerges A., 155–179. Cambridge: Cambridge University Press.

Chalcraft, John. 2016. *Popular Politics in the Making of the Modern Middle East*. Cambridge: Cambridge University Press.

Chaudhry, Kiren A. 1997. *The Price of Wealth: Economies and Institutions in the Middle East*. Ithaca: Cornell University Press.

Cheibub, Jose A. 2007. *Presidentialism, Parliamentarism, and Democracy*. Cambridge: Cambridge University Press.

Cimbala, Stephen J., ed. 2012. *Civil-Military Relations in Perspective: Strategy, Structure, and Policy*. Burlington, VT: Ashgate.

Clément, Françoise. 2009. "Workers Protests Under Economic Liberalisation in Egypt". In *Political and Social Protest in Egypt*, edited by N.S. Hopkins, 135–154. Cairo: American University in Cairo Press.

Clement, Henry M., and Robert Springborg. 2011. "Why Egypt's Military Will Not Be Able to Govern". *Foreign Affairs* 2, 21 February 2011. www.foreignaffairs.com/articles/67475/clement-m-henry-and-robert-springborg/a-tunisian-solution-for-egypts-military.

Collier, Ruth B. 1999. *Paths Toward Democracy*. Cambridge: Cambridge University Press.

Collier, Ruth B., and David Collier. 1991. *Shaping the Political Arena*. Princeton: Princeton University Press.

Collombier, Virginie. 2012. "Egypt in 2011: A Regime that No Longer Knows How to Adapt? Fluid Conjunctures and Regime Transformations in Perspectives". *EUI Working Paper MWP* 2012/03.

Colombo, Silvia. 2011. "The Southern Mediterranean. Between Changes and Challenges to Its Sustainability". In *The Challenges of State Sustainability in the Mediterranean*, edited by Silvia Colombo and Nathalie Tocci, 15–58. Rome: IAI Research Papers 3.

Cook, Steven A. 2007. *Ruling But Not Governing: The Military and Political Development in Egypt, Algeria and Turkey*. Baltimore: The Johns Hopkins University Press.

Cook, Steven A. 2011. *The Struggle for Egypt: From Nasser to Tahrir Square*. New York: Oxford University Press.

Coram, Bruce T. 1996. "Second Best Theories and Institutional Design". In *Theory of Institutional Design*, edited by Robert E. Goodin, 90–102. Cambridge: Cambridge University Press.

Corfield, Penelope J. 2007. *Time and the Shape of History*. New Haven/London: Yale University Press.

Cox, Gary. 1999. "Electoral Rules and Electoral Coordination". *Annual Review of Political Science* 2: 145–161.

Croissant, Aurel, and Stefan Wurster. 2013. "Performance and Persistence of Autocracies in Comparison: Introducing Issues and Perspectives". *Contemporary Politics* 19 (1): 1–18.

Dahl, Robert. 1965. *A Preface to Democratic Theory*. Chicago: University of Chicago Press.

Dawisha, Karen, and Bruce Parrott, eds. 1997. *The Consolidation of Democracy in East-Central Europe*. Cambridge: Cambridge University Press.

Della Porta, Donatella, and Michael Keating, eds. 2009. *Approaches and Methodologies in the Social Sciences*. Cambridge: Cambridge University Press.

Democracy Reporting International. 2013. "Egypt's Elections: More Legal Roadblocks". *Briefing Paper* 36. www.democracy-reporting.org/files/bp_36_more_roadblocks_1.pdf.

Diamond, Larry. 1999. *Developing Democracy: Towards Consolidation*. Baltimore: Johns Hopkins University Press.

Diamond, Larry, and Leonardo Morlino, eds. 2005. *Assessing the Quality of Democracy*. Baltimore: Johns Hopkins University Press.

Di Palma, Giuseppe. 1990. *To Craft Democracies: An Essay on Democratic Transitions*. Berkeley: University of California Press.

Dunne, Michele. 2006. "Evaluating Egyptian Reform". *Carnegie Endowment for International Peace*. http://carnegieendowment.org/2006/01/24/evaluating-egyptian-reform/26xo.

Ehteshami, Anoushiravan. 2007. *Globalization and Geopolitics in the Middle East: Old Games, New Rules*. New York, NY: Routledge.

Ekin, Stephen L., and Karol E. Soltan, eds. 1993. *A New Constitutionalism: Designing Political Institutions for a Good Society*. Chicago: University of Chicago Press.

El-Adawy, Adel. 2013. "The Future of Egypt's Electoral System". *Policywatch* 2142, The Washington Institute. www.washingtoninstitute.org/policy-analysis/view/the-future-of-egypts-electoral-system.

El-Din Haseeb, Khair. 2012. "The Arab Spring Revisited". *Contemporary Arab Affairs* 5 (2): 185–197.

El Fegiery, Moataz. 2012. "Crunch Time for Egypt's Civil-Military Relations". *FRIDE Policy Brief* 134. www.fride.org/publication/1054/crunch-time-for-egypt%E2%80%99s-civil-military-relations.

El-Ghobashy, Mona. 2011. "Politics by Other Means: In Egypt, Street Protests Set the Agenda". *Boston Review*, November/December 2011: 39–44.

El-Ghobashy, Mona. 2011. "The Metamorphosis of the Egyptian Muslim Brothers". *International Journal of Middle East Studies* 37 (3): 373–395.

Elgie, Robert, and Sophie Moestrup, eds. 2008. *Semi-Presidentialism in Central and Eastern Europe*. Manchester: Manchester University Press.

Elkins, Zachary, Tom Ginsburg, and Justin Blount. 2008. "Citizen as Founder: Participation in Constitutional Design". *Temple Law Review* 81 (3): 361–382.

Elster, Jon. 1995. "Forces and Mechanisms in the Constitution-Making Process". *Duke Law Journal* 45: 364–396.

Elster, Jon. 2006. "Legislatures as Constituent Assemblies". In *The Least Examined Branch: The Role of Legislatures in the Constitutional State*, edited by Richard W. Bauman and Tsvi Kahana, 181–197. Cambridge: Cambridge University Press.

Elster, Jon, Claus Offe, and Ulrich K. Preuss. 1998. *Institutional Design in Post-Communist Societies: Rebuilding the Ship at Sea*. Cambridge: Cambridge University Press.

Emirbayer, Mustafa, and Ann Mische. 1998. "What Is Agency?". *American Journal of Sociology* 103 (4): 962–1023.

Erdle, Steffen. 2004. "Tunisia: Economic Transformation and Political Restauration". In *Arab Elites: Negotiating the Politics of Change*, edited by Volker Perthes, 207–236. Boulder, CO/London: Lynne Rienner Publishers.

Eskander, Wael. 2011. "How Are Seat Winners Determined in the Egyptian Elections?". *Jadaliyya*, 1 December 2011. www.jadaliyya.com/pages/index/3361/how-are-seat-winners-determined-in-the-egyptian-el.

Euro-Mediterranean Human Rights Network (EMHRN). 2010. "Inconsistent European Policies Fail to Address Human Rights Abuses in Tunisia". *Copenhagen: Euro-Mediterranean Human Rights Network*. www.euromedrights.org/files/EUTUN_ReportENFinal_2011_926562157.pdf.

Fahmy Menza, Mohamed. 2013. *Patronage Politics in Egypt: The National Democratic Party and Muslim Brotherhood in Cairo*. Abingdon/New York: Routledge.

Farag, Mona. 2012. "Egypt's Muslim Brotherhood and the January 25 Revolution: New Political Party, New Circumstances". *Contemporary Arab Affairs* 5 (2): 214–229.

Faris, David M. 2012. "Constituting Institutions: The Electoral System in Egypt". *Middle East Policy* 19 (1): 140–154.

Filiu, Jean-Pierre. 2011. *The Arab Revolution: Ten Lessons From the Democratic Uprising*. London: C. Hurst.

Frisch, Hillel. 2013. "The Egyptian Army and Egypt's 'Spring'". *Journal of Strategic Studies* 36 (2): 180–204.

Forster, Anthony, Timothy Edmunds, and Andrew Cottey, eds. 2001. *Democratic Control of the Military in Post-Communist Europe: Guarding the Guards*. New York: Palgrave Macmillan.

Forster, Anthony, Timothy Edmunds, and Andrew Cottey, eds. 2002. *The Challenge of Military Reform in Post-communist Europe: Building Professional Armed Forces*. New York, NY: Palgrave Macmillan.
Fukuyama, Francis. 2011. "Political Order in Egypt". *The American Interest* 6 (5): 7–12.
Galal, Ahmad. 2003. "Social Expenditure and the Poor". *Economic Research Forum Paper* 89. Cairo: Egyptian Centre for Economic Studies.
Geisser, Vincent, and Eric Gobe. 2003. "Le président Ben Ali entre les jeux de coteries et l'échéance présidentielle de 2004". In *Chronique politique Tunisie, Annuaire de l'Afrique du Nord 2003*, 291–300. Paris: Editions du CNRS.
Geisser, Vincent, and Eric Gobe. 2005. "Des fissures dans la "Maison Tunisie"? Le régime Ben Ali face aux mobilisations protestataires". In *L'Année du Maghreb*. Paris: Editions du CNRS.
Gellner, Ernest, and John Waterbury, eds. 1977. *Patrons and Clients in Mediterranean Societies*. London: Duckworth.
Gerges, Fawaz A. 2015. *Contentious Politics in the Middle East: Popular Resistance and Marginalized Activism Beyond the Arab Uprisings*. New York, NY: Palgrave Macmillan.
Gobe, Eric. 2009. "Deceptive Liberal Reforms: Institutional Adjustments and the Dynamics of Authoritarianism in Tunisia (1997–2005)". In *Democracy Building and Democracy Erosion: Political Change in North and South of the Mediterranean*, edited by Eberhard Kienle, 93–111. London: Saqi.
Godec, Robert F. 2010. "Corruption en Tunisie: Ce qui est à toi m'appartient". *Tunisia Watch*, 14 December 2010.
Goertz, Gary. 2006. "Assessing the Trivialness, Relevance, and Relative Importance of Necessary or Sufficient Conditions in Social Sciences". *Studies in Comparative International Development* 41 (2): 88–109.
Goldberg, Ellis. 2011. "Mubarakism Without Mubarak – Why Egypt's Military Will Not Embrace Democracy". *Foreign Affairs*, 11 February 2011. www.foreignaffairs.com/articles/67416/ellis-goldberg/mubarakism-without-mubarak.
Goldberg, Ellis. 2013. "Whatever Happened to Egypt's Democratic Transition?". *Jadaliyya*, 3 March 2013. www.jadaliyya.com/pages/index/10444/whatever-happened-to-egypts-democratic-transition.
Guazzone, Laura, and Daniela Pioppi, eds. 2009. *The Arab State and Neo-Liberal Globalization: The Restructuring of State Power in the Middle East*. London: Ithaca Press.
Guirguis, Dina. 2009. "Egypt's NGO Bill Imperils Civil Society Funding". *Carnegie Endowment for International Peace*. http://carnegieendowment.org/2009/02/03/egypt-s-ngo-bill-imperils-civil-society-funding/few4.
Gunther, Richard, Nikiforos P. Diamandouros, and Hans-Jurgen Puhle, eds. 1995. *The Politics of Democratic Consolidation: Southern Europe in Comparative Perspective*. Baltimore: The Johns Hopkins University Press.
Hachemaoui, Mohammed. 2013. "*Tunisia at a Crossroads*. Which Rules for Which Transition?". *SWP Research Paper* 6. www.swp-berlin.org/en/publications/swp-research-papers/swp-research-paper-detail/article/tunisia_which_rules_for_which_transition.html.
Hackett, James, ed. 2010. *The Military Balance 2010*. International Institute for Strategic Studies. London: Routledge.
Haerpfer, Christian W., Patrick Bernhagen, Ronald F. Inglehart, and Christian Welzel. 2009. *Democratization*. Oxford: Oxford University Press.
Hakimian, Hassan, and Ziba Moshaver, eds. 2001. *The State and Global Change: The Political Economy of Transition in the Middle East and North Africa*. Richmond, Surrey: Curzon.

Bibliography 179

Hall, Peter A. 1986. *Governing the Economy: The Politics of State Intervention in Britain and France*. New York: Oxford University Press.
Hall, Peter A., and David Soskice. 2001. *Varieties of Capitalism*. Oxford: Oxford University Press.
Hall, Peter A., and Rosemary C. R. Taylor. 1996. "Political Science and the Three New Institutionalisms". *Political Studies* 44: 936–957.
Hamid, Shadi. 2011a. "Tunisia. Birthplace of the Revolution". In *The Arab Awakening: America and the Transformation of the Middle East*, edited by Kenneth M. Pollack et al., 111–116. Washington, DC: Brookings Institution Press.
Hamid, Shadi. 2011b. "Egypt. The Prize". In *The Arab Awakening: America and the Transformation of the Middle East*, edited by Kenneth M. Pollack et al., 102–110. Washington, DC: Brookings Institution Press.
Hamid, Shadi. 2011c. "Islamists and the Brotherhood. Political Islam and the Arab Spring". In *The Arab Awakening: America and the Transformation of the Middle East*, edited by Kenneth M. Pollack et al., 29–38. Washington, DC: Brookings Institution Press.
Hamzawy, Amr. 2009. "Rising Social Distress: The Case of Morocco, Egypt, and Jordan". *Carnegie Middle East Centre*. www.carnegieendowment.org/2009/06/17/rising-social-distress-case-of-morocco-egypt-and-jordan/1q9f.
Hanlon, Querine. 2012. "Security Sector Reform in Tunisia. A Year After the Jasmine Revolution". *United States Institute of Peace*. www.usip.org/sites/default/files/SR304.pdf.
Harb, Imad. 2003. "The Egyptian Military in Politics: Disengagement or Accommodation". *Middle East Journal* 57 (2): 269–290.
Harik, Iliya. 1992. "Subsidization Policies in Egypt: Neither Economic Growth Nor Distribution". *International Journal of Middle East Studies* 24: 481–499.
Harrigan, Jane, and Hamid El-Said. 2009. *Economic Liberalisation, Social Capital and Islamic Welfare Provision*. Basingstoke: Palgrave Macmillan.
Harris, Christina P. 1964. *Nationalism and Revolution in Egypt: The Role of the Muslim Brotherhood*. Stanford: Mouton.
Hashemi, Nader. 2009. *Islam, Secularism, and Liberal Democracy: Toward a Democratic Theory for Muslim Societies*. New York, NY: Oxford University Press.
Hashim, Ahmed. 2011. "The Egyptian Military, Part Two: From Mubarak Onward". *Middle East Policy* 18 (4). www.mepc.org/journal/middle-east-policy-archives/egyptian-military-part-two-mubarak-onward.
Haouari, Ibrahim. 2011. "Ces chiffres qu'on ne nous a jamais révélés", *La presse de Tunisie*, 6 February 2011.
Haugbølle, Rikke H., and Francesco Cavatorta. 2011. "Will the Real Tunisian Opposition Please Stand Up? Opposition Coordination Failures Under Authoritarian Constraints". *British Journal of Middle Eastern Studies* 38 (3): 323–341.
Hawthorne, Amy. 2005. "Is Civil Society the Answer?". In *Uncharted Journey: Promoting Democracy in the Middle East*, edited by Thomas Carothers and Marina Ottaway, 81–114. Washington, DC: Carnegie Endowment for International Peace.
Hedi Bchir, Mohamed, Mohammed A. Chemingui, and Hakim Ben Hammouda. 2009. "Ten Years After Implementing the Barcelona Process: What Can Be Learned From the Tunisian Experience". *Journal of North African Studies* 14 (2): 123–144.
Hellyer, Hisham A. 2012. "Military or President: Who Calls the Shots in Egypt?". *RUSI Analysis*. www.rusi.org/analysis/commentary/ref:C50379EA7E956C/#.UtuU7vso_Mw.
Henry, Clement M., and Robert Springborg. 2001. *Globalization and the Politics of Development in the Middle East*. Cambridge: Cambridge University Press.

Bibliography

Herrera, Linda, and Asef Bayat. 2010. *Being Young and Muslim: New Cultural Politics in the Global South and North*. New York: Oxford University Press.

Heydemann, Steven. 2004. *Networks of Privilege in the Middle East: The Politics of Economic Reform Revisited*. New York, NY: Palgrave Macmillan.

Heydemann, Steven. 2007a. *Upgrading Authoritarianism in the Arab World*. Washington, DC: Brookings Institution, Saban Centre.

Heydemann, Steven. 2007b. "Social Pacts and the Persistence of Authoritarianism in the Middle East". In *Debating Arab Authoritarianism*, edited by Oliver Schlumberger, 21–38. Stanford: Stanford University Press.

Heydemann, Steven, and Reinoud Leenders. 2011. "Authoritarian Learning and Authoritarian Resilience: Regime Responses to the 'Arab Awakening'". *Globalizations* 8 (5): 647–653.

Hibou, Béatrice. 2004. *Privatising the State*. London: Hurst & Company.

Hibou, Béatrice. 2011. *The Force of Obedience: The Political Economy of Repression in Tunisia*. Cambridge: Polity Press.

Higley, John, and Michael G. Burton. 1989. "The Elite Variable in Democratic Transitions and Breakdowns". *American Sociological Review* 54 (1): 17–32.

Higley, John, and Richard Gunther, eds. 1992. *Elites and Democratic Consolidation in Latin America and Southern Europe*. Cambridge: Cambridge University Press.

Hinnebusch, Raymond A. 1990. *Authoritarian Power and State Formation in Ba'thist Syria*. Boulder, CO: Westview Press.

Hinnebusch, Raymond A. 2006. "Authoritarian Persistence, Democratization Theory and the Middle East: An Overview and Critique". *Democratization* 13 (3): 373–395.

Hite, Katherine, and Leonardo Morlino. 2004. "Problematizing the Links Between Authoritarian Legacies and 'Good' Democracy". In *Authoritarian Legacy and 'Good' Democracy*, edited by Paola Cesarini and Katherine Hite, 25–83. Indiana: University of Notre Dame Press.

Hopkins, Nicholas S., ed. 2009. *Political and Social Protest in Egypt, Political and Social Protest in Egypt*. Cairo: American University in Cairo Press.

Horowitz, Donald L. 2002. "Constitutional Design: Proposals Versus Processes". In *The Architecture of Democracy: Constitutional Design, Conflict Management, and Democracy*, edited by Andrew Reynolds, 15–36. Oxford: Oxford University Press.

Huntington, Samuel P. 1968. *Political Order in Changing Societies*. New Haven/London: Yale University Press.

Huntington, Samuel P. 1981. *The Soldier and the State: The Theory and Practice of Civil-Military Relations*. Cambridge, MA: Harvard University Press [1957].

Huntington, Samuel P. 1991. *The Third Wave: Democratisation in the Late Twentieth Century*. Norman: University of Oklahoma Press.

Hyden, Goran, and Denis Venter, eds. 2001. *Constitution-Making and Democratisation in Africa*. Pretoria: Africa Institute of South Africa.

International Crisis Group. 2012. "Lost in Transition: The World According to Egypt's SCAF". *Middle East Report* 121. www.crisisgroup.org/en/regions/middle-east-north-africa/egypt-syria-lebanon/egypt/121-lost-in-transition-the-world-according-to-egypts-scaf.aspx.

International Monetary Fund. 2007. *Regional Economic Outlook: Middle East and Central Asia*. Washington, DC: International Monetary Fund.

Jervis, Robert. 2000. "Timing and Interaction in Politics: A Comment on Pierson". *Studies in American Political Development* 14: 93–100.

Joffé, George. 2011. "The Arab Spring in North Africa: Origins and Prospects". *The Journal of North African Studies* 16 (4): 507–532.
Johnston, Hank. 2011. *States and Social Movements*. London: Polity.
Kaldor, Mary. 2011. "Civil Society in 1989 and 2011". *OpenDemocracy*, 7 February 2011. www.opendemocracy.net/mary-kaldor/civil-society-in-1989-and-2011.
Kallander, Amy A. 2011. "Tunisia's Post-Ben Ali Challenge: A Primer". *Middle East Research and Information Project*. www.merip.org/mero/mero012611.
Kandil, Hazem. 2012. *Soldiers, Spies and Statesmen: Egypt's Road to Revolt*. London/ Brooklyn, NY: Verso.
Kandil, Mahmoud. 2012. "The Judiciary in Egypt. Pursuing Reform and Promoting Independence". *Arab Reform Initiative*. www.arab-reform.net/judiciary-egyptpursuing-reform-and-promoting-independence.
Karl, Terry L. 1990. "Dilemmas of Democratization in Latin America". *Comparative Politics* 23: 1–21.
Karl, Terry L., and Philippe Schmitter. 1991. "Modes of Transition in Latin America, Southern and Eastern Europe". *International Social Science Journal* 128: 269–284.
Karshenas, Massoud, and Valentine M. Moghadam. 2006. *Social Policy in the Middle East: Economic, Political and Gender Dynamics*. Basingstoke: Palgrave Macmillan.
Kassem, Maye. 2004. *Egyptian Politics: The Dynamics of Authoritarian Rule*. Boulder, CO: Lynner Rienner.
Kausch, Kristina. 2009. "Tunisia: The Life of Others. Project on Freedom of Association in the Middle East and North Africa". *FRIDE Working Paper* 85. www.fride.org/publication/631/tunisia:-the-life-of-others.
Kechichian, Joseph, and Jeanne Nazimek. 1997. "Challenges to the Military in Egypt". *Middle East Policy* 5 (3). www.mepc.org/journal/middle-east-policy-archives/challenges-military-egypt.
Khatib, Lina, and Ellen Lust, eds. 2013. *Taking to the Streets: Activism, Arab Uprisings, and Democratization*. Baltimore: Johns Hopkins University Press.
Kienle, Eberhard. 1998. "More Than a Response to Islamism: The Political Deliberalization of Egypt in the 1980s". *Middle East Journal* 52 (2): 219–235.
Kienle, Eberhard. 2001. *A Grand Delusion: Democracy and Economic Reform in Egypt*. London: I.B. Tauris.
King, Stephen J. 2003. *Liberalization Against Democracy*. Bloomington: Indiana University Press.
Kiser, Larry L., and Elinor Ostrom. 1982. "The Three Worlds of Action: A Metatheoretical Synthesis of Institutional Approaches". In *Strategies of Political Inquiry*, edited by Elinor Ostrom, 179–222. Beverly Hills: Sage.
Klau, Arne. 2010. *Impact of the Economic Crisis on Trade, Foreign Investments, and Employment in Egypt*. Cairo: International Labour Organisation.
Koopmans, Ruud. 2004. "Protest in Time and Space: The Evolution of Waves of Contention". In *A Blackwell Companion to Social Movements*, edited by David A. Snow *et al.*, 19–46. Malden, MA: Blackwell.
Landolt, Laura K., and Paul Kubicek. 2013. "Opportunities and Constraints: Comparing Tunisia and Egypt to the Coloured Revolutions". *Democratization*, April 2013: 1–23.
Lang, Anthony F. 2013. "From Revolutions to Constitutions: The Case of Egypt". *International Affairs* 89 (2): 345–363.
Laremont, Ricardo, eds. 2014. *Revolution, Revolt and Reform in North Africa: The Arab Spring and Beyond*. London: Routledge.

Bibliography

Lasswell, Harold D. 1936. *Politics: Who Gets What, When, How*. New York/London: Whittlesey House.

Lawson, George. 2006. "The Promise of Historical Sociology in International Relations". *International Studies Review* 8 (3): 397–423.

Layachi, Azzedine. 2000. "Reform and the Politics of Inclusion in the Maghrib". *The Journal of North African Studies* 5 (3): 15–42.

Lerner, Daniel. 1958. *The Passing of Traditional Society: Modernizing the Middle East*. Glencoe, IL: The Free Press.

Levitsky, Steven, and Lucan A. Way. 2002. "Elections Without Democracy: The Rise of Competitive Authoritarianism". *Journal of Democracy* 13 (2): 51–65.

Lijphart, Arend. 1991. "Constitutional Choices for New Democracies". *Journal of Democracy* 2 (1): 72–84.

Linz, Juan J. 1964. "An Authoritarian Regime: Spain". In *Cleavages, Ideologies and Party Systems: Contributions to Comparative Political Sociology*, edited by Erik Allardt and Yrjo Littunen, 291–341. Helsinki: Westermarck Society.

Linz, Juan J. 1990. "The Perils of Presidentialism". *Journal of Democracy* 1 (1): 51–69.

Linz, Juan J. 1994. "Presidential Versus Parliamentary Democracy: Does It Make a Difference?". In *The Failure of Presidential Democracy*, edited by Juan J. Linz and Arturo Valenzuela, 3–87. Baltimore: Johns Hopkins University Press.

Linz, Juan J. 2000. *Totalitarian and Authoritarian Regimes*. Boulder, CO: Lynne Rienner.

Linz, Juan J., and Alfred C. Stepan, eds. 1978. *The Breakdown of Democratic Regimes*. Baltimore: Johns Hopkins University Press.

Linz, Juan J., and Alfred C. Stepan. 1996. *Problems of Democratic Transition and Consolidation: Southern Europe, South America, and Post-Communist Europe*. Baltimore: John Hopkins University Press.

Lipset, Seymour M. 1959. "The Social Requisites of Democracy: Economic Development and Political Legitimacy". *American Political Science Review* 53 (1): 69–105.

Luciani, Giacomo. 1988. "Economic Foundations of Democracy and Authoritarianism: The Arab World in Comparative Perspective". *Arab Studies Quarterly* 10 (4): 437–465.

Luciani, Giacomo. 1995. "Resource, Revenues, and Authoritarianism in the Arab World: Beyond the Rentier State?". In *Political Liberalization and Democratization in the Arab World: Theoretical Perspectives*, edited by Rex Brynen, Bahgat Korany, and Paul Noble, 205–226. Boulder, CO: Lynne Rienner.

Luethold, Arnold. 2004. "Security Sector Reform in the Arab Middle East: A Nascent Debate". In *Reform and Reconstruction of the Security Sector*, edited by Alan Bryden and Heiner Hänggi, 93–120. Geneva: Geneva Centre for Democratic Control of Armed Forces.

Lufti Al-Sayyid Marsot, Afaf. 1977. *Egypt's Liberal Experiment: 1922–1936*. Berkeley, CA: University of California Press.

Lust-Okar, Ellen. 2004. "Divided they Rule: The Management and Manipulation of the Political Opposition". *Comparative Politics* 36: 159–179.

Lust-Okar, Ellen. 2008. *Political Participation in the Middle East*. Boulder, CO/London: Lynne Rienner.

Lust-Okar, Ellen. 2009. "Competitive Clientelism in the Middle East". *Journal of Democracy* 20 (3): 122–135.

Lutterbeck, Derek. 2012. "After the Fall: Security Sector Reform in Post-Ben Ali Tunisia". *Arab Reform Initiative*. www.arab-reform.net/after-fall-security-sector-reform-post-ben-ali-tunisia.

Lynch, Marc. 2011. "After Egypt: The Promise and Limitation of the Online Challenge to the Authoritarian Arab State". *Perspectives on Politics* 9 (2): 301–310.

Magen, Amichai, and Leonardo Morlino, eds. 2008. *International Actors, Democratization and the Rule of Law: Anchoring Democracy?*. London: Routledge.

Mahjoub, Azzam. 2010. "Labour Markets Performance and Migration Flows in Tunisia". In European Commission Directorate-General for Economic and Financial Affairs, *Labour Markets Performance and Migration, Tunisia, Morocco and Algeria*. Occasional Papers 60 (2), Brussels.

Mahoney, James, Erin Kimball, and Kendra L. Koivu. 2009. "The Logic of Historical Explanation in the Social Sciences". *Comparative Political Studies* 42 (1): 114–146.

Mahoney, James, and Dietrich Reuschemeyer. 2003. *Comparative Historical Analysis in the Social Sciences*. Princeton: Princeton University Press.

Mahoney, James, and Kathleen Thelen, eds. 2010. *Explaining Institutional Change: Ambiguity, Agency, and Power*. Cambridge: Cambridge University Press.

Maravall, José M., and Adam Przeworski, eds. 2003. *Democracy and the Rule of Law*. Cambridge: Cambridge University Press.

March, James G., and Johan P. Olsen. 1989. *Rediscovering Institutions: The Organizational Basis of Politics*. New York/London: The Free Press and Collier MacMillan.

Marshall, Shana, and Joshua Stacher. 2012. "Egypt's Generals and Transnational Capital". *Middle East Report* 262 (42). www.merip.org/mer/mer262/egypts-generals-transnational-capital.

Marshall, Thomas H., and Tom Bottomore. 1992. *Citizenship and Social Class*. London: Pluto Press.

Mashaw, Jerry L. 2006. "Accountability and Institutional Design: Some Thoughts on the Grammar of Governance". In *Public Accountability: Designs, Dilemmas and Experiences*, edited by Michael W. Dowdle, 115–156. Cambridge: Cambridge University Press.

Masoud, Tarek. 2011. "The Upheavals in Egypt and Tunisia: The Road to (and from) Liberation Square". *Journal of Democracy* 22: 20–34.

Mayfield, James B. 1996. *Local Government in Egypt: Structure, Process, and the Challenges of Reform*. Cairo: American University in Cairo Press.

McAdam, Doug, John D. McCarthy, and Mayer N. Zald, eds. 1996. *Comparative Perspectives on Social Movements: Political Opportunities, Mobilizing Structures, and Cultural Framings*. Cambridge: Cambridge University Press.

Meir, Hatina. 2003. "Historical Legacy and the Challenge of Modernity in the Middle East: The Case of al-Azhar in Egypt". *The Muslim World* 93 (1): 51–68.

Migdal, Joel. 1988. *Strong Societies and Weak States: State-Society Relations and State Capabilities in the Third World*. Princeton: Princeton University Press.

Miller, Laurel E., ed. 2010. *Framing the State in Times of Transition: Case Studies in Constitution Making*. Washington, DC: USIP Press.

Mitchell, Timothy. 1991. "The Limits of the State: Beyond Statist Approaches and their Critics". *American Political Science Review* 85 (1): 77–96.

Moore, Pete W. 2004. *Doing Business in the Middle East*. Cambridge: Cambridge University Press.

Moore, Pete W., and Bassel F. Salloukh. 2007. "Struggles under Authoritarianism: Regimes, States, and Professional Associations in the Arab World". *International Journal of Middle East Studies* 39 (1): 53–76.

Morlino, Leonardo. 1998. *Democracy Between Consolidation and Crisis: Parties, Groups and Citizens in Southern Europe*. Oxford: Oxford University Press.

Morlino, Leonardo. 2003. *Democrazie e Democratizzazioni*. Bologna: Il Mulino.

Bibliography

Morlino, Leonardo. 2011. *Changes for Democracy: Actors, Structures, Processes*. Oxford: Oxford University Press.

Moustafa, Tamir. 2002. "The Dilemmas of Decentralization and Community Development in Authoritarian Contexts". *Journal of Public and International Affairs* 13 (4): 123–144.

Moustafa, Tamir. 2012. "Drafting Egypt's Constitution: Can a New Legal Framework Revive a Flawed Transition?". *Brookings Doha Center – Stanford Project on Arab Transitions*. http://arabreform.stanford.edu/publications/drafting_egypts_new_constitution_policy_paper/.

Mulderig, M. Chloe. 2011. *Adulthood Denied: Youth Dissatisfaction and the Arab Spring*. Boston: Frederick S. Pardee Center for the Study of the Longer-Range Future.

Murphy, Emma. 1999. *Economic and Political Change in Tunisia: From Bourguiba to Ben Ali*. New York/London: St Martin's Press.

Murphy, Emma. 2011. "The Tunisian Uprising and the Precarious Path to Democracy". *Mediterranean Politics* 16 (2): 299–305.

Murphy, Emma. 2013. "The Tunisian Elections of October 2011: A Democratic Consensus". *The Journal of North African Studies* 18 (2): 231–247.

National Democratic Institute (NDI). 2011. *Final Report on the Tunisian National Constituent Assembly, October 23, 2011*. www.ndi.org/files/tunisia-final-election-report-021712_v2.pdf.

Niblock, Tim, and Emma Murphy. 1993. *Economic and Political Liberalisation in the Middle East*. London: British Academic Press.

Nonneman, Gerd. 2001. "Rentier and Autocrats, Monarchs and Democrats, State and Society: The Middle East Between Globalisation, Human Agency, and Europe". *International Affairs* 77 (1): 141–162.

Norris, Pippa. 1997. "Choosing Electoral Systems: Proportional, Majoritarian and Mixed Systems". *International Political Science Review* 18 (3): 297–312.

North, Douglass C. 1990. *Institutions, Institutional Change and Economic Performance*. Cambridge: Cambridge University Press.

North, Douglass C. 1991. "Institutions". *The Journal of Economic Perspectives* 5 (1): 97–112.

North, Douglass C. 1999. "In Anticipation of the Marriage of Political and Economic Theory". In *Competition and Cooperation: Conversations With Nobelists About Economics and Political Science*, edited by James E. Alt, Margaret Levi, and Elinor Ostrom, 314–317. New York: Russell Sage Foundation.

Norton, Augustus R., ed. 1995. *Civil Society in the Middle East*. Leiden: E.J. Brill.

O'Donnell, Guillermo. 2001. "Democratic Theory and Comparative Politics". *Studies in Comparative International Development* 36 (1): 7–36.

O'Donnell, Guillermo, Philippe C. Schmitter, and Laurence Whitehead, eds. 1986. *Transition From Authoritarian Rule: Comparative Perspectives*. Baltimore: The Johns Hopkins University Press.

Okruhlik, Gwenn. 1999. "Rentier Wealth, Unruly Law, and the Rise of Opposition: The Political Economy of Oil States". *Comparative Politics* 31 (3): 295–315.

Olsen, Johan P. 2010. *Governing Through Institution Building: Institutional Theory and Recent European Experiments in Democratic Organization*. New York, NY: Oxford University Press.

Osman, Tarek. 2010. *Egypt on the Brink: From Nasser to Mubarak*. New Haven/London: Yale University Press.

Ottaway, Marina. 2013. "Learning Politics in Tunisia". *Viewpoints* 26. Washington: Woodrow Wilson Center. www.wilsoncenter.org/publication/learning-politics-tunisia.

Ottaway, Marina, and Amr Hamzawy. 2011. "Protest Movements and Political Change in the Arab World". *Carnegie Endowment for International Peace*. http://carnegieendowment.org/2011/01/28/protest-movements-and-political-change-in-arab-world/1xu.

Owen, Roger. 2004. *State, Power and Politics in the Making of the Modern Middle East*. London: Routledge.

Owen, Roger. 2012. *The Rise and Fall of Arab Presidents for Life*. Cambridge, MA/London: Harvard University Press.

Pace, Michelle, and Francesco Cavatorta. 2012. "The Arab Uprisings in Theoretical Perspective – An Introduction". *Mediterranean Politics* 17 (2): 125–138.

Paciello, M. Cristina. 2010. "The Impact of the Economic Crisis on Euro-Mediterranean Relations". *The International Spectator* 45 (3): 51–69.

Paciello, M. Cristina. 2013. "Post-uprising Socio-economics in Tunisia and Egypt". *The International Spectator* 48 (4): 7–29.

Perthes, Volker, ed. 2004. *Arab Elites: Negotiating the Politics of Change*. Boulder, CO/London: Lynne Rienner.

Pfeifer, Karen. 1999. "How Tunisia, Morocco, Jordan, and Even Egypt Became IMF Success Stories". *Middle East Report* 210: 23–27.

Picard, Elizabeth. 1990. "Arab Military in Politics: From Revolutionary Plot to Authoritarian State". In *The Arab State*, edited by Giacomo Luciani, 189–219. London: Routledge.

Pickard, Duncan. 2012. "Lessons From Constitution-Making in Tunisia". *Rafik Hariri Center for the Middle East, Atlantic Council*. www.atlanticcouncil.org/publications/issue-briefs/lessons-from-constitutionmaking-in-tunisia.

Pickard, Duncan. 2013. "Electoral Politics Under Tunisia's New Constitution". *Rafik Hariri Center for the Middle East, Atlantic Council*. www.atlanticcouncil.org/publications/issue-briefs/electoral-politics-under-tunisias-new-constitution.

Pierson, Paul. 2000. "Increasing Return. Path Dependence and the Study of Politics". *American Political Science Review* 94 (2): 251–267.

Pierson, Paul. 2004. *Politics in Time: History, Institutions, and Social Analysis*. Princeton/Oxford: Princeton University Press.

Pierson, Paul, and Theda Skocpol. 2002. "Historical Institutionalism in Contemporary Political Science". In *Political Science: State of the Discipline*, edited by Ira Katznelson and Helen V. Milner, 693–721. New York, NY: W.W. Norton.

Pridham, Geoffrey, ed. 1991. *Encouraging Democracy: The International Context of Regime Transition in Southern Europe*. New York, NY: St. Martin's Press.

Pridham, Geoffrey. 2000a. *The Dynamics of Democratization: A Comparative Approach*. London: Continuum.

Pridham, Geoffrey. 2000b. "Confining Conditions and Breaking With the Past: Historical Legacies and Political Learning in Transitions to Democracy". *Democratization* 9: 36–64.

Pridham, Geoffrey. 2001a. "Comparative Reflections on Democratisation in East-Central Europe: A Model of Post-Communist Transformation?". In *Prospects for Democratic Consolidation in East-Central Europe*, edited by Geoffrey Pridham and Attila Ágh, 1–24. Manchester/New York: Manchester University Press.

Pridham, Geoffrey. 2001b. "Rethinking Regime Change Theory and the International Dimension of Democratisation: Ten Years After in East-Central Europe". In *Prospects for Democratic Consolidation in East-Central Europe*, edited by Geoffrey Pridham and Attila Ágh, 56–65. Manchester/New York: Manchester University Press.

Pripstein Posusney, Marsha. 2002. "Multi-party Elections in the Arab World". *Studies in Comparative International Development* 36 (4): 34–62.

Przeworski, Adam. 1991. *Democracy and the Market: Political and Economic Reforms in Eastern Europe and Latin America*. Cambridge: Cambridge University Press.

Quandt, William B. 1998. *Between Ballots and Bullets: Algeria's Transition From Authoritarianism*. Washington, DC: Brookings Institution Press.

Ragin, Charles. 2006. "Set Relations in Social Research: Evaluating their Consistency and Coverage". *Political Analysis* 14 (3): 291–310.

Remmer, Karen L. 1997. "Theoretical Decay and Theoretical Development. The Resurgence of Institutional Analysis". *World Politics* 50 (3): 34–61.

Roberts, Hugh. 2013. "The Revolution that Wasn't". *London Review of Books* 35 (17): 3–9. www.lrb.co.uk/v35/n17/hugh-roberts/the-revolution-that-wasnt.

Rubin, Barry, ed. 2010. *The Muslim Brotherhood: The Organization and Policies of a Global Islamist Movement*. New York, NY: Palgrave Macmillan.

Rueschemeyer, Dietrich, Evelyne H. Stephens, and John D. Stephens. 1992. *Capitalist Development and Democracy*. Chicago: University of Chicago Press.

Rustow, Dankwart A. 1970. "Transitions to Democracy: Toward a Dynamic Model". *Comparative Politics* 2 (3): 337–363.

Sadiki, Larbi. 2002. "The Search for Citizenship in Ben Ali's Tunisia: Democracy Versus Unity". *Political Studies* 50 (3): 497–513.

Sadiki, Larbi. 2003. "Political Liberalization in Ben Ali's Tunisia: Façade Democracy". *Democratization* 9 (4): 122–141.

Sadiki, Larbi. 2015. *Routledge Handbook of the Arab Spring*. London: Routledge.

Salamé, Ghassan, ed. 1994. *Democracy Without Democrats? The Renewal of Politics in the Muslim World*. London: I.B. Tauris.

Samuels, Kirsti. 2006. *Constitution Building Processes and Democratization: A Discussion of Twelve Case Studies*. Stockholm: International IDEA.

Sartori, Giovanni. 1997. *Comparative Constitutional Engineering: An Inquiry into Structures, Incentives and Outcomes*. Basingstoke, Hants: Macmillan.

Sayigh, Yezid. 2007. "Security Sector Reform in the Arab Region: Challenges to Developing and Indigenous Agenda". *Arab Reform Initiative*. www.arab-reform.net/security-sector-reform-arab-region-challenges-developing-indigenous-agenda-0.

Sayigh, Yezid. 2012. "Above the State: The Officers' Republic in Egypt". *Carnegie Endowment for International Peace*, August 2012. http://carnegieendowment.org/2012/08/01/above-state-officers-republic-in-egypt/d4l2.

Sayigh, Yezid, et al. 2011. "Roundtable: Rethinking the Study of Middle East Militaries". *International Journal of Middle East Studies* 43 (3): 391–407.

Schattschneider, Elmer E. 1960. *The Semisovereign People: A Realist's View of Democracy in America*. New York, NY: Holt, Rinehart, and Winston.

Schedler, Andreas, ed. 2006. *Electoral Authoritarianism: The Dynamics of Unfree Competition*. Boulder, CO/London: Lynner Rienner Publishers.

Schlumberger, Oliver. 2006. "Rents, Reform and Authoritarianism in the Middle East". *Internationale Politik und Gesellschaft* 2: 43–57.

Schlumberger, Oliver, ed. 2007. *Arab Authoritarianism: Debating the Dynamics and Durability of Nondemocratic Regimes*. Stanford, CA: Stanford University Press.

Schmitter, Philippe C. 1995. "The International Context of Contemporary Democratisation". In *Transitions to Democracy: Comparative Perspectives From Southern Europe, Latin America and Eastern Europe*, edited by Geoffrey Pridham, 499–532. Dartmouth: Aldershot.

Schwedler, Jillian. 2007. "Democratization, Inclusion and the Moderation of Islamist Parties". *Development* 50: 56–61.

Schwedler, Jillian. 2011. "Can Islamists Become Moderates? Rethinking the Inclusion-Moderation Hypothesis". *World Politics* 63 (2): 347–376.
Shorbagy, Manar. 2007. "Understanding Kefaya: The New Politics in Egypt". *Arab Studies Quarterly* 29: 39–60.
Shugart, Matthew S., and John M. Carey. 1992. *Presidents and Assemblies: Constitutional Design and Electoral Dynamics*. Cambridge: Cambridge University Press.
Skach, Cindy. 2005. *Borrowing Constitutional Designs: Constitutional Law in Weimar Germany and the French Fifth Republic*. Princeton: Princeton University Press.
Skocpol, Theda. 1979. *States and Social Revolutions: A Comparative Analysis of France, Russia and China*. Cambridge: Cambridge University Press.
Söyler, Mehtap. 2013. "Informal Institutions, Forms of State and Democracy: The Turkish Deep State". *Democratization* 20 (2): 310–334.
Springborg, Robert. 2011a. "Whither the Arab Spring? 1989 or 1848?". *The International Spectator* 46 (3): 5–12.
Springborg, Robert. 2011b. "The Political Economy of the Arab Spring". *Mediterranean Politics* 16 (3): 427–433.
Stepan, Alfred C. 1988. *Rethinking Military Politics: Brazil and the Southern Cone*. Princeton: Princeton University Press.
Stepan, Alfred C. 2012. "Tunisia's Transition and the Twin Tolerations". *Journal of Democracy* 23 (2): 89–103.
Stepan, Alfred C, and Cindy Skatch. 1993. "Constitutional Frameworks and Democratic Consolidation". *World Politics* 46: 1–22.
Storm, Lise. 2009. "The Persistence of Authoritarianism as a Source of Radicalization in North Africa". *International Affairs* 85 (5): 997–1013.
Sullivan, Denis. 2009. "Will Egypt's Muslim Brotherhood Run in 2010?" *Carnegie Endowment for International Peace*, 5 May 2009, https://carnegieendowment.org/publications/23057.
Taagepera, Rein. 2002. "Designing Electoral Rules and Waiting for an Electoral System to Evolve". In *The Architecture of Democracy: Constitutional Design, Conflict Management, and Democracy*, edited by Andrew Reynolds, 248–265. New York: Oxford University Press.
Tadros, Mariz. 2006. "State Welfare in Egypt Since Adjustment: Hegemonic Control With a Minimalist Role". *Review of African Political Economy* 33 (108): 237–254.
Tadros, Mariz. 2008. *The Muslim Brotherhood and Islamist Politics in the Middle East*. London: Routledge.
Tanneberg, Dag, Christoph Stefes, and Wolfgang Merkel. 2013. "Hard Times and Regime Failure: Autocratic Responses to Economic Downturns". *Contemporary Politics* 19 (1): 115–129.
Tavana, Daniel. 2012. "The Future of Egypt's Electoral Law". *Carnegie Endowment for International Peace*, 11 September 2012. http://carnegieendowment.org/2012/09/11/future-of-egypt-s-electoral-law/dt37.
Thelen, Kathleen. 2003. "How Institutions Evolve. Insights From Comparative Historical Analysis". In *Comparative Historical Analysis in the Social Sciences*, edited by James Mahoney and Dietrich Reuschemeyer, 208–239. Princeton: Princeton University Press.
Thelen, Kathleen, and Sven, Steinmo. 1992. "Historical Institutionalism in Comparative Politics". In *Structuring Politics: Historical Institutionalism in Comparative Politics*, edited by Sven Steinmo, Kathleen Thelen, and Frank Longstreth, 1–32. Cambridge: Cambridge University Press.

Treisman, Daniel. 2007. *The Architecture of Government: Rethinking Political Decentralization*. Cambridge: Cambridge University Press.

Tripp, Charles. 2013. *The Power and the People. Paths of Resistance in the Middle East*. Cambridge: Cambridge University Press.

Tsebelis, George. 2002. *Veto Players: How Political Institutions Work*. Princeton, NJ: Princeton University Press.

Valbjørn, Morten. 2012. "Upgrading Post-Democratization Studies: Examining a Re-Politicized Arab World in a Transition to Somewhere". *Middle East Critique* 21 (1): 25–35.

Valenzuela, J. Samuel. 1992. "Democratic Consolidation in Post-Transitional Settings: Notion, Process, and Facilitating Conditions". In *Issues in Democratic Consolidation: The New South American Democracies in Comparative Perspective*, edited by Scott Mainwaring, Guillermo O'Donnell, and J. Samuel Valenzuela, 57–104. Notre Dame, Ind.: University of Notre Dame Press.

Vermeule, Adrian. 2007. *Mechanisms of Democracy: Institutional Design Writ Small*. New York, NY: Oxford University Press.

Volpi, Frédéric. 2013. "Explaining (and Re-explaining) Political Change in the Middle East During the Arab Spring: Trajectories of Democratization and of Authoritarianism in the Maghreb". *Democratization* 20 (6): 969–990.

Volpi, Frédéric, and Francesco Cavatorta, eds. 2007. *Democratization in the Muslim World: Changing Patterns of Power and Authority*. Abingdon/New York: Routledge.

von Beyme, Klaus. 2001. "Parties in the Process of Consolidation in East-Central Europe". In *Prospects for Democratic Consolidation in East-Central Europe*, edited by Geoffrey Pridham and Attila Ágh, 138–156. Manchester/New York: Manchester University Press.

Ware, Lewis B. 1985. "The Role of the Tunisian Military in the Post-Bourghiba Era". *Middle East Journal* 39 (1): 27–47.

Way, Lucan. 2011. "Comparing the Arab Revolts: The Lessons of 1989". *Journal of Democracy* 22: 17–27.

Wegner, Eva. 2007. "Islamist Inclusion and Regime Persistence: The Moroccan Win-Win Situation". In *Debating Arab Authoritarianism*, edited by Oliver Schlumberger, 75–93. Stanford: Stanford University Press.

Whitehead, Laurence, ed. 1996. *The International Dimensions of Democratisation: Europe and the Americas*. Oxford: Oxford University Press.

Whitehead, Richard. 2002. "In Debate: The Casual Focus of Historical Institutionalism". Paper presented at Temple University Course Seminar on Authoritarian Regimes. Philadelphia, October 2002.

Widner, Jennifer. 2007. "Proceedings". Workshop on Constitution Building Processes. Bobst Center for Peace and Justice, Princeton University in cooperation with Interpeace and International IDEA. Princeton University, 17–20 May 2007.

Willis, Michael J. 2002. "Political Parties in the Maghreb: The Illusion of Significance". *The Journal of North African Studies* 7 (2): 1–22.

Wood, Elisabeth J. 2001. "An Insurgent Path to DemocracyPopular Mobilization, Economic Interests, and Regime Transition in South Africa and El Salvador". *Comparative Political Studies* 34 (8): 862–888.

World Bank. 2010. *Global Economic Prospects 2010*. Washington, DC: World Bank.

Wurzel, Urlich G. 2009. "The Political Economy of Authoritarianism in Egypt: Insufficient Structural Reforms, Limited Outcomes and a Lack of New Actors". In *The Arab State and Neo-Liberal Globalization: The Restructuring of State Power in the Middle East*, edited by Laura Guazzone and Daniela Pioppi, 97–123. London: Ithaca Press.

Zartman, William I. 1988. "Opposition as a Support of the State". In *Beyond Coercion: The Durability of the Arab State*, edited by Adeed Dawisha and I. William Zartman, 61–87. London: Croom Helm.

Zielonka, Jan, ed. 2001. *Democratic Consolidation in Eastern Europe 1: Institutional Engineering*. New York, NY: Oxford University Press.

Zielonka, Jan, and Alex Pravda, eds. 2001. *Democratic Consolidation in Eastern Europe 2: International and Transnational Factors*. New York, NY: Oxford University Press.

Zlitni, Sami. 2012. "Social Networks and Women's Mobilization in Tunisia". *Journal of International Women's Studies* 13 (5): 46–58.

Index

6 April Movement 49, 138n8
50-member constituent assembly (Egypt) 76–77
2012 constitution (Egypt) 71–79, 91n29, 101–103, 127, 131, 151–153
2014 constitution (Egypt) 78

Aboul Fotouh, Abdul Moneim 99, 113n11
accountability 4–6, 21–26, 37–38, 118, 133, 143, 146–157
Al-Azhar 72–77, 89n17
Al-Ghad party (Egypt) 39–40
Al-Nour party (Egypt) 72, 78, 96–97, 99, 113n9
Al-Sisi, Abdel Fattah 126, 138n5
Ammar, Rashid (General) 47, 110, 116n40, 134
Arab uprisings: agency 50–52; causes of 5, 23, 35, 37, 42, 118, 147; contingency 44–48; literature on 160–167; transition processes 4, 6, 12, 56–57, 142; unsustainability 33; youth 31–32
authoritarian breakdown 11–12, 19, 56
authoritarian legacy 13, 163
authoritarian resilience 4, 154

bargaining 12, 66, 77, 82, 145, 156
Ben Ali, Zine El-Abidine 2, 30, 38, 41–43, 44–50, 53n7, 57, 104, 106–111, 133–136, 140n23, 165
Bouazizi, Mohamed 30, 50–51
Bourghiba, Habib 80, 111, 115n31, 133

citizenship 37–38, 57, 157; see also civil rights; political rights; social rights
civilian-military relations 9, 23–24, 61, 117–134
civil rights 37–38, 146
communication technologies 31–32, 95
comparative political analysis 2; see also comparative politics

comparative politics 2, 14, 161
Congrès pour la République (CPR) (Tunisia) 81, 106–107
constituent assembly (Egypt) 61, 64–81, 88n6, 89n17, 91n30, 103, 123, 156
constitutional committee (Tunisia) 83, 92n41
Constitutional Court (*Cour Constitutionnelle*) (Tunisia) 93n54, 137
constitutional referendum (Egypt, March 2011) 63–64, 91n26, 125, 155
constitution-making process: constitution and time 21, 74, 156, 158; constitution drafting 59, 152, 155; Egypt 65–71, 76–79, 89n12, 122, 125, 138n5, 138n7, 138n9, 151; role of the constitution 20, 24, 61; Tunisia 80–87, 92n45, 92n48, 92n51, 109
contagion 10, 50
contentious politics 57
contingency 18–19, 44–52, 143, 157, 162
corruption 2, 12, 41–42, 49–53, 66, 107–109, 130, 139–140n15
Council of Representatives (Egypt) 72, 100

democratic consolidation 9, 151
democratic installation 11, 144–152
democratisation literature 3, 8, 12
demonstration effect 10, 50, 54n22; see also contagion

Eastern and Central Europe 4, 8, 11, 164
electoral authoritarianism 94–95; see also 'electoralist fallacy'
electoral formula 21, 105; see also electoral laws
'electoralist fallacy' 21, 147
electoral laws 7, 21, 34, 94–104, 114n18, 114n23, 131
electoral politics 3, 94–96
elites 7–9, 12–18, 25–26, 28nn8–9, 34, 45, 54n24, 66, 80, 85, 118, 150, 163, 165

Index

Ennahda (Tunisia) 81–87, 92n41, 92n52, 105–111, 116nn36–37, 137, 151, 163
Ettakatol (Tunisia) 81, 87, 106–108, 111
extractive institutions 25, 26, 157; *see also* predatory institutions

founding elections 19, 21, 143
Freedom and Justice Party (FJP) (Egypt) 66–67, 77, 96–97, 113n6, 113n11, 113n14, 156

Gamal, Mubarak 45–49, 54n16, 121–122
Ghannouchi, Rashid 110
global financial and economic crisis 2

Higher Commission for Political Reform (Tunisia) 104–105
historical institutional literature 4, 15–20, 27, 84, 143, 158, 161, 163; *see also* neo-institutionalism
House of Representatives (Egypt) 77

Ikhwanisation 75, 132
inclusive institutions 20, 151–163
inequality 32, 42
informal institutions 16–20, 57, 79, 110, 124, 128, 131, 154
Instance Supérieure Indépendantepour les Elections (ISIE) (Tunisia) 105–107, 116nn32–33
institutional engineering 20–23, 162
institutional inertia 15; *see also* institutional legacy
institutional layering 17
institutional legacy 15–18, 83, 162
institutional logics 2, 16
institutional structures 2, 15, 16, 151
International Monetary Fund (IMF) 34, 42, 43, 53n12, 75

'Judges' Club' 39, 130
judicial system 22, 24, 41, 122, 130, 136, 140n17
judiciary 3–5, 13, 22–24, 40–42, 70, 75, 79, 88n5, 99, 117–119, 125, 128–132, 135–137, 139n10, 140nn16–19, 148, 150, 156; *see also* judicial system
July 2013 constitutional declaration (Egypt) 76–79, 91n36, 103
June 2012 constitutional declaration (Egypt) 68, 90n20, 91n37, 124–126; *see also* June declaration
June declaration (Egypt) 68–69

Kifaya! Movement 39–40, 49

Lasswell, Harold 3–4, 87
Leagues for the Protection of the Revolution (Tunisia) 109
legitimacy: attribute of democracy 4, 23–25, 37–38, 74, 119, 128, 146–157; authoritarianism 5, 6, 13, 34, 45; constitution making 58, 59, 67–68, 71, 80, 81, 84–87, 88n6, 109, 123; elections 21, 78, 103, 115nn26–27; Islamists 82; military 126, 134; 'revolutionary' 64

Mansour, Adly 103
March 2011 constitutional declaration (Egypt) 64–68, 79, 89n14, 98, 123
marginalisation 32, 35, 134
military budget 24, 123, 135
military courts 122, 124, 127–128, 139n10
military institutionalization 23
military's interests 31, 47, 54n16, 64, 88n4, 119–132, 134
Morsi, Mohammed 69–76, 86, 91n30, 91nn34–35, 99, 102–103, 113n6, 113n10, 124–129, 138n5, 140n19, 148
Mubarak, Hosni 2, 30–32, 39–49, 62–64, 89n15, 113n9, 120–122, 130, 139n9, 140n17, 149–150
Muslim Brotherhood: alliance with the military 62–64, 138n8; conflict with the judiciary 130–132; conflict with the military 118, 122, 125–129, 148, 166; constituent assembly 67; constitution making 70; lack of inclusiveness 76, 89n12, 101, 113n14, 150–151, 156, 163; under Mubarak 40–41; parliamentary elections 66, 97–98, 100; participation in the uprisings 32; party 96; presidential elections 69, 99

National Constituent Assembly (NCA) (Tunisia) 80–87, 92n39, 92n41, 92n47, 92n50, 104–112, 156
National Defence Council (Egypt) 123, 125
National Democratic Party (NDP) (Egypt) 39, 95, 149
National Dialogue (Tunisia) 85–87, 111
National Salvation Front (NSF) (Egypt) 86, 101, 110, 114nn20–21
National Security Council (Egypt) 123
neo-authoritarianism 6–7, 28–29n15, 33–36, 38–42
Neo-Dustur 80, 133
neo-institutionalism 3, 14–16, 161
Nidaa Tounes 92n50, 111
November 2012 constitutional declaration (Egypt) 70, 90n22, 91n30, 114n20

Index   193

pactism 9, 13
path-dependence 18–19, 27, 60, 86, 156, 158–159, 162, 164
People's Assembly (Lower House of parliament) (Egypt) 65, 68, 70, 72, 89n17, 90n19, 96, 98, 100; *see also* Council of Representatives
polarisation 21, 24, 64–74, 75–87, 89n9, 96, 101, 110, 127, 148, 155
political development 4–10, 23, 27, 28–29n15, 53n3, 87, 142–166
political rights 10–11, 37–43, 95, 102, 146, 148
popular mobilisation 2, 13, 30, 32, 46, 48, 50–53, 54n23, 63, 76, 81, 86, 134; *see also* popular protests; popular unrest
popular protests 2, 37, 51
popular unrest 2, 44, 91n31
poverty 2, 43, 53n13, 157
predatory institutions 32, 33, 38, 42
process tracing 4, 164

Quartet 87; *see also* Tunisian General Labour Union (*Union Générale Tunisienne du Travail*, UGTT); *Union Tunisienne de l'Industrie, du Commerce et de l'Artisanat* (UTICA)

Rassemblement Constitutionnel Démocratique (RCD) (Tunisia) 41, 57, 95, 135, 150
regime change 6, 8, 9, 11, 54–55n24
rentier state 28–29n15, 33–34, 53n3
repression 2, 12, 34–52, 53n10, 54–55n24, 107, 148, 165, 166
responsiveness 4, 21, 23–25, 37–38, 142–150, 163
rule of law 8, 21–22, 37, 41–42, 66, 118, 130, 137, 139n11, 146, 152–153

Salafists 58, 72, 96–98, 113n9, 166
security sector reform (SSR) 128, 139n11
sequencing 4–7, 18–20, 59–64, 78, 86–87, 98, 111, 143, 156–164
Shafiq, Ahmed 99
Sharia 72–77, 81–82, 113n12, 151–152, 167
Shura Council (Upper House of parliament) (Egypt) 65, 70, 72, 77, 96, 100, 102, 114n18, 115nn25–26, 131

social contract 45
social media 12, 50–52
social rights 36–38, 42–43, 146, 157
stability 2, 6–7, 15, 20, 33, 36, 44–45, 52, 119, 137, 166
state of emergency 39–40, 63, 71
state-society relations 10
succession (Egypt) 7, 45–47, 52, 124
Supreme Constitutional Court (SCC) (Egypt) 67–69, 77, 98, 101, 123
Supreme Council of Magistrates (*Conseil Supérieur de la Magistrature*) (Tunisia) 136
Supreme Council of the Armed Forces (SCAF) (Egypt) 31, 62, 65, 96, 122, 155
Supreme Organisation to Realise the Goals of the Revolution, Political Reform and Democratic Transition (SORGR) (Tunisia) 80, 85, 104, 154; *see also* Higher Commission for Political Reform
Supreme Police Council (Egypt) 128
sustainability 36–38

Tahrir Square 32, 48, 54n19, 54n23, 118, 124
Tamarrod 76, 121
Tantawi, Mohamed Hussei (Field Marshall) 47, 122, 126–127
timing 4–5, 7, 18–20, 51, 59, 62–66, 78, 86–87, 98, 111, 131, 143, 156–161, 163–164
Troika (Tunisia) 81, 83, 108, 116n40
Tunisian General Labour Union (*Union Générale Tunisienne du Travail*, UGTT) 53n7, 85–87, 92nn49–50, 110–112
Tunisian League of Human Rights (*Ligue Tunisienne des Droits de l'Homme*) 38, 87, 137
turning points 19, 143

unemployment 2, 25, 36, 42–43, 53–54n13, 75, 84; *see also* youth unemployment
Union Tunisienne de l'Industrie, du Commerce et de l'Artisanat (UTICA) (Tunisia) 87, 110–111

World Bank (WB) 34

youth unemployment 32, 149